Troubleshooting Your PC For Dummies, 3rd Ed

D0691241

Useful Information

This computer's manufacturer: _____

Manufacturer's Web page: _____

Tech-support number: _____

Customer number: _____

Computer serial number: _____

Computer dealer: _____

Computer dealer's number: _____

Computer purchase date: _____

Other handy numbers

Guru's phone number: _____

ISP's phone number: _____

Other: _____

Other: _____

About My Computer

My version of Windows: _____

My optical drive letter: _____

Key (or keys) to enter Setup program: _____

Quick Things to Check

❏ Is the cable connected at both ends?

❏ Is it plugged in?

❏ Is it turned on?

❏ Is it getting power?

❏ Does the computer recognize it in the Device Manager?

❏ Have you installed any new software or hardware recently?

❏ Is the keyboard or mouse dead?

Stuff to Try First

❏ Press Ctrl+Z to undo a bad file operation.

❏ Try pressing the Esc key.

❏ Will restarting the program fix things?

❏ Did restarting Windows solve the problem?

❏ Did you run System Restore?

❏ Swap out the keyboard, mouse, or monitor with another PC's keyboard, mouse, or monitor or with a second keyboard, mouse, or monitor, to narrow down what's at fault.

For Dummies: Bestselling Book Series for Beginners

Troubleshooting Your PC For Dummies, 3rd Edition

Cheat Sheet

Handy Tools

The Device Manager

Open the Control Panel's Device Manager icon.

From the Run dialog box: **DEVMGMT.MSC**

The System Configuration Utility

From the Start menu, choose Run (or press Win+R to instantly summon the Run dialog box). Type **MSCONFIG** into the box and click OK.

Bonus tip: The Tools menu in the System Configuration utility contains a list of almost every common troubleshooting tool you will ever need.

System Restore

From the Start menu, choose All Programs⇨Accessories⇨System Tools⇨System Restore.

Registry Editor

Choose the Run command from the Start menu (or press Win+R) and type **REGEDIT** into the box. Click the OK button. Do *not* use the Registry unless you're directed to do so. It's not a place to be wandering around.

The System Information Utility

From the Start menu, choose Programs or All Programs⇨Accessories ⇨System Tools⇨System Information.

Stuff to Remember

- It's not your fault.
- Computers crash.
- Often, a simple restart fixes things.
- Upgrading or adding new software typically introduces new problems.
- Backing up your data is an excellent way to ensure that your stuff is safe.
- Windows doesn't come with antivirus software, so you need to get your own.
- The computer harbors no insidious intelligence, and it's not out to get you.
- "Stuff" happens.

For Dummies: Bestselling Book Series for Beginners

Troubleshooting Your PC

FOR

DUMMIES®

3RD EDITION

by Dan Gookin

WILEY

Wiley Publishing, Inc.

Troubleshooting Your PC For Dummies®, 3rd Edition

Published by
Wiley Publishing, Inc.
111 River Street
Hoboken, NJ 07030-5774

www.wiley.com

WILEY

About the Author

Dan Gookin has been writing about technology for way, way too long. He has contributed articles to numerous high-tech magazines and written over 110 books on personal computers, many of them accurate.

Dan combines his love of writing with his gizmo fascination to create books that are informative, entertaining, and not boring. Having sold more than 14 million titles translated into over 30 languages, Dan can attest that his method of crafting computer tomes seems to work.

Perhaps his most famous title is the original *DOS For Dummies,* published in 1991. It became the world's fastest-selling computer book, at one time moving more copies per week than the *New York Times* #1 bestseller (though, as a reference, it could not be listed on the *NYT* bestseller list). That book spawned the entire line of *For Dummies* books, which remains a publishing phenomenon to this day.

Dan's most popular titles include *Word 2007 For Dummies*, *Laptops For Dummies*, and *PCs For Dummies* (all published by Wiley). He also maintains the vast and helpful Web page www.wambooli.com.

Dan holds a degree in communications/visual arts from the University of California, San Diego. Presently, he lives in the Pacific Northwest, where he enjoys spending time with his sons in the gentle woods of Idaho.

Publisher's Acknowledgments

We're proud of this book; please send us your comments through our online registration form located at www.dummies.com/register/.

Some of the people who helped bring this book to market include the following:

Acquisitions, Editorial

Senior Project Editor: Mark Enochs

Executive Editor: Greg Croy

Copy Editor: Rebecca Whitney

Technical Editor: Lee Musick

Editorial Manager: Leah Cameron

Editorial Assistant: Amanda Foxworth

Sr. Editorial Assistant: Cherie Case

Cartoons: Rich Tennant
(www.the5thwave.com)

Composition Services

Project Coordinator: Katie Key

Layout and Graphics: Stacie Brooks, Reuben W. Davis, Alissa D. Ellet, Melissa K. Jester, Christine Williams

Proofreader: Penny L. Stuart

Indexer: Broccoli Information Management

Publishing and Editorial for Technology Dummies

    Richard Swadley, Vice President and Executive Group Publisher

    Andy Cummings, Vice President and Publisher

    Mary Bednarek, Executive Acquisitions Director

    Mary C. Corder, Editorial Director

Publishing for Consumer Dummies

    Diane Graves Steele, Vice President and Publisher

    Joyce Pepple, Acquisitions Director

Composition Services

    Gerry Fahey, Vice President of Production Services

    Debbie Stailey, Director of Composition Services

Contents at a Glance

Table of Contents

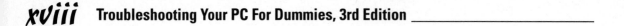

Introduction

· ·

*W*ho would believe that there's so much trouble out there in PC land that this book would evolve into a third edition? Golly!

Well, trouble looms. Anyone who has used a PC for any length of time suddenly realizes what scientists in white lab coats have known since the 1950s: Computers sometimes don't work right. Even without a degree from MIT, it's obvious. And, unlike those bespectacled, clipboard-toting geniuses of the Eniac era, you most likely have no training in how to troubleshoot, let alone manage and maintain, that expensive piece of computer hardware sitting on your desk (or lap).

Well, do not fret! Troubleshooting is something I do well, which is why I wrote this book. And, this is a *For Dummies* book, so you know that it's easy to understand, full of good advice, and spiced throughout with a modicum of humor and good taste.

You know, computers aren't supposed to die or crash or hang or bomb or toss a hissy fit for no apparent reason. But, as any computer owner knows, computers often don't do what they're told. Unpredictable behavior from a PC is predictable. You can have problems ranging from the *it-was-working-yesterday* syndrome to the *who-owns-the-problem?* issue. You'll have to decide whether the printer isn't working because of the printer itself or because of Windows or because of the application that's trying to print. I won't even bore you with random Internet-disconnect problems, dead mice, monitors thrust into stupid mode, and a myriad of other problems — because these and other issues are all adequately covered, cured, and remedied throughout this handy little book.

About This Book

My approach here is simple: The idea is to help you find out what's wrong with your PC. Most computer trouble follows a logical (surprise!) pattern. When you recognize the pattern, you can better deal with the solution. After all, had I just chickened out and listed *every* possible problem that you could have with your computer, this book would be several millions of pages long and have far fewer cartoons.

You can use the index to discover where solutions to specific problems lie, or you can just browse through Part II, which covers many solutions based on the particular piece of PC hardware that's being troubled. Each section within a chapter mentions the problem and covers potential solutions. Sample sections include

- ✔ What do to about "restart guilt"
- ✔ Before you call tech support
- ✔ Removing documents from the File menu
- ✔ Missing Internet passwords
- ✔ The bane of Sticky Keys
- ✔ Hard drive failure warning signs
- ✔ Forcing the power button to turn off the computer
- ✔ Stopping a naughty program

And many, many more. You don't have to learn anything. You don't have to complete worksheets or take quizzes or follow flowcharts. Just find your problem, look up the answer, and follow a few quick and easily explained steps, and you're back on your way with a working computer in no time.

How This Book Works

This book explains how to do things in a step-by-step manner. Occasionally, solutions have a large number of steps, or sometimes you have only one or two things to do, but, fortunately, it's all numbered and explained in a cheerful and entertaining manner.

Whenever you're told to type something, that something appears in **special** type. For example:

1. Type **WINVER** in the box.

This instruction tells you to type the text **WINVER** into the box. The next step may be to click the OK button with the mouse or press the Enter key. But all you need to worry about for this step is to type **WINVER**.

The steps tell you exactly which button to click or which gizmo to tickle with the mouse:

2. Click the OK button.

Sometimes these steps are shortened:

3. Click OK.

This line still means "Click the OK button with the mouse."

    4. Press the Enter key.

Don't press the Enter key until you're told to do so. Often this is to give you time to review what you've typed.

Keyboard shortcuts or key-combination commands are given like this:

    Press the Alt+F keys on the keyboard.

This line means to press and hold the Alt key on your keyboard and then tap the F key. Release the Alt key. It works the same way as pressing Shift+F to type a capital letter *F,* but the Alt key is used rather than Shift.

Likewise, you may use the Ctrl key in combination with other keyboard characters.

The key between the Ctrl and Alt keys in the lower-left corner of your keyboard is the Windows key, which is abbreviated as *Win* throughout this book. So, whenever you see

    Win+F

it means to press and hold the Win key and then tap the F key.

Choosing items from the menu works like this:

    Choose Edit⇨Paste.

This line means to use the mouse to click the Edit menu and then click again to choose the Paste item from that menu. (You can also use the keyboard to work the menus, in which case you press the Alt key and then the underlined letter of the menu or command to choose that command.)

The Start menu's All Programs menu works differently from the standard menus in Windows. In that case, items are separated by commas because you don't really open a submenu:

    Choose All Programs, Accessories, Command Prompt.

The above command directs you to choose the All Programs item from the bottom of the Start menu, and then click once to choose Accessories and once to choose the Command Prompt item. (Double-clicking is not necessary to open an item from the Start menu.)

What You're Not to Read

I just can't help being technical at times. So, when I break into a high-tech ballad, I let you know. Reading that material may increase your knowledge for playing computer trivia, but, otherwise, such asides and tidbits are written because — after 20 years of writing computer books — *I just can't help myself!*

The trivia and asides are always marked as optional reading. Don't bother about trying to figure out what's important and what's just the author babbling.

Foolish Assumptions

I must assume a few things about you, O dear, gentle reader: You use a computer. Specifically, you use a computer (or PC) that runs the Windows operating system, Windows Vista. You can have any version of Windows Vista, though be aware that the Windows Vista Home version may not sport all the nifty features mentioned in this book.

Further, I assume that your computer is set up and configured with Windows. This is not a Windows book, and if you need help with basic PC stuff, then get my book, *PCs For Dummies.* You'll enjoy it, especially the uplifting conclusion and moral message it drives home.

Windows Vista can be configured in a number of ways. The figures and steps in this book assume that you've not configured anything, though if you've customized Windows, it should be easy to figure out what's what. Further, this book presents information about using the Control Panel in both the Home and Classic views.

Finally, this book doesn't cover previous versions of Windows. If you're using Windows XP, try to find this book's second edition. For information on Windows 98 and Windows Me, try to find this book's first edition.

How This Book Is Organized

This book contains five major parts to whet your troubleshooting appetite. Each part contains chapters that help further explain the part subject. Then, each chapter is divided into individual sections that address specific issues. Everything is cross-referenced. You don't have to read the entire book, from front to back. You may start reading anywhere and receive the full enjoyment that you would if you were to start on the first page or wherever the binding falls open when you try to lay this book on its back.

Part 1: What the @#$%&*!?

The chapters in this part of the book serve as a handy introduction to the entire notion of troubleshooting your PC. I give you some explanations, some quick things to try, plus helpful tips and advice on where to go when you can't find the answers.

Part II: Troubleshooting Minor Irks and Quirks

The chapters in this part make up the book's core. Each chapter covers a specific aspect of the computer, either some piece of hardware or something you do, such as use the Internet. Each chapter contains general troubleshooting information and some specific (and common) questions and answers along with their possible solutions.

Part III: Woes, Wows, Windows

The four chapters in this part of the book deal specifically with Windows itself. Yes, one chapter covers those problems that Windows causes. But other chapters tell you how to interact with Windows and your programs as well as offering up the exciting and useful smorgasbord of new Windows Vista troubleshooting tools and utilities.

Part IV: Preventive Maintenance

Nothing beats being prepared. The chapters in this part tell you how to best prepare for the potential of PC peril and how to optimize your system, and you get some general good advice on what to do "just in case."

Part V: The Part of Tens

The traditional *For Dummies* Part of Tens contains several chapters with some good advice, all bundled into neat lists of ten.

Icons Used in This Book

This icon flags something I would consider a tip (though just about all the information in this book falls into the Tip category).

This icon serves as a special reminder to do something or to remember something.

This icon serves as a special reminder not to do something.

This infamous icon alerts you to the presence of highly technical stuff discussed in the text nearby. It's optional reading only!

Where to Go from Here

Read on! If you don't know where to start, start at Chapter 1, which is why I made that text Chapter 1 and not Chapter 4.

The first part of the book serves as a basic orientation, and Chapter 2 is an excellent introduction to some immediate troubleshooting fixes you can try. Otherwise, look up the problem and find the solution. It's in here somewhere.

As an author, I enjoy supporting my own books. If you have any questions about this book or need something explained further, you can e-mail me at dgookin@ wambooli.com. That's my real e-mail address, and I do respond to every e-mail sent to me. I cannot, however, troubleshoot your computer for you, nor do I provide free technical support. This book will help you troubleshoot, and your computer dealer provides you with the support you need. But I can help answer questions about the book or just say "Hello, thank you for writing," if that's all you want.

Enjoy the book!

Part I

What the @#$%&*!?

The 5th Wave

By Rich Tennant

Arthur inadvertently replaces his mouse pad with a Ouija board. For the rest of the day, he receives messages from the spectral world.

YOU WILL FORGET YOUR PASSWORD. YOUR HARD DISK WILL CRASH AAAHAHAHAHA

In this part . . .

*H*ow old is the oldest working computer? It's difficult to obtain an answer. I suppose some primal fear prevents one of those dusty old vacuum tube behemoths from the 1940s and 1950s from being powered up in their cozy museum displays. In fact, there probably isn't an electrical grid available today that can handle 13 million vacuum tubes coming to life at once.

Certainly there are old PCs, some still used in back offices around the world. But no, the computer that has been working the longest cannot be found on planet Earth. That's because the world's oldest continually operating computer is found onboard the *Voyager 1* spacecraft, which is some 10 *billion* miles away from the sun.

After more than 30 years of continuous operation, the *Voyager* computer is definitely a record holder, but it's not without problems of its own. Specifically, it's so old that it's difficult to maintain the ancient Earth-based computers that communicate with *Voyager.* So, frankly, there's really no such thing as the eternal, flawless computer. PC fatality is inevitable. Computers wheeze. They crash. They die. The chapters in this part of the book show you how to deal with it.

Chapter 1

Dealing with Disaster (While Keeping Your Sanity)

In This Chapter

▶ Discovering whether it's your fault
▶ Investigating what causes PC problems
▶ Emotionally dealing with a crash

*W*hen you notice that something is wrong with your computer, my guess is that the first thing you do is to blame yourself. Don't.

It's natural for any human to think, "What did I do?" any time that the computer goes wacky. Unlike the car, which people refer to as a "stupid thing" when it refuses to start or does something else unexpected, the computer seems to stare back at you innocently when trouble looms. With a sad face and an angelic disposition, the PC seems to sob, "Look what *you* did to me!" And the human feels the instant pang of guilt.

Yet, in over 20 years of dealing with a computer, I've discovered that only a few odd times have I either intentionally or accidentally caused my computer ill. In fact, I recommend that you adopt the same attitude I have when it comes to dealing with those inevitable computer boo-boos. It helps to know and recite my PC troubleshooting mantra:

> *Oh, my. The computer is behaving in a random and unexpected manner. I suppose that I shall have to look into this to see what can be done to remedy the situation.*

In only 32 words (and 32 is a Holy Number in computerdom because it's twice the Holy Number 16), the mantra lets you profess a neutral observation about the computer's sickly state. Accepting this positive attitude allows you to better fix the problem rather than futilely fix the blame.

Computers shouldn't crash, of course. They're not designed to. Really! But they do, for two reasons, neither of which is really your responsibility:

- ✔ The software has bugs in it.
- ✔ There is an utter lack of cooperation.

Most of all, the main reason that things go wrong in a computer is because

- ✔ Something has changed.

Dealing with that change and its consequences is the topic of this entire book.

The Jargon File: When the PC Screws Up

BSOD, the Blue Screen of Death: The BSOD is specifically a Microsoft Windows issue. Even today, when Windows walks off a cliff, the computer reverts to a text-screen mode and displays a cryptic error message. Whatever. Don't bother reading the message; the computer is dead, and resuscitation is out of the question.

bug: A *bug* is an error in a computer program. Despite the efforts of the best programmers, most computer software is riddled with bugs. Bugs cause computers to do the unexpected. Bad bugs can cause a computer to *hang*, or *crash*. Note that most of the worst bugs happen when you mix two programs together and they interact in some new and unexpected way. The term comes from the early days of computing, when a real bug (a moth) got stuck in the circuitry.

crash: *Crash* is a spectacular term describing how a computer surprisingly enters a nonworking state. Naturally, nothing on the computer actually crashes or even makes noise. There's no tearing of metal or popping and tinkling of broken glass, nor does anything explode. (I hope.) The crash is merely on a computer that suddenly stops operation, or it may even

continue, but in a sluggish manner or while exhibiting odd behavior.

freeze: See *hang*.

glitch: Whenever the computer does something strange or unexpected or behaves in a manner inconsistent with normal operation, that's a *glitch*. Glitches happen to everyone. Often, you fail to notice a glitch unless it does something that directly affects what you're doing. For example, you don't notice a sound glitch until you try to make your computer squawk. The sound may have not been working for weeks, but you notice it missing only when you otherwise would expect it. Such is the agony of the glitch.

hang: A totally unresponsive computer is said to be *hung*, or *hanged*. You could also use the term *frozen*, though *hang* is the accepted term used by computer nerds for generations.

infinite loop: Also called "stuck in a loop," the *infinite loop* is a bug where a program devises a situation that the computer cannot calculate its way out of. The result is a *hang*. Often times, recovery is possible by killing off the stuck program.

Why do computers have bugs?

In the real world, bugs — or, more accurately, *insects* — are a necessary part of the ecosystem. In a computer system, bugs are evil and entirely unnecessary. Yet they exist.

A *bug* is an error in a computer program. It's an accident (caused by an oversight on the part of the programmer), sloppy programming, or a lack of anticipation. For example, a programmer may not anticipate that a user may have a last name that's more than 25 characters long and that when you type the 26th character, the program waltzes off into La-La Land. Or, the programmer may type `variable_AM1` when he really meant to type `variable_AM2` or something similar.

No programmer creates bugs on purpose. In fact, most programming involves *removing* bugs as opposed to writing new code. So, a programmer types a set of instructions, runs them, fixes them, runs them, fixes them, and back and forth until all the bugs are (hopefully) worked out. Programmers even invite others *(beta testers)* to check their programs for bugs. After all, the programmers can't possibly figure out every possible way their software will be used. The object is to make the final product as bug free as possible.

When you discover a bug, which is the case with most PC trouble, you should report it to the software developers. They're the ones — not you — responsible for fixing the bug!

Why It's Not Your Fault

The only way a computer hardware or software problem could ever be your fault is when you built the hardware or wrote the software yourself. In fact, if you ever bother to read the software license that comes with any program, you'll discover that it's your fault that there are bugs in the software because you, the human, are actually running the program. That's weird, but so is our legal system. I rest my case.

And I reopen the case: Consider that when you're running a program, you're *using* your computer. You stumble across a bug. Thunk! The program crashes, and your data is gone, and you attempt seppuku with a USB flash drive. Did you cause the error? No. You were the trigger, but the fault isn't your own. Put that flash drive away!

In addition to bugs is the lack-of-cooperation issue. Software and hardware vendors test their products to ensure that things run properly. But they just cannot test every possible PC configuration. Chances are very good that somehow you will stumble across some software-hardware combination that wreaks havoc in the computer. Is that your fault? Technically, no, because the manufacturer should build reliable stuff.

So there you have it. The computer is a device that's not designed to crash, but through the odd chance of a software bug or some weird software-hardware mixture, it does crash, and crash often. Yes, I would quite agree that the reason it happens is *not* your fault.

How It Possibly Could Be Your Fault

You're not off the hook!

Rarely in my travels have I found someone who has somehow influenced the computer to go wacky. In fact, only a few things have been known to be directly related to human problems. These causes are covered in this section.

You did something new to the computer

Computers are very conservative; they don't like change. The most stable computer I have in my office has only Microsoft Word installed on it. Nothing else is used on that computer — not the Internet, no games, no nothing! The computer still crashes, but not as often as other systems I use.

The key to having a more stable computer is *not* to install new software or hardware. Unfortunately, this advice is nearly impossible to follow. It's not that the mere act of installing something new causes the computer to crash. No, it's just that installing something new introduces another combination into the system — a new potion into the elixir, so to speak — and an incompatibility or conflict may come from that. It's what I call the it-was-working-yesterday syndrome.

For example, one of my readers writes in and says, "The sound is gone from my computer! I had sound yesterday, but today it's all gone!" The first thing I ask is whether the person installed any new hardware or software. The answer is generally "Yes," and that's what prompted the problem.

Sometimes, you can forget that you have installed new stuff, which makes the problem seem random. After all, the computer is acting goofy, and it's easy to overlook that you downloaded some corny animation from the Internet yesterday. Yet that lone change was enough to alter the system.

- ✔ Yes, if you had one computer for every program, you would probably live a relatively crash-free, high-tech existence. But I don't recommend spending your money that way.

- ✔ Try to keep track of the times that you add, update, or change the hardware and software in your computer system.

- ✔ If possible, do research to determine the new stuff's compatibility with your existing computer system. Do that *before* you install. Heck, do it before you *buy*! The manufacturer's or developer's Web page lists known technical issues.

✔ I recommend that you get used to checking Windows logs, which keep track of any change to your computer system, whether you made the change or Windows did so behind your back. See Chapter 23 for more information about using the Event Viewer.

✔ These types of new hardware and software installations are why utilities such as System Restore are so popular. For more information, see the section in Chapter 4 about using System Restore.

You were bad and deleted files you shouldn't have deleted

Delete only those files you created yourself. It's when people go on file-hunting expeditions that they can get into trouble. In fact, deleting a swath of files is typically the *only* reason I recommend reinstalling Windows. After all, if you surgically remove a great portion of your operating system, reinstalling is the only way to get it back. (For all other problems, you generally have a solution *other than* reinstalling Windows.)

Here is what's okay to delete:

✔ Files (icons), folders, subfolders, and any files in those subfolders that exist in the Account Profile folder — the main folder where you save stuff

✔ Shortcut files on the desktop

✔ Files, folders, and subfolders that you created in the Public folder

✔ Compressed (Zip) files you have downloaded and installed

That's it!

Never, ever, delete any other files anywhere else on your computer, or on the computer network. I know that you may want to! The urge may be irresistible! You may go on a "cleaning" binge and yearn to mow down files like some crazed gardener with a multispeed weed whacker. Don't!

✔ You can also delete items from the Start menu, but I recommend doing that only for organizational purposes.

✔ No, I don't ever recommend reinstalling Windows. See Chapter 21 for the reasons.

Things to say when the computer crashes

Frack! A wonderful, forceful, yet completely G-rated term. Sounds like you-know-what, but utterly non-offensive. Bonus: It meets the qualifications for a genuine, English-language swear word:

✔ It must be a single syllable.

✔ It could be German.

✔ It's easy to say when intoxicated.

Oh, come on. . . . As if the computer could hear you, but you at least you shift the blame from yourself to the device. (My personal variation is "Come on, you pig!" for when the computer is stubbornly slow.)

Please! Please! Please! Pleading with the computer is very emotional, but it really doesn't help. Most users typically follow the pleading with "Oh, you sorry son-of-a-[female dog]."

What the —? A natural and common response to an unexpected situation. Can be followed by "Frack" or the true English-language swear word.

You stupid @#$%&!? piece of @#$%!! Very definitely getting it out of your system; this satisfying phrase just feels good to say. Note how blame is placed entirely on the computer. That's keeping the proper perspective. Good.

Other ways to remove files you didn't create yourself

The main complaint I get with my "Delete only those files you created yourself" maxim is that people find on the computer other files that they're just itching to delete themselves. These files include

✔ Internet cookies

✔ Temporary files (especially temporary Internet files)

✔ Wallpapers and extra media files

✔ Programs that are unwanted or no longer used

✔ Pieces of Windows they want to get rid of

✔ Teaser programs that come "free" with a new computer

✔ Stuff I can't think of right now

Avoid the temptation to manually delete these files! It gets you into trouble!

"But, Dan!" you whine, "A friend said that it's okay to manually delete my Internet cookies!"

Well . . . there are proper ways to delete the cookies, rid yourself of temporary files, clean and scour unwanted programs, and remove things you don't need.

Use those proper ways! Do not attempt to manually delete things yourself. You will get into trouble if you do.

  ✔ See Chapter 18 for information on dealing with cookies.

  ✔ Also see Chapter 25 for information on properly removing unwanted files from your computer.

  ✔ It's not your fault that the computer crashes — especially if you follow my advice in this section!

How old is your PC?

The older your computer is, the more likely it is to crash. I have no idea why. Systems that run stable for years may suddenly experience a growing number of glitches. It happens so often that I refer to it as "tired RAM." And, alas, no electronic equivalent of Geritol is available for your PC's tired RAM.

When your PC gets old, you have to prepare for inevitable quirkiness from it. You can try replacing the parts piece by piece, but eventually you wind up spending more on parts than you would for an entirely new system. No matter how much you love your computer, when it comes time for it to go, let it go.

  ✔ The average computer lives between four and six years.

  ✔ If you're in business, plan on replacing your PCs at or near the end of their lifespans. The boost in productivity from the new models alone is worth the expense.

  ✔ In government or in public schools, demand to replace computers every two years. (Other people's money is so much easier to spend.)

  ✔ For the home, keep your PC as long as you can. If it still works, great! Even if you do buy a new system, you can still use the old system for the kids to do homework or play games.

  ✔ I have a "bone yard" full of old computer pieces and parts. It's not all junk either; recently, I used parts from several old computers to create a file server for my network. I call him Franken-server.

  ✔ The main problem with older computers: parts! I have an older PC that can only "see" 8GB of hard drive storage, yet the smallest hard drive I can find for sale is 20GB. Oops.

  ✔ The first things to fail on any old PC are the things that move the most, such as disk drives, mice, and keyboards.

  ✔ A failing hard drive is typically the sign of a PC entering its twilight years. You will notice that the disk drive takes longer to access files and that Check Disk (or a similar disk utility) begins to report more disk errors and bad sectors. See Part IV for information on what to do next.

✔ Mice can fail long before the rest of the computer. This problem may not be a portent of the PC's ultimate demise; see Chapter 13 for more mouse information.

✔ When your PC dies, bid it adieu. Salvage what you can; no point in tossing out the monitor, mouse, keyboard, modem, or other "pieces parts" that could work on another computer. Properly dispose of the rest of the computer according to the PC disposal laws of your locality.

What You Can Do about It

Whether a computer glitch is your fault or not, it's your job to do something about it. This book is your best tool for helping you find a solution, so the next step is to continue reading.

Before you do, be aware that you go through certain emotional phases as you experience and deal with your computer's often irrational behavior. I have categorized these phases in chronological order:

✔ **Guilt:** Despite what you know or have read about computers, just about everyone feels guilty when the thing fouls up. "Is it my fault?" "What did I do?" Even after years of troubleshooting other people's computers, I still blame myself. It must be a human gene or an instinct we have — probably proof that mankind was created by robots from Dimension IX in 70,000 BC.

✔ **Anger:** Yeah, hit the monitor! Get it out of your system. "Stupid PC! Stupid PC! Why do you *always* crash when I'm doing something important! Arghghgh!" Yes, you have a right to expect obedience from your personal electronics. Too bad the drones in the manufacturer's Human Usability Labs don't express their anger so readily.

✔ **Fear or depression:** "This dumb thing will never work." Wrong! This book helps you eliminate your fear and get over the depression phase.

✔ **Acceptance:** Hey, it's a computer. It crashes. It could be your fault, but chances are that it's something else. You must deal with the problem. Be stronger and wiser than the computer.

✔ **Confidence:** "I have *Troubleshooting Your PC For Dummies!* I can solve any problem!" This book lists many solutions to many common glitches, but also helps you to troubleshoot just about any problem. And I have rarely met a PC problem that cannot be solved — some, by simply restarting your computer.

✔ **Success:** Your computer is back to normal, and everything is right with the universe. World peace is just around the corner! It's raining money! And bluebirds will help you get dressed in the morning. Let's all sing.

Chapter 2

Do This First

*T*hat feeling is pretty universal. Whether the computer sniffles or simply falls over dead, the icy grip of panic reaches out and tickles your chest. It's not a happy time, but it's not quite the end of the world. As a somewhat sane and seasoned expert, I present you with this chapter chock-full of my tried-and-true techniques for immediately dealing with pressing PC peril.

Some Quick Keyboard Things You Can Do

If the computer had ears, they would look like your PC's keyboard. Just as you would ask a human "Are you okay?" you can theoretically shout at your computer by doing some typing. Unlike real shouting (which you can feel free to try, but I'm not advising it), the computer may actually "hear" your typing and signal that it's okay. Well, unless the keyboard is dead. But there are ways around that as well!

Test the keyboard

To see whether the keyboard is responding, press the Caps Lock key. If the keyboard is alive and well, the Caps Lock light blinks on or off as you tap the Caps Lock key. It shows you that the keyboard is alive and paying attention.

On most PCs, the Caps Lock light is right on the Caps Lock key. In some cases, it might be near the key or along the top of the keyboard, marked with the text *Caps Lock* or the letter *A*. For wireless keyboards, the Caps Lock key might even be on the wireless dongle that hangs from the back of the PC's console.

✔ If the keyboard is dead, use the mouse to restart the computer, a subject covered later in this chapter. Restarting the computer awakens most snoozing keyboards.

✔ Alas, in some cases the keyboard can be alive, yet the computer is ignoring what it's saying. I have seen this situation more often with USB keyboards than with the keyboards that plug directly into a keyboard port on the PC. In these cases, the Caps Lock light does indeed blink on and off, but the computer is still deader than the dodo. Time to restart the computer.

✔ More keyboard troubleshooting information is offered in Chapter 13.

Press Ctrl+Z for immediate file relief

If you ever botch a file operation — moving, deleting, copying, renaming — *immediately* press the Undo key combination, Ctrl+Z. That undoes just about any file operation you can imagine.

✔ You must be prompt with the Ctrl+Z key press. The Undo command, also known as Edit⇔Undo, undoes only the most recent file operation. If you delete a file and then rename a file, the Undo command undoes only the renaming. You have to find another solution for any earlier problems that need fixing.

✔ Most people forget that editing an item or a submenu on the Start menu is really a *file* operation. When you screw up something on the Start menu, such as dragging an icon off the Start menu and onto the desktop, pressing Ctrl+Z fixes it right away. Remember that!

✔ Whoops! You cannot undo a Shift+Delete file operation. That's why Windows warns you that deleting a file in that manner renders the file permanently deleted.

✔ If Ctrl+Z, or the Undo command, doesn't work, give up. Either it's too late to undo the operation or the operation wasn't undoable in the first-place. You have to try something else.

Escape! Escape!

The Esc key on your keyboard is called Escape for a reason: It often gets you out of tight situations! Most scary things that happen on a PC can instantly be canceled or backed away from by pressing the handy Esc key.

Using the keyboard in Windows when the mouse doesn't work

Windows needs a mouse, so if you can't get your mouse to work, you need to rely on the keyboard to finish up whatever tasks you can and then restart the computer. Here are some handy key combinations you can use in place of some mouse techniques:

Ctrl+S: Saves a document to disk. Always save! If you can't work the commands in the Save As dialog box, just save the file wherever you can; you can move it to a better location the next time you start Windows or recover the mouse.

Esc: Cancels a dialog box; closes some windows.

Enter: Does the same thing as pressing the OK, or "default," button in a dialog box.

Tab: Moves between various gizmos in a dialog box. Try using the arrow keys or spacebar to activate the gizmos.

Shift+Tab: Moves you *backwards* between gizmos, opposite of the Tab key.

Ctrl+W or Alt+F4: Closes a window.

Win (the Windows key): Can be used to pop up the Start menu. You can then use the arrow keys and Enter to select items from the menu.

Ctrl+Esc: Pops up the Start menu when you have an older computer keyboard without a Windows key.

You can use other keys all throughout Windows to do just about anything the mouse can do, but that's missing the point here: When something is amiss, you should try to save your stuff and then restart Windows. Don't use a dead mouse as an excuse to show off your keyboard skills.

See the later section on restarting Windows when the mouse doesn't work. That typically fixes most mouse problems.

The Drastic Measure of Restarting Windows (Yet It Works)

Drastic is perhaps too severe a word. To me, it conjures up images of amputation or — worse — having to drink a barium shake. Ick. Yet, for some cosmic reason, the "drastic" step of restarting Windows tends to work out many of the more frustrating and seemingly devious computer foibles.

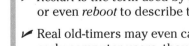

✔ *Restart* is the term used by Microsoft. Old-timers may use the term *reset* or even *reboot* to describe the same thing.

✔ Real old-timers may even call it a *warm boot.* Boots were popular with early computer users, though many of them chose to wear sandals.

Restarting Windows

Believe it or not, a simple restart of Windows can fix most problems: mouse, keyboard, modem, network, or graphics. Try it! If it doesn't work, you can move on to other solutions offered later in this book.

To restart Windows, follow these steps:

1. **Click the Start button.**
2. **Click the Shutdown menu button.**

   The Shutdown menu appears, as shown in Figure 2-1.

3. **Choose Restart.**

Start menu

Figure 2-1:
Various
options for
quitting
Windows.

Shutdown menu

Start button   Start menu power button   Shutdown menu button   Lock button

Maybe you want to wait for that download

If you're connected to the Internet and down-loading a program, you may want to wait a bit before restarting Windows. Even if the keyboard is dead and the mouse doesn't work, sit back and watch the download. If the data is still moving, you're okay. Wait for the download to complete. Then, after the information is fully received (or sent), you can attempt to restart Windows.

The reason this strategy works is that Windows can do several things at once. Although the mouse or keyboard may be dead and other programs running amok, the Internet connection may not be affected. Information may still fly in or out despite other parts of the computer playing possum. If you're lucky, you may get that file downloaded and not have to start over.

To determine whether the download is working, keep an eye on the progress meter. If it's moving, the data is flying. Good. Otherwise, if the meter is still for a few minutes, go ahead and restart Windows.

After you successfully complete these steps, Windows shuts down everything and immediately restarts. Hopefully, that clears up whatever dilemma existed.

- ✔ If you have any unsaved documents open, you're asked to save them before Windows restarts.

- ✔ If you're connected to the Internet, the act of restarting Windows disconnects you. That means if you're doing anything on the Internet, such as downloading a file, the task is interrupted and you have to start over when the computer comes back on.

- ✔ If the computer alerts you that others are connected to your computer and asks whether you're *sure* you want to restart, go ahead. Those "other users" are network connections, and if your computer is having a conniption, odds are good that those network users can't use your computer either.

- ✔ You must restart Windows! Don't just log off or switch users. You must choose the Restart option as described in this section.

- ✔ Sometimes, you may even have to turn off the computer to fix the problem. See the later section "Restarting when everything is dead."

- ✔ Some older programs running in command-prompt (DOS) windows may prevent the computer from shutting down. You must properly quit the command-prompt program and then try to restart Windows.

- ✔ Refer to Chapter 8 for more solutions to startup problems.

Restarting Windows when the mouse is dead but the keyboard is alive

If the mouse pointer is stuck to the screen like it was painted on, you have to rely on the keyboard to restart Windows. This task isn't as hard as it seems (and I suppose I'm saying that because of my years of experience in doing this):

1. **Press the Win key to pop up the Start menu.**

   If your keyboard lacks a Win key, press the Ctrl+Esc key combination.

2. **Press → three times.**

   That's the right-arrow key: Click, click, click. The third click pops up the Shutdown menu.

3. **Use the ↑ key to highlight the Restart menu option.**

4. **Press the Enter key.**

If you're prompted to save any documents, do so. Don't fret if you can't work the Save As dialog box; just save the document to disk and worry about relocating the file after the computer starts (and the mouse is, hopefully, back in action).

✔ You can also follow the steps in this section when the mouse is behaving in a stubborn or slow manner.

✔ If you have a USB mouse (one that connects to the PC by using a USB port rather than the mouse port), the problem may be with another USB device misbehaving. Consider disconnecting the USB scanner, disk drive, or other USB device to see whether that action remedies the stuck or sluggish mouse.

✔ You can use the computer's hard drive light as a way to read its pulse. When the hard drive light is flashing, the computer is still alive and working. If the light is dead, or if the light pulses regularly over a *long* period, the computer most likely is locked up.

✔ Be patient! The computer may be unbearably slow. Even so, as long as you're getting a response, it's better to shut down properly than to just unplug the sucker.

Restarting when everything is dead

Ah, life at the end of Dismal Street! The keyboard is clacking, but the computer is slacking. You could roll the mouse to the North Pole and back, but the mouse pointer on the screen is possessed by the devil. Time to be severely drastic:

1. **Press the computer's Power button to turn it off.**

   If briefly pressing the power button doesn't work, press and hold it for several seconds. On most modern computers, this press-and-hold action turns off the power.

   Yes, if things appear hopeless, just unplug the PC. Or — better still — flip the switch on the surge protector (or power strip or UPS).

2. **After the computer is off, wait a few seconds.**

   Honestly, I don't know why you wait, but you should. One tech guy told me that you wait to ensure that the hard drives properly "spin down," which is analogous to my washing machine, which I definitely don't want to stick my hand in until the thing has done its spin-down.

Why is just turning off a PC such a "bad thing?"

Back in the old days, it was common practice to turn a PC off and on again as a way to stop one program and start another. No one said not to. And it was fast: When you were using WordPerfect or Lotus 1-2-3, you reached around to the side of the PC and *thunk-thunk*, the off-on action stopped the program and restarted the computer. Simple and consistent.

The problem with the *thunk-thunk* technique was that it left bits and pieces of dead files all over a computer's hard drive. I once fixed a PC that had 40 percent of its total disk space occupied by dead and useless file fragments. Such detritus caused the computer to slow down dramatically, yet no one in that office had been told

of the proper way to quit a program, let alone shut down the computer.

Today's computers are smarter than the beasts of yesterday, plus a lot more is going on inside. The complexity of the modern computer requires that it be properly shut down, that various programs or *services* be stopped, and that any data waiting to be saved is properly saved.

If worse comes to worst and you need to turn off a computer manually, Windows is smart enough to recognize the improper shutdown, and it does the best job it can of fixing things back up when the computer starts again (which explains why Windows may take longer to start after you do disaster recovery).

Another techy type told me that you have to wait for the RAM to drain. I don't recall whether he was intoxicated, but I'll accept his reasoning.

Finally, I think that the wait period prevents some people from doing a quick on-off double flip of the power switch, which has the potential of damaging some of the computer's components. No, it's just best to wait a tad before turning the thing on again.

3. Turn the computer back on.

Punch the button on the computer or turn the power strip or UPS back on. If you do the latter, you may still have to thump the computer's Power button to wake it up.

Hopefully, the restart resurrects your keyboard or mouse and gets you back on your way. If not, you can try ever more things, as covered in this book.

- ✔ Older PCs had big red switches or on-off rocker buttons that really, really did turn off the power. Amazing.

- ✔ Some older PCs even had reset buttons, which you could use rather than power switches to wake up dead or even catatonic PCs. I miss reset buttons.

- ✔ Yes, I know: Some computer cases still have reset buttons on them. But the buttons don't seem to work like they did in the old days. Alas.

What to do about "restart guilt"

Many people feel this pang of guilt when they're forced to restart their computers — even when they have no other course of action. I call it *restart guilt*. It most likely occurs because older versions of Windows came back to life with an ominous message:

```
Windows was not shutdown properly.
```

Oh, no! Which computer gods have ye offended? Peril! Doom!

Happily for everyone, the folks at Microsoft recognized restart guilt and removed the "Windows was not shutdown properly" message from the most recent versions of Windows. Even so, the computer recognizes that it was improperly shut down and performs a quick check of the system to ensure that everything is okay. (Specifically, the Check Disk program is run to ensure that no file or disk damage occurred.)

Don't feel guilty about restarting! If you're forced to unplug the computer to get its attention, so be it. I'm sure that computer scientists in the 1950s eventually had to resort to unplugging their mammoth systems to wrest control when something went haywire. You're no different. (Well, you may not be wearing a white lab coat while you compute.)

✔ The Check Disk program (or utility) scans the computer's hard disks for errors, missing files, corrupted data, and other annoying problems. In the case of shutting down a computer improperly, Check Disk locates the lost file clusters that inevitably appear during an improper shutdown. The lost file clusters are deleted, which is the best course of action to take.

✔ Also see Chapter 20 for soothing words of advice when you just can't get the computer to quit all by itself.

✔ If the computer starts in Safe mode, a hardware glitch or some other anomaly may need fixing. Flip on over to Chapter 24 for more information.

✔ No, it's not required or necessary to restart in Safe mode after every crash or system reset.

Chapter 3

Is It a Hardware Problem or a Software Problem?

• •

In This Chapter

▶ Finding the criminal — hardware or software

▶ Discovering how things fail

▶ Asking yourself some questions

▶ Checking the hardware

▶ Using diagnostic tools

• •

I call it the runaround, and nearly everyone who has a PC has experienced it at one time or another: You have a printer problem, so you phone up technical support for your printer. After wading through the bog of voice-mail menus, you finally reach a tech person who says "Oh, that's a Windows problem." So you phone Microsoft, and someone there says "You really need to call your computer dealer because you didn't buy Windows directly from us." And then you phone your dealer, who says "That's a printer problem." And so it goes.

So, can anyone solve your problem, or is technical support all about passing the buck? Don't answer just yet! That's because there's a valid issue here, and that is whether your problem is related to software or hardware. A computer system is composed of both, so it helps to know whether you have a software or hardware problem first and then ask for the proper technical support if you're unable to resolve the problem on your own. This chapter is about telling the difference between software sorrows and hardware hardships.

Whose Problem Is It?

Step 1 in any troubleshooting investigation should be eliminating the possibility that you have a hardware problem. After all, if the device is working properly, you can fairly assume that it's the software controlling the device that's fouling things up.

✔ *Hardware* is anything physical in your computer. If you can touch it, it's hardware.

✔ Storage media — disk drives, flash memory, media cards, CDs, and DVDs, for example — are all hardware. The programs *(software)* are encoded on the storage media, but that doesn't transform the media into software.

✔ Software controls the hardware. Specifically, a program called a *driver* is used to control every bit of hardware in the PC. If the hardware itself functions fine, the real problem lies in the driver. Either the driver needs updating, or other software in the computer is conflicting with the driver.

✔ Drivers are also known as *device drivers.*

Is it a hardware problem?

Specific examples of hardware and software problems (plus their solutions!) are located throughout Part II of this book. Generally speaking, however, hardware problems crop up suddenly and are not random.

For example, when the printer breaks, it stops working. That's a hardware problem. However, if you cannot print when you use Windows Mail but you can print in every other program, that's a software problem. The printer is being affected by one particular program, Windows Mail. Otherwise, the hardware apparently works just fine.

If the computer shuts itself off half an hour after you start using it — no matter which programs you run — that's a hardware problem. It isn't random. It's generally one half-hour, and it's most likely caused by something getting too hot inside the case — again, hardware.

If the tray on the optical drive no longer slides open — yup: hardware.

The Enter key doesn't work. Hardware.

Only when the problem seems more random or unpredictable is the software to blame, though that's not a hard-and-fast rule (which is one reason that troubleshooting is so tough).

How hardware fails

Hardware can fail electronically or physically. Both ways are fairly easy to spot.

Electronic failure of hardware usually happens within one month of purchase. If the electronics don't work or were cheap or improperly assembled or installed, or if the hardware is just bad, it fails right away. That's good because the warranty on just about any computer electronics covers such failures, and whatever goes kaput is replaced free of charge.

The physical failure of hardware happens only when the hardware moves. Fortunately, a PC has few moving parts on it: the disk drives and keyboard.

When a disk drive stops spinning, it's dead! It needs replacement. Fortunately, the disk drive usually has a period of intermittent errors, stops and starts, and hits and misses before this happens, which gives you plenty of warning.

Removable disk drives may have problems with their doors or eject mechanisms, which are obvious to spot.

Finally, the keyboard can fail. Cheap ones can go quickly, usually all at once. The better-made keyboards may lose a key here and there, but they can be fixed. Well, better than fixing, any keyboard can be replaced, and it's inexpensive to do so.

✔ A cheap keyboard is one that utterly lacks a "clack" or "click" when you type; the keys feel mushy. That's because the keyboard is most likely a touch-membrane model with spring-activated keys. If the membrane, which is like a flimsy rubber sheet, breaks, the keyboard is finished.

✔ Nearly all hardware is replaceable, which is often cheaper than fixing things. For example, an optical drive can be fixed, but often it's just cheaper to get another optical drive as a replacement.

✔ Avoid repair outfits that attempt to fix electronic components. Yes, even electronic components (the motherboard or plug-in cards, for example), can easily and cheaply be replaced if they're damaged. With modern computers, it's often easier to replace things than to repair them.

Is it a software problem?

Of the two types of problems — hardware and software — software is more common because it's the software that does everything in a computer.

Alas, software trouble is more devious than hardware trouble. Consider that most software has unknown bugs in it, and no software developer fully tests programs in all possible configurations. Tracking the problem can be *tough.*

The good news is that software problems can be predictable. If you find that choosing an option in a program causes the computer to lock up — and it behaves that way time and time again — it's a software bug. If the mouse stops working in only one program, it's a software problem.

The insidious thing, of course, is that it may not be that particular program causing the problem. For example, Internet Explorer may lock up tight whenever you visit a certain Web page, but it may be a Web plug-in that's causing the thing to crash — very nasty, but at least you have properly identified the problem as software and not as hardware.

Some good questions to ask yourself

To help determine whether you have a software problem or a hardware problem, ask yourself some basic questions:

- ✔ Have you installed any new hardware recently?
- ✔ Have you installed any new software recently?

Remember that computers don't like change. Change introduces new elements into the mix. Sometimes, changing something works without a hitch. But, if you have a busy computer — one with lots of software installed and many peripherals — adding something new may be that final pebble in the gears that grinds your PC to a halt.

- ✔ Adding something new introduces the it-was-working-yesterday syndrome.
- ✔ The reason for the popularity of such utilities as System Restore in Windows XP and Windows Vista is that they effectively uninstall new hardware and software and restore your computer to the state it was in when it last worked best.
- ✔ See Chapter 4 for more information on using the System Restore utility.

- ✔ Remember that adding new hardware also adds new software. Most hardware requires device drivers in order to work. This explains why it's tough sometimes to determine whether it's the hardware that doesn't work or whether it's just the software not cooperating.

Hardware Things to Check When You Smell Trouble

The first things to check when you suspect hardware trouble are the connections, cables, and whatnot that link all the various pieces and parts of your PC:

- ✔ Is everything properly plugged in and receiving power? (Are the power strip on-off switches in the On position, for example?)
- ✔ Are cables snuggly plugged into their sockets?

✔ Are cables snuggly plugged into the *proper* sockets? (The Line In and Microphone jacks look identical on every PC, but *there is a difference!*)

✔ Are *both ends* of the cable connected?

Let me relate a story from my old computer consulting days: Once upon a time, I made $60 in two minutes by plugging a modem's phone cord into a phone jack in the wall. The business wasn't happy paying my fee, but the people there learned an expensive lesson.

Listen!

Is the computer making noise? All computers have internal fans designed to regulate the temperature inside the box. If the fan goes, the computer gets too hot and fails.

Do you hear the fan? Poke your head around the back to see whether the fan is spinning, just to be sure. If not, you have hardware trouble.

✔ Not all PCs have a fan. The Apple iMac computer comes without a fan. I know that some older microcomputers and laptops come without internal fans. I suppose that a PC here or there could be without a fan, so if you know of one, please don't write in to tell me that I'm wrong.

✔ Some PCs can get hot even with their fans spinning. For such systems, you can get fan "upgrades" by adding a second fan to the PC's case.

✔ Laptops have internal fans, but they still run notoriously hot. To help keep your laptop cool, consider an external cooling pad. The pad contains several fans, and you set your laptop atop the thing. The result is a cooler-running and much happier laptop.

✔ Sometimes, the fan is integrated into the power supply. In that case, you need to buy a new power supply to replace the fan.

Another unfortunate software problem: Malware

A sad fact of computing is that some software programs are specifically designed to do nasty things to your computer. These programs are viruses or worms or spyware, but they all fall under the general software category of *malware,* which means *mal*icious soft*ware.*

Malware arrives in a number of ways, mostly sneaking in from the Internet, either from a suspicious Web page or riding piggyback on a simple e-mail message. The unwanted program then opens like a mushroom cloud, distributing havoc and chaos throughout your computer system.

There are a variety of ways to fight malware, many of which are provided within Windows itself. Refer to Chapter 24 for more information.

✔ If you have to wait for a fan or new power supply to arrive in the mail but you still need to use the computer, you can operate it without the case's lid, as shown in Figure 3-1. See how I used a little fan to help keep the PC's innards cool? I don't recommend this solution for the long term.

Touch!

Is the computer hot? Electronics do get hot, but they're designed to dissipate the heat. Heat is a Bad Thing for electronics. It causes errors. In fact, your computer manual probably has a "recommended operating temperature" guide somewhere — maybe even on the console's back panel.

✔ If the computer is hot, turn it off. Get it fixed.

✔ Also check a peripheral's power brick to see whether it gets too hot. Power bricks (more properly, *transformers*) get warm but should never be hot. If they're hot, they need to be replaced.

✔ Heat also refers to the room temperature. Generally speaking, the hotter the room, the more likely the computer is to malfunction. If it's hotter than 80 degrees where your computer sits, turn the thing off.

Figure 3-1:
Don't try this
at home.

Check the monitor

To do a quick check of the monitor, first ensure that it's properly connected and turned on: A monitor plugs into both a power source and the computer. A CRT, or "glass," monitor plugs directly into a socket. An LCD monitor typically plugs into a power brick (transformer) and then into the wall socket.

The monitor may look dead, but the brightness may just be turned down all the way. Fiddle with the knobs to try to get a reaction.

Modern monitors are quite smart. If yours doesn't receive a signal from the computer, it displays a message telling you so. It says No input or No signal or something equally cryptic or obtuse, but conveys the general meaning of "I'm not connected to anything sending me a signal."

Some monitors have more than one input. My Mitsubishi monitor has an A-B switch for viewing output from more than one source. Some high-end monitors have both VGA and BNC connectors for the signal, plus corresponding buttons on the panel to choose either input.

- ✔ It's quite common for the power light on a monitor to turn green when the monitor is up and running. When the monitor isn't receiving a signal, the light turns yellow or flashes.

- ✔ The light also turns yellow when the computer is in Sleep, Stand By, or Hibernate mode.

  Speaking of which, tap the Ctrl or Enter key on the keyboard to see whether the computer is just sleeping and has shut down the monitor.

- ✔ On some computers, you have to punch the Power/Sleep button to wake it up.

- ✔ If you still have your hearing, most CRT (glass) monitors make a high-pitched whistle, to indicate that they're on. The top of the CRT monitor is also warm to the touch.

Other hardware tricks to try

This book is full of hardware tricks and tests you can use to determine whether your problem is hardware or software. See the proper chapter in Part II for more information on specific pieces of hardware.

Using Software to Check for Hardware Problems

It's quite possible to use software to test the computer's hardware. Smart software knows where to poke around and which kind of responses are expected. If something is amiss, software can generally report it. After all, why not make the computer do the work? Isn't that what it's for?

The Device Manager

Windows comes with a handy tool called the *Device Manager,* which you can use to detect any hardware errors that are bugging Windows. You see, despite its lousy reputation, Windows is quite tolerant of sloppy hardware. Many claim that it's a fault of Windows — and it may be, but that's not my point: Checking with the Device Manager generally confirms that you have a hardware problem.

To display the Device Manager window, heed these steps:

1. **Open the Control Panel.**

   You may find a link to the Control Panel from the Start button's menu.

2. **Open the Device Manager icon.**

3. **Type the administrator's password or click the Continue button, if necessary.**

   The Device Manager is a sensitive area, so you need administrator privilege to access it.

The Device Manager is shown in Figure 3-2.

In Figure 3-2, you see the telltale sign that something is wrong with the computer: The sound adapter in this computer isn't working properly. The triangle (which is yellow) flags any misbehaving hardware right there in the Device Manager window. Further examination shows that a new driver is needed to make the sound adapter functional.

Close the Device Manager window when you're done looking at it.

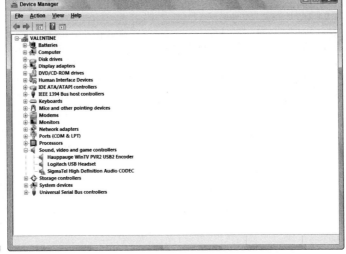

Figure 3-2:
The Device
Manager
flags a mis-
behaving
doodad.

So, does the Device Manager disclose hardware or software problems? Potentially both. In Figure 3-2, a software fix is required to get the hardware gizmo working, but you could also remove the offending hardware and install something more compatible, which also addresses the problem. But between software and hardware, the audio program illustrated in Figure 3-2 is really a software issue.

✔ See Chapter 24 for more information on how to use the Device Manager.

✔ You can find information on how to reinstall a device driver (software) in the various chapters of Part II that deal with specific devices (video and sound, for example).

Diagnostic tools

In addition to using the Device Manager (see the preceding section), you can use software diagnostic tools to determine the status of just about any hardware component in your system. So, when you suspect trouble, you can run the diagnostic program to determine whether your hardware is operating properly.

Because these tools are a hardware thing, they generally come with the hardware itself and are not a part of Windows. To find the tools, look for the bonus disks that came with your computer when it was new. Otherwise, you can find the disks with the hardware device inside the box it came in.

One diagnostic tool that comes with Windows is the DirectX Diagnostic Tool, shown in Figure 3-3. This tool displays information about the DirectX driver, which is used by games, graphics, and audio programs in Windows.

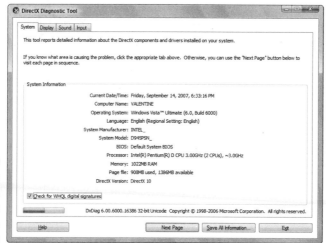

Figure 3-3:
The DirectX
Diagnostic
Tool.

To run the DirectX Diagnostic Tool, follow these steps:

1. **Summon the Run dialog box.**

   Choose Run from the Start menu, or press Win+R on the keyboard.

2. **Type dxdiag.**

3. **Click OK.**

The DirectX Diagnostic Tool scans your computer, displays several screens of information, and notes any errors or problems along the way. Click the Next Page button to peruse the information. Click the Exit button when you're done.

Your computer may come with a hardware diagnostic tool, accessed from the PC's *Setup* program, the program that's run when the computer first starts. A message appears, such as `Press the <F2> key to enter Setup`. (The key to press can be any key. Commonly, the Delete key or F1 is also used.) Inside the Setup program, you may find a diagnostic tool you can use to test all the PC's components.

✔ One thing you cannot test for in most PCs is the RAM. Programs must run in RAM, so a diagnostic program that tests RAM is a questionable thing in the first place. How can the program test memory if the program must reside in memory to begin with?

✔ Computers with failing RAM are generally a total mess anyway. It's best to have your dealer or the manufacturer test your PC's RAM; those people have the proper equipment to give your computer's memory a good once-over.

✔ Diagnostic programs were all the rage in the early 1990s — not that anyone needed them suddenly; it was just one of those computer crazes. (And, it's probably why the TV show *Star Trek: The Next Generation* used the word *diagnostic* more than any other computer term of the day.)

✔ You can get two types of diagnostic programs. One is only a report program; it simply reports which hardware resources you have in your computer. The program doesn't test anything. The other type of diagnostic program tests your hardware and displays the results along with suggestions and recommendations.

✔ It's funny how the word *diagnostic* tends to lose its meaning the more you say it.

Chapter 4

The R Chapter (Reinstall, Restore, Recycle, Recover)

*F*or some reason, many useful troubleshooting tools start with the letter *R*. This is most likely related to the rich resource of words in English that deal with happy things and also start with the letter *R: rescue, recovery, repair, restore, refund, recline, resolve, remember, refresh, rejoice, rich, recreation, redhead, rum, Rio,* and the *rest. Really!*

With computers, the R retinue repeats: Restore, Reinstall, Recycle, and Recover. With those fine utilities, you can assist your PC in respite from a range of ravages and risks. Indeed, this chapter is brought to you by the letter *R*.

Restoring from the Recycle Bin

To ease the panic that sets in when you can't find a file, you need to do two things: First, use the Search command to try to locate the file (this topic is covered in Chapter 9); second, check the Recycle Bin to see whether the file was accidentally deleted:

1. **Open the Recycle Bin icon on the desktop.**

   If the Recycle Bin icon cannot be found on the desktop, open a Windows Explorer window (press Win+E on the keyboard) and choose the Recycle Bin from the list of folders displayed on the left side of the window.

2. Choose Details from the toolbar's View button menu.

The Recycle Bin window, shown in Figure 4-1, displays information about deleted files in several columns: Name, Original Location, Date Deleted, and Size, for example. The number of columns you see depends on the width of the window. (You can pick and choose which columns to display; see the nearby sidebar, "Showing more columns in the Recycle Bin".) Use the column headings to help you quickly locate files you have deleted, as covered in the sections that follow.

✔ To recover a deleted file, click it and choose the toolbar button titled Restore This Item.

✔ To recover more than one file, press the Ctrl key and hold it down as you click the files you want to restore.

✔ Files are restored to their original location. To restore a file to another folder, you must first restore it to its original folder and then move the file after it's restored. (Make a note of the location to where the file is restored.)

✔ You cannot restore files that were deleted using the Shift+Delete keystroke. Those files cannot be recovered by using any of the tools in Windows. (Various third-party tools, such as Norton Utilities, might be able to recover these files.)

✔ *Rubbish* is yet another R word, underused by Americans but right at home in the commonwealth.

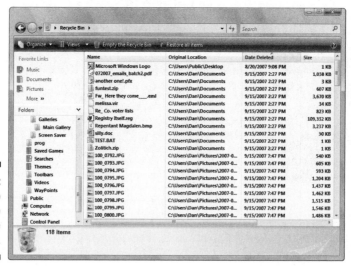

Figure 4-1:
Setting up the Recycle Bin for file recovery.

Showing more columns in the Recycle Bin

For some reason, I don't feel that pretty icons show me enough information when it comes to the serious issue of restoring a file. That's one reason I prefer Details view for the Recycle Bin (refer to Figure 4-1). If you want even more information displayed about dormant files, you will be pleased to know that the number of columns displayed, and therefore the information about each file, is adjustable.

To see more columns in the Recycle Bin window, such as the Type or Date Created columns, right-click any column heading. A pop-up menu appears, listing all the potential columns displayed in Details view. To add a column, choose it from the menu. Columns currently displayed have a check mark by them. Or, you can choose the More item from the bottom of the pop-up menu, to use the Choose Details dialog box to select columns as well as change the order in which the columns appear. Click OK when you're done with your selections.

Restoring a file you deleted recently

To find a file that you suspect was just deleted, click the Date Deleted heading in the Recycle Bin window (refer to Figure 4-1). When the triangle next to Date Deleted points *down,* the most recently deleted files appear at the *top* of the list: Scroll to the top of the list and pluck out the files you want recovered.

Restoring a deleted file when you know its name

To locate a file by name, click the Name heading in the Recycle Bin window. That sorts the files alphabetically by name, either from A to Z or from Z to A, depending on how many times you click the Name heading.

To quickly scroll to a given filename, type its first letter on the keyboard. To find all files beginning with *N,* for example, press the N key.

Restoring a deleted file when you know which application created it (by file type)

Searching for files by type allows you to locate a file when you don't know its name but you do remember which program created it. To do so, click the Type heading in the Recycle Bin window to sort the files by their file types (or by which programs created them).

Using System Restore

The System Restore utility in Windows is an excellent way to recover from just about any mishap, but specifically it works best for those it-was-working-yesterday situations. With System Restore, you can turn back the clock on your entire computer system — yes, back to the good old days when things were working normally.

Working magic with System Restore

The System Restore utility works by setting various restore points. A *restore point* is a record of your computer's settings, from settings made in Windows to options set for various pieces of hardware and all sorts of potentially mischievous things.

In Windows Vista, restore points are set regularly, at least once a day. A restore point is also set when you install new software or whenever Windows updates itself.

You can, optionally, set your own restore points. For example, if you plan to upgrade or change hardware, mess around with network settings, modify your Internet or network settings, edit the Start menu, rearrange files, uninstall programs — or do just about anything other than get your work done — set a restore point. You will thank yourself later.

Setting a restore point

Suppose that you're about to install that new wireless router. Yep, that sounds like an example of a good time to set a new restore point. Here's what you would do *before* setting things up:

1. **Open the Control Panel.**

2a. **From the Control Panel Home, choose System and Maintenance and then System.**

2b. **From the Control Panel Classic view, open the System icon.**

   Either way, you get to the System window.

3. **Choose Advanced System Settings.**

   You find the Advanced System Settings link on the left side of the window.

4. **Enter an administrator's password or click the Continue button if you're prompted to do so.**

   The good old System dialog box appears, familiar to Windows users of days gone by.

5. **Click the System Protection tab.**

   Ah, finally.

6. **Click the Create button.**

7. **Enter a restore point description.**

   The restore point description appears when you later use System Restore. Therefore, it helps to be descriptive here.

   Good restore point descriptions are `Installing new hard drive`, `Changing resolution for new monitor`, `Green ooze emitting from console`, or anything else that may remind you in the future of what the problem could be.

   Bad restore point descriptions are `Installing` and `Stuff` and `This will certainly make it appear to the boss that I'm actually working and not just messing with the computer again`.

8. **Click the Create button.**

   The new restore point is created. Sit back and be entertained by the simplistic, time-passing Windows thermometer animation.

9. **Click OK.**

   You're done. System Restore closes its window and sneaks off. You can, optionally, close any other windows you have lying open after this operation.

Now you can proceed to mess with your system. Those are the times when the system may not behave as you have expected. Not to worry! You have the safety net of a recent restore point, which you can bring the system back to if things don't work as expected.

✔ Windows automatically sets restore points when you install new software, so there's no need to do so manually.

✔ Setting a restore point is done in the System Properties dialog box, not in the System Restore program itself. This is a major change from previous versions of Windows.

✔ Get creative with that restore point description! It's valuable information that may come in handy later if something goofs up.

✔ Windows attempts to create automatic restore points as long as you leave the system on for a length of time. I leave my computers on 24 hours a day, so I notice restore points created just about every day, typically around midnight.

✔ Windows may not, however, create restore points if System Restore has been disabled by you or by a computer virus. See Chapter 23 for information on what to do in that case.

Restoring the system

When your PC suffers from it-was-working-yesterday syndrome or whenever evil electrons from the planet Woe thwart your attempts to ""fix"" the computer, you can attempt a system restore. (My first advice is to restart Windows, which is covered in Chapter 2, and then run System Restore.)

Follow these steps to restore your system:

1. **Close any open windows or programs, to safely save any unsaved information.**

   Restoring the system restarts the computer, so it's best to close and save now, before you begin the restore process. See Chapter 22 for a nifty tip on shutting down programs.

2. **Start System Restore.**

   From the Start menu, choose Programs⇨Accessories⇨System Tools⇨System Restore.

   If a problem occurs or System Restore doesn't start, see Chapter 23 for help.

3. **If prompted, enter an administrator's password or click the Continue button to proceed.**

   The System Restore window presents two options for restoring the computer. The first one is the most recent restore point set by Windows. That's probably your best choice, unless you set another restore point or need to restore your PC to an earlier time.

4. **Choose either Recommended Restore or Choose a Different Restore Point.**

5. **Click the Next button.**

   If you chose Recommended Restore, skip to Step 8.

6. **Choose a restore point.**

   A list of restore points is displayed, listed by date and time as well as by description, similar to what's shown in Figure 4-2.

If necessary, select the Show Restore Points Older Than 5 Days check box to see some ancient restore points.

Select the restore point that works best for you.

7. Click the Next button.

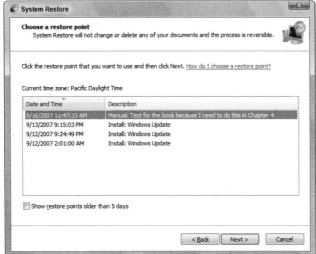

Figure 4-2:
Choose the
restore
point here.

8. Click the Finish button.

Read the scary warning. The bottom line is that the System Restore process is fully reversible, so if System Restore makes things worse, you can undo its changes.

9. Click Yes to confirm the scary warning.

Windows restores and. . . .

Don't be fooled! Your computer must restart, even when it seems like it's just sitting there.

10. Log in after Windows restarts.

After Windows starts again, you must log in and then wait for another message from System Restore before you can start your work. Be patient! When the operation is fully complete, you see a message saying `System Restore completed successfully`, with a summary of what happened.

11. Click the Close button.

Hopefully, things wind up just fine, and the kinks are worked out of the system.

I have suggested this operation to many of my readers with computer problems, and most of the time it meets with tremendous success. If not, further troubleshooting is needed. In fact, if System Restore doesn't fix the problem, it's most likely a hardware problem that needs further attention (replacement, for example).

Undoing a System Restore

If the System Restore operation fails to address the issue or you just would rather have not performed the operation in the first place, you can undo the changes. Heed these steps, and do so right after performing a System Restore:

1. **Start System Restore.**

   Complete Steps 1 and 2 from the preceding section.

2. **Choose the first option, which is now titled Undo System Restore.**

3. **Click the Next button.**

4. **Click the Finish button.**

Heed the directions on the screen, and watch as your computer is restored to its previous state.

Restoring Files from a Backup

The second half of the computer backup operation is Restore. Hopefully, you never have to restore. Despite that, you definitely should back up your computer's data regularly. Having that *backup,* or safety copy of your data, is a good thing. The copy is a guarantee that you're better able to recover lost or damaged files — a better guarantee than any other troubleshooting tool available to Windows.

Information in the sections that follow describes how to restore files from a backup. This information is based on the Windows Vista Backup program, though it's similar in philosophy to all backup programs.

  ✔ *Backing up* is the process of creating a duplicate of the information on your computer's hard drive. The backup itself is the copy. See Chapter 26 for more detailed information.

  ✔ Tools such as System Restore would be completely unnecessary now if more people made backups of their hard drives.

  ✔ For Restore to work, you must have a recent backup handy.

Restoring a single file, folder, or more

If you can't find a particular file or you lose it or permanently delete it, you can always recover it from a recent backup. Follow these steps:

1. **From the Start menu, choose All Programs⇨Accessories⇨System Tools⇨Backup Status and Configuration.**

   The Backup Status and Configuration window materializes.

2. **Click the button on the left, Restore Files.**

3. **Choose Restore Files from the two options presented on the left.**

   The Restore Files window appears. The option to restore files from the most recent backup is preselected for you. That's probably the best option for now; if not, you can repeat these steps later.

4. **Click the Next button.**

   The next window lists the files or folders you selected to restore to your computer — for example, a file you deleted or lost or one that was corrupted, mangled, folded, spindled, or mutilated.

5. **Click the Add Files button to restore an individual file; click the Add Folders button to recover entire folders (and contents).**

   Either way, a dialog box appears that works just like either an Open or Browse dialog box. The dialog box peers into the contents of the most recent (or older) backup and displays the files that were backed up.

6. **Use the dialog box to locate a folder or file to restore.**

   Choose the file by manipulating the dialog box's controls.

7. **When you find the file or folder, click to select it.**

   You can choose a folder only when you've begun your search by clicking the Add Folders button.

8. **Click the Add button.**

   The file or folder appears in the list of files to restore.

9. **Repeat Steps 5 through 8 until you pluck out all the files or folders to restore.**

10. **Click the Next button.**

11. **Choose to restore the files in their original location.**

   The only time you select a new location is when you're recovering a previous edition of a file to compare with the current edition. That way, the older, recovered file (or folder) doesn't overwrite the present one.

12. **Click the Start Restore button.**

    The Restore process works through the backup archive, by pulling out those files or folders you selected and replacing them to their original locations.

    If the original file still exists, you're prompted on what to do. If in doubt, choose the option to copy but keep both files. Then make a note of things so that you can review the files later, to see which is best to keep.

13. **Click the Finish button.**

    You're done. You can, optionally, close the Backup Status and Configuration window.

I would say that, of all the utilities I have ever used on any computer, the restore half of Backup is the most satisfying. It's not enough knowing that you have the backup copy. It's a great feeling when you actually get to restore a file and recover something that you thought was lost forever.

Restoring an application

Alas, it's fairly difficult to pluck out a single application from a backup disk. Applications in Windows don't really install themselves in a specific place. Therefore, trying to locate all the bits and pieces of a program that may be scattered all over a hard drive is a questionable operation.

Rather than restore an application, just reinstall it. See the section "Reinstalling Stuff," later in this chapter.

Restoring the entire hard drive

When disaster strikes, you can use your backup to restore your entire hard drive — for example, if your computer is infected with one of those nasty, nonremovable viruses. Or, suppose that your 12-year-old "computer genius" cousin decides to "optimize" your Windows folder. It's those severe times that call for a full hard drive restore operation.

Restoring the entire hard drive requires that you have backed it up first by using Windows Complete PC Backup. Refer to Chapter 26 for details. If you have not backed up your entire hard drive, refer to the nearby sidebar, "More R words: Reconstruct and rebuild."

More R words: Reconstruct and rebuild

When total disk disaster strikes, you do one of two things. First, you cry like a baby. Although that may sate you emotionally, it doesn't really fix the problem with the computer. So, moving on, the second thing you do is begin the process of reconstructing the information on your computer's hard drive.

The first step is to reinstall the operating system, Windows. You do this with a recovery disc that came with the PC or with the original Windows disc. If possible, try the Repair option that comes up when you first start the computer from the recovery disc. If that doesn't work, reinstall Windows just as you would on a new computer.

The second step is to reinstall your programs. As I recommend in my book *PCs For Dummies,* you should have the discs that came with any software purchased for your computer. I keep the discs in their original boxes. Reinstall your software, one application at a time.

The final step is to recover your data. If you have a backup, you can recover from it. If not, basically you're screwed, and you have to re-create all your data files or just start all over. If that sounds depressing — it is! Bone up on backing up your computer by reading Chapter 26 right now!

To recover the entire hard drive, you need to start the computer by using a Windows CD or DVD. After a spell, you see an option titled Repair Your Computer. Choose it. Then run Windows Complete PC Restore to reinstall Windows, your software, and all your stuff from the Windows Complete PC Backup you made earlier.

Any subsequent backups you make after you complete your Windows Complete PC Backup can then be installed after you cover your entire computer.

If your computer didn't come with restore discs or the original Windows disc, contact the manufacturer.

Restoring a Previous Version of a File or Folder

A new trick with Windows Vista is the Restore Previous Version command. It allows you to wind back the clock on your files, by recovering an older version of a file that you may have deleted, changed, or even overwritten. Using the Restore Previous Version command is the quickest way to get your data back. Here's how it works:

1. **Open the folder containing the file or folder you want to restore.**

2. **Right-click the file or folder to restore.**

Suppose it's a file you just overwrote with a new file of the same name. Oops! But there's hope. . . .

3. **Choose Restore Previous Version from the pop-up menu.**

   The file's Properties dialog box appears, with the Previous Versions tab forward, as shown in Figure 4-3. The dialog box lists previous versions of the file.

4. **Choose a previous version.**

5. **Click the Restore button.**

   If prompted, decide whether to replace or merely copy the restored version of the file.

6. **Click the Finish button when you're done.**

7. **Close the file's Properties dialog box.**

Note that whereas Restore Previous Version may seem like a godsend, it isn't a 100 percent reliable replacement for Backup and Restore. I still highly recommend that you regularly back up your PC's data. See Chapter 26.

Previous Versions works only when System Restore has been activated for the drive. See Chapter 23 for information on enabling or disabling System Restore.

Figure 4-3:
Restore
Previous
Version
lurks here.

Reinstalling Stuff

Sometimes, the solution to a problem is as easy as reinstalling software. You just find the original copy or distribution discs, pop 'em in the computer, and reinstall. Problem fixed (most of the time).

Consider reinstalling an application for any of the following reasons:

- ✔ The application is behaving in a manner inconsistent with the way it once behaved.

- ✔ All files "owned" by that application are now owned by some other application, and that new ownership is vexing you.

- ✔ Files belonging to the application were deleted so that the application no longer runs or it displays error messages as it starts.

- ✔ The application was accidentally uninstalled.

- ✔ The application was infected with a virus.

- ✔ The application decided to go bohemian and teach English as a second language in Prague for a semester.

There may be even more reasons. In my experience, I have had to reinstall only two programs. One was a graphics program that apparently didn't like another graphics program I later installed. Reinstalling the first program fixed the incompatibilities. The second instance was an older program that no longer worked, but reinstalling it somehow fixed things up nicely.

To reinstall your application, simply insert the Install or Setup disc in the optical drive. Go ahead and install the program over itself; you rarely need to remove or uninstall the original from the hard drive. (Only if the Setup program tells you that the original needs to be removed do you need to do so.)

- ✔ Generally speaking, consider visiting the Web page for the application's developer. Check for a FAQ list or any tech support you can find online that maybe has a specific solution to your problem.

- ✔ The support Web page for all Microsoft products is `http://support.microsoft.com`.

- ✔ No, you probably don't ever need to reinstall Windows. See Chapter 21 for my many insistent reasons.

- ✔ Another thing to reinstall is a *device driver*. That's the software used by Windows to control a piece of hardware. Because reinstalling a device driver is specific to the hardware you're troubleshooting, that information is located elsewhere in this book. Use the index to locate the hardware for which you need a new device driver.

Chapter 5

Help! I Need Somebody!

*H*elp is something you paid for. You deserve it. Whenever you buy a computer, purchase software, or sign an agreement for online service, you should get some form of support. You don't have to use it, but when you need it, it's there. And, if everything goes as planned, help should actually *help*.

Regretfully, the quality of technical support has dwindled over the past several years: I'm sure the bean counters would have most companies do away with support. Those bottom-line people just don't see the value, the obligation, and the necessity of support. Although you can find good support here and there, the general consensus is that good technical support is a rare thing. Sad. It shouldn't be.

This chapter shows you the ups and downs of technical support, where to find it, and when to use it.

When to Use Tech Support

This advice is simple: Use tech support as a last resort, if at all.

✔ Most problems are easily "fixable" without having to call support.

✔ Use this book to help you troubleshoot many of the common computer foibles that everyone experiences.

✔ Technical support is also available for any peripheral or add-on hardware you may buy. In that case, call the manufacturer, as listed in your manual or on your invoice.

- In the computer biz, there's a difference between technical support and customer service. *Customer service* deals with sales, sale support, product questions before purchase, and product return. *Technical support* is where to go when you have questions about, or problems with, a product. Know the difference before you make the call!

- Above all, you *paid* for support when you bought the product. They owe it to you. If you can fix it yourself, great. But don't feel guilty about calling support when you need it.

Boring tech-support history that you don't have to read

In the old days, technical support was purely technical. By that, I mean that the only people who would call tech support were technicians themselves, office computer gurus, programmers, or hackers. They knew computers. And, the folks giving the technical support were typically the software programmers or product engineers themselves. They knew the answers, and, more importantly, the people calling knew the right questions to ask. The system worked rather well.

Yes, there's a time limit

Technical support is often "farmed out" to businesses other than the original manufacturer or developer. So, although you may think that you're calling the software developer, hardware manufacturer, or online service, you really end up being connected to some third-party company, one that specializes in handling technical support.

For the most part, the people answering the tech-support phones are knowledgeable about the product and capable of solving the problems. Unfortunately, because they base their business on the number of calls answered per hour (or per shift), their financial goal is beating the clock, as opposed to really solving your problem.

The average amount of time a typical tech-support person has to deal with your problem is 12 minutes, more or less. After that, he's under tremendous pressure to "dump" you. I have experienced this situation too often myself. And, my readers have related to me the disappointing results of being dumped: After 12 minutes, the person simply says "Reinstall Windows" or "Reformat the hard drive" and then hangs up. Most definitely, that is *not* the solution to your problem. It's the solution to *his* problem, which is to get rid of you before the 12 minutes are up.

When you phone tech support, keep an eye on the clock. If you have spent more than 12 minutes and no solution is working or if the tech-support person suggests reinstalling Windows or reformatting the hard drive, you should protest. Ask to speak to a supervisor. Often, supervisors aren't under the same time limitations as the grunts who have to answer the phones. That should lead to an answer.

As computers became more of a consumer commodity, tech support changed to accommodate more beginners. In fact, the folks at the old (early 1990s) WordPerfect toll-free tech-support line told me that the most common phone call they received was from someone who hadn't yet taken the product out of the box. Sure, those people needed help, and in those days the WordPerfect folks were willing to help them. *That* was good technical support and one of the reasons WordPerfect dominated the market back then.

In the profit-motivated 1990s and 2000s, technical support has been deemed negative to the bottom line, and many companies therefore offer poor or no tech support. The toll-free numbers are almost gone. Free support has dried up except for the first 90 days. After that, you have to pay a flat-rate toll, a per-call fee, or a per-minute fee. Even then, paying the fee doesn't guarantee that your problem gets solved or even that you won't grow a beard while you wait on hold.

Before you call tech support

Yeah, they lied to you when they said that computers are easy to use. Such bunk! A computer is a complex device. Anything can and does go wrong. The tech-support people know this, and they brace themselves for anything. Callers range from the timid beginner who still has the computer in the box to the hacker whose computer has been utterly disassembled and desoldered. You can make the tech-support person's job easier by doing a little research before you call. Follow my suggestions:

Find out who owns the problem. Narrow things down. Is it hardware or software? That way, you can call the proper place. Refer to Chapter 3 for help on making this determination.

Try as many solutions yourself as possible. Use this book to help you troubleshoot as much as possible. Tech-support people are blown away if you have already looked in the Device Manager or worked in the System Configuration Utility. They may have you look there again — if so, be patient. (They're typically following a script and must check things off before taking you to the next level.)

Determine whether the problem is repeatable. Be prepared to demonstrate to tech support that the bug isn't random and can be reproduced. I did this once, and the tech-support guy was amazed when the same foul-up happened on his computer.

Be prepared to give information, and lots of it. Do your homework before you call. This book tells you many places to look for solving problems. Complete those steps and gather as much information as possible. You don't have to spill it all at once to the tech-support person, but have it ready when you're asked.

Finally, it pays to know which number to call. This is something I find frustrating: The tech-support number is typically hidden somewhere in the manual. Sometimes, it's right up front or in a tech-support index. But most often it's in a not-so-obvious place.

- ✔ When you find the tech-support phone number, flag it! Highlight it. Better still, write it in the front of the manual. Add it to your address book. You can even spray-paint it on the wall.
- ✔ See Chapter 24 for more information on the Device Manager and other useful programs and troubleshooting tools in Windows Vista.

Finding your version of Windows

One important piece of information to relate to tech support is which version of Windows you have. It also helps to know the version of any application or utility that you figure is causing the problem.

To find out the Windows version, open the System icon in the Control Panel: From the Control Panel Home, choose System and Maintenance and then System. From the Control Panel Classic view, open the System icon. Or, right-click the My Computer icon on the desktop (if it's visible), and choose Properties from the pop-up menu.

The System window lists, well — it says it right there at the top of the screen — "basic information about your computer." As shown in Figure 5-1, the computer is running Windows Vista Ultimate Edition.

Figure 5-1:
Windows
version
information.

You also find in the System window other useful information for technical support, including information about your PC's processor and memory and other trivia.

You don't have to cough up *all* the information displayed in the System window. Offer only what the tech-support person asks for.

Finding the version number in an application program

Windows may not be the problem. It may be some other program you run. In that case, you may need to tell the tech-support person which version of that program you're running. This information is *not* the same thing as the version number for Windows; each piece of software has its own version number.

To find out the version of any specific application, choose the Help⇨About command. (The About command is usually followed by the program's name.) That command displays a dialog box with the program's full name, release, and version information — and maybe even a quick button to click for connecting to tech support.

Making the call

Phone up tech support. Wait on hold. Listen to the silly music.

Be prepared to talk to a screener before you get true tech support. Sometimes, a person breaks in initially and records your name, phone number, customer ID, and serial or registration number, and then a description of the problem before you speak with a live "tech."

Do some doodling in the Paint program while you wait.

When the tech answers, calmly and politely explain the problem. Then follow the instructions as best you can. Don't bother saying, "But I already tried this." Just follow along and, hopefully, your problem will be solved.

- ✔ For some reason, when you opt to pay for tech support, it happens sooner and faster than when it's "free" support.

- ✔ Keep an eye on the clock. Do this for two reasons. First, if you're paying for the call, you probably want to check the amount of time you spend waiting on hold. Second, after the call starts, you need to keep an eye out for the 12-minute limit to elapse and then see whether tech support is giving you the brush-off. (See the sidebar "Yes, there's a time limit," earlier in this chapter.)

Tech Support on the Web (Better than You Think)

As long as your problem isn't with getting on the Internet in the first place, you can find some excellent tech support freely available on the Web. Most software developers and hardware manufacturers have support areas on their Web sites. There, you can review common questions and answers, troubleshoot products, e-mail questions, or download new software solutions. In fact, only after checking the Web do I bother contacting tech support by phone.

Finding the manufacturer's Web site

After you discover whether the problem is hardware or software, your next step is to find a Web site to seek out technical support. Sometimes, this part is easy: Choose Help⇨About or Help⇨Support from the menu, and often the developer's Web page is listed right there. Neat-o.

For hardware manufacturers, the problem is a bit rougher. First, if the hardware came with your computer, contact the computer manufacturer. You may be lucky and find the manufacturer's contact information in the System window (refer to Figure 5-1, though it's not shown in that figure), in the System area. The manufacturer name might even be a link you can click to get support. (Refer to the earlier section "Finding your version of Windows" for information on summoning the System window.)

Another way to hunt down the hardware manufacturer is by using a search engine, like Google:

```
www.google.com/
```

Type the manufacturer name into the Search box, and click the Search button on the Google main page. Scan the results for something likely to be the manufacturer's Web page.

When you get to the manufacturer's page, look for a technical-support link. Then you can begin the process of searching for the information you need.

✔ Be sure to use as few words as possible when you search for information on the Internet. Be direct: Type S3 graphics driver upgrade or missing icon, for example.

✔ Another tip: If you search broadly at first, check to see whether any options can refine your search or "search within results." For example, if the search results on the tech-support Web page yield 400 answers, consider searching through those answers for something more specific to your situation.

✔ You should also use these steps for finding support information for any extra hardware you buy for your computer. If the tech-support Web page isn't listed in the manual, use the Internet to search for the Web page.

✔ When you find the support page, drop a bookmark! In Internet Explorer, press Ctrl+D. That's one page you want to remember.

✔ If you bought your computer locally, just phone the dealer for support. This is one case where it's easier to call and bug them than to use a Web page. But, for manufacturers, going to the Web page is easier by far.

✔ Also, check on the manufacturer's Web page for an FAQ — Frequently Asked Questions — list.

Using the Microsoft Knowledge Base

Microsoft has perhaps the most extensive and exhaustive troubleshooting database on the Internet. It's called the Microsoft Knowledge Base, and it's similar to information that the Microsoft tech-support people use when you phone them (and pay) for an answer.

Visit the Knowledge Base by typing this address:

```
http://support.microsoft.com/
```

Type a brief, punchy question or problem description; for example, `Windows shutdown` or `Missing toolbar`. Click the button, and soon a list of potential solutions appears, perhaps one of which will save your butt.

✔ Definitely, definitely, most definitely use the Microsoft Knowledge Base *first,* before phoning up Microsoft.

✔ Much of the information in the Knowledge Base is a rehash from what you find in the Windows Help system. To use the Help system in Windows, choose Help and Support from the Start button menu.

✔ Note that some problems have multiple solutions. Each one is for a different system configuration, so try to match your computer's configuration to the best possible solution.

✔ It helps to know Microsoft-ese when you're typing questions for the Knowledge Base. For example, you may use the word *hang,* but the Knowledge Base uses the word *freeze.* Be sure to try another, similar word if your initial search yields no results.

Downloading a new driver

Occasionally, your Internet search ends with the task of installing new software to make things work right. For example, to fix that video glitch, you may need new software — a *driver*. To get rid of a printer problem or to make your printer happy with other software, you may need a new printer driver. Whatever the reason, your task is to download and install new software. Here's my advice for getting that done:

- As long as the site is the manufacturer's legitimate Web page, it's okay to download and install software from that site. Refer to Chapter 24 for information on Internet Explorer's Phishing Filter, to ensure that you have a legitimate Web page.

- If the download fails or Windows tells you that it's "corrupted," you have to try again. If the file is still corrupted after the second download, contact the developer and tell someone there that something is wrong with the file.

- Bookmark the Web page! Press the Ctrl+D key combination to add the Web page to your Favorites list. You do this just in case things go wrong and you need to return.

- Print any instructions for installing the new software. In Internet Explorer, choose File➪Print to print the current Web page.

- Drivers should be free. I have found only one Web site where they wanted to charge me for a new driver — and for hardware I already owned. I immediately tossed out the hardware and bought something else. I wrote a letter to the hardware manufacturer's president — not that it did any good. Don't be suckered into paying for a driver or software upgrade.

Windows Remote Assistance

I have answered technical and troubleshooting questions from my readers for more than a dozen years now. The biggest hurdle in trying to help someone is not being able to see what that person sees on the screen.

For example, someone may write, "The buttons are wrong; they're all over the screen." After two or three exchanges of e-mail, I discovered that the reader's taskbar was on the top edge of the screen, not on the bottom. Now, had I been standing right there looking at the screen, it would have been a click and a swipe of the mouse to fix things. But, via e-mail, it took four or five messages to get things right.

Seeing things is a big part of getting proper tech support. To help out, Windows Vista has a feature named Remote Assistance. By using Remote Assistance, you can allow anyone on the Internet who also has Windows

Vista to take control of your computer and see what you see on the screen. That makes it a heck of a lot easier to fix things, as this section demonstrates.

✔ I recommend using this feature only if you really, really trust the person who's looking at your computer. If so, you may find a ready solution for some of your PC's problems.

✔ Remote Assistance isn't worth diddly-squat if your computer cannot connect to the Internet.

✔ Speaking of the Internet, the faster the connection, the more effective Remote Assistance is. I have done it with 56K modems at about 49 Kbps true speed, and it was tolerable but not ideal.

✔ Remote Assistance isn't the same thing as Remote Desktop, though the two are similar. Remote Desktop allows you to access your PC from another location, similar to Remote Assistance, but it's designed more for working away from home than for troubleshooting.

Setting up your system for remote assistance

Before asking for remote assistance, ensure that the Remote Assistance option is turned on. After all, you can't let anyone else in when your computer lacks a door for someone to walk through. Follow these steps to ensure that Remote Assistance is activated:

1. **Open the Control Panel's System icon.**

   From the Control Panel Home, choose System and Maintenance, and then choose System. From the Control Panel Classic view, open the System icon.

2. **From the Tasks list on the left side of the System window, choose Remote Settings.**

3. **(Optional) Enter the administrator's password or click Continue.**

4. **Click to put a check mark by the item labeled Allow Remote Assistance Invitations to Be Sent from This Computer.**

5. **Click the OK button.**

   The System Properties dialog box bows out.

Your PC is now set up for remote assistance, but to actually get help, you need to run the Windows Remote Assistance program, which is the topic of the next section.

You can disable the Remote Assistance feature by repeating these steps and removing the check mark. I recommend doing this after you get remote help, to keep your computer secure.

Getting someone to help you

Obviously, you don't want just anyone barging into your PC to give you "assistance." The person must be properly invited. Follow these general steps:

1. **From the Start menu, choose All Programs⇨Maintenance⇨Windows Remote Assistance.**

2. **Click the top button, Invite Someone You Trust to Help You.**

   The next screen lists options for inviting someone. You can send an invitation by e-mail, send the invite as a file, or reuse a previous invitation.

3. **If you choose to send an invitation by e-mail, proceed with Step 5; if you choose to send the invitation as a file, go to Step 4.**

4. **Use the Browse button to save the invite file in a location where the other user can grab it.**

   For example, pick a common spot on the network, a safe place to exchange files on the Internet, or a removable storage media, like a USB flash drive. Name the file appropriately.

5. **Enter a password for your connection; type it twice.**

   Do not use your regular Windows, Internet, or e-mail password here! Instead, make up a special password just for getting help. Then, to help keep your computer secure, do not use that password again.

6. **For the file invitation, you're done; click the Finish button. If you're sending an e-mail invitation, click the Next button and proceed to Step 7.**

   If you're sending an invite via e-mail, the e-mail program's message-sending window appears, listing the contents of your plea-for-help invitation.

7. **For an e-mail invitation, fill in the To field and click the Send button to send the message.**

When you're done sending out the e-mail invitation or you've created the invite file, the Windows Remote Assistance toolbar appears on the screen, as shown in Figure 5-2. This toolbar is used to control your Remote Assistance session.

The next step is to wait until the other person connects.

You must keep Windows Remote Assistance open until someone connects, or else the other person cannot help you!

Figure 5-2:
The Remote
Assistance
toolbar.

A connection is made!

When your pal makes a connection, you see a warning, such as the one shown in Figure 5-3. Click Yes to let the person help you, or click No when the cold fear of suspicion grips your soul.

Figure 5-3:
Who's that
knocking at
my door?

At this point, the other person merely sees what you see on your screen. For example, using the Chat button on the Remote Assistance toolbar, or over an Internet voice connection, that person can direct you to do things over the phone and then can watch to see what happens. For higher-level support, you can let the person have full control over your PC.

Giving them full control

To give your helper more power than just observation, he must ask for "full control" (see the next section). When the request is made, you see a warning dialog box, similar to the one shown in Figure 5-4. Click Yes to give the other user full control; No to deny.

After the other person is given control, he can move your mouse pointer and type things that affect your PC's input — just as though he's running the computer. In fact, that person *is* running your computer and can help you (you hope) find a solution to whatever problem you have.

Figure 5-4:
Granting full
computer
access to
some nerd.

> **Windows Remote Assistance**
>
> Would you like to allow Dan Gookin to share control of your desktop?
>
> To stop sharing control, in the Remote Assistance dialog box, click Stop sharing or press ESC.
>
> ☐ Allow Dan Gookin to respond to User Account Control prompts   [Yes]   [No]
>
> What are the privacy and security concerns?

Saying bye-bye

To release full control, click the Stop Sharing button on the toolbar. You can also merely press the Esc key on the keyboard.

To disconnect the other user, click the Disconnect button on the toolbar. Then click Yes to confirm.

You can then close the Windows Remote Assistance window.

- ✔ To properly use the Remote Assistance e-mail invitation, the recipient must have Windows Vista. The directions for using the information that's sent are in the e-mail message itself.

- ✔ No one can get into your computer unless they're invited, and even then you have to grant that person access to your computer.

- ✔ Only by clicking the Yes button when you're prompted can someone else see what you see on your computer screen. Only by your allowing them full access to your PC can they actually change things.

- ✔ When the other person can see your desktop but not control it, the text on the Remote Assistance toolbar says

      Your helper can now see your desktop

  When the other person has full control, the text in the toolbar reads

      Your helper is sharing control of your computer

- ✔ Even though the other person can manipulate your PC, you still have control on your end: You can use the keyboard or mouse at any time.

- ✔ If you don't want the person to meddle with certain areas of your hard drive, such as your Personal Finance folder, make that known ahead of time.

- ✔ Yes! It's *slow* over dialup modems, but workable.

Giving help with Windows Remote Assistance

When some poor soul has begged for help, you can chip in your talent and time by having that person buy this book, read to this very section, and then wait for you to complete the following steps:

1. **Ensure that the other person has completed the steps listed in the preceding section.**

   The other computer must be running Windows Remote Assistance and be ready to accept an incoming link. Further, you're going to need an invitation.

2. **If you received an invitation by e-mail, save the invitation attachment to disk.**

3. **Locate the saved invitation file (which can be a file saved on the network, on a USB drive, or on the Internet) or the file you saved from the e-mail invite, and open that file.**

   Opening the file automatically starts Windows Remote Assistance in "offer to help" mode.

4. **Type the password and click the OK button.**

   You have to wait while the other person accepts your invitation. When that happens, you see that person's desktop screen in the Windows Remote Assistance window on your desktop, as shown in Figure 5-5.

At this point, you're merely looking at the other user's screen; you cannot control what you see. You can use the Chat button to start a chat conversation, or phone up the other person and tell them to work while you watch.

To actually use the other person's computer, click the Request Control button. You see the request appear on the other user's screen and then watch as the user clicks Yes or No to allow or deny your access.

When you get control, your computer mouse controls the mouse pointer on the other user's screen. You can even type on your keyboard and have the text appear on the other person's screen. Some keys, such as Alt+Tab, do not pass through to the other computer, but you should have enough control to help the other person troubleshoot. And don't expect things to happen quickly; you're controlling another PC across the Internet, which is only as fast as your Internet connection.

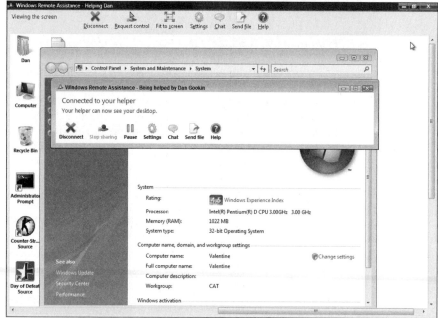

Figure 5-5:
Helping
someone
else looks
like this.

To release control over the other PC, click the Stop Sharing button. Or, the other user may do this for you.

To stop viewing the other PC, click the Disconnect button, and then click the Yes button to confirm.

Close the Windows Remote Assistance window when you're done.

Part II
Troubleshooting Minor Irks and Quirks

The 5th Wave   By Rich Tennant

Maintenance is chagrined to find out the squeak in Clark's disk drive is really a whistle in Clark's nose.

In this part . . .

Face it: Even at times of brutal desperation, human beings are essentially lazy. It's nothing to feel guilty about and nothing worth "getting over." It's just one of those random and ugly facts about people. For example, only in the movies does the good guy go back and rescue his stumbling girlfriend when the monster is chasing them. In real life, the guy runs to the shelter and bends over all red-faced, panting and wheezing. Then, only after someone hands him a cold beer does he wonder, "Hey! Where's Linda?"

Why experience the solution when you can just look it up instead? It's human nature to prefer the ready-made solution. After all, so many computer problems are common or similar enough that someone somewhere must have had the same thing happen to them. Then, all you need to do is look up that answer and get on with your life. That's the function of the chapters in this part of the book. They're organized into problem areas, scenarios, or specific hardware or software issues. Look up a common question. Get an answer. Get on with your life.

Chapter 6

This Just Bugs Me!

. . . .

In This Chapter

▶ Hearing weird things

▶ Fixing the display's "dumb mode" resolution

▶ Dealing with the notification area

▶ Diagnosing sleep and hibernation woes

▶ Checking the battery

▶ Opening unusual files (or not)

▶ Undoing a file's read-only persuasion

▶ Installing weird DVD software

. . . .

*I*n the hall of computer weirdness, there is a special section for things that just don't fit anywhere else. Call it the anomaly closet. Call it the *special* collection. I call it This Just Bugs Me, and it's, coincidentally, the title of this chapter.

✔ Seriously, I couldn't list *everything* that bugs you with your computer; there aren't enough trees in the world to produce the paper needed to print *that* particular book.

✔ Yes, even though a particular problem may be on your personal This Just Bugs Me list, it may not be in this chapter.

✔ See the index or use the table of contents to discover in which chapter the problem and solution lie.

Funny Startup Noises

Yeah, I'm sure the computer could accuse *you* of making various funny noises when you start your day. But this book isn't titled *Troubleshooting Humans For Dummies*. No, this book helps you deal with *unexpected* noises that your computer makes when it starts. If the noises were really funny, you probably wouldn't be alarmed about the situation, which doesn't aid in the troubleshooting process.

Officially, the computer makes only the following noises when it starts (I leave it up to you to determine whether there's any humor in the following):

- ✔ The fan inside the computer case whirs to life and makes a soft, warbling drone. The fan (and sometimes you have more than one) is responsible for keeping the console's internal components cool.

- ✔ The hard drive spins up to speed, which makes a high-pitched humming sound that few people over 40 can hear.

- ✔ The computer beeps once as it comes to life. The single beep means that everything is okay. It's like the computer gets all excited and — golly, gee! — if this were an MGM musical from the 1940s, the computer would burst into song and have a big dance number with all the other office equipment. But, no: It's just a beep (a Paramount Studios beep).

The computer could make additional noises, funny or no:

- ✔ The monitor may honk when it comes to life. Especially for larger CRT (glass, not LCD) monitors, you may hear a loud honking noise. Actually, it's more of an "UNK" noise than a car horn tootling. This sound is normal.

- ✔ CRT monitors generally make a high-pitched whistling sound. Again, if you're over 40, there's no point in trying to hear it.

- ✔ The printer may hum a few bars of "oink-grunt-oink" as it comes to life.

- ✔ External disk drives honk and whir when they're first initialized.

- ✔ The scanner may also power up and play "Clink, grindily grind."

That's pretty much it for the early-morning computer cacophony. You are most likely familiar with all these noises and will note that something's wrong when a noise goes missing or a new noise gets introduced.

- ✔ No, sadly, wearing earplugs merely only masks the symptoms. It doesn't solve any noise-related problems.

- ✔ Refer to Chapter 10 for information on troubleshooting sound problems other than startup sounds.

In the presence of unwanted noises

Noise problems are invariably hardware related, especially at startup. New noises generally indicate a problem with whichever device seems to be causing the noise. Alas, these problems must be fixed by your computer dealer or manufacturer. Especially if the computer is still under warranty, avoid a homebrew solution.

✔ If the computer beeps more than once, the beeps indicate a problem with the computer's startup electronics. This problem must be fixed by your dealer or the manufacturer. Tell them what the beep pattern was: several short beeps or long-short beeps, for example.

✔ Beeps may also sound off after you upgrade some hardware, typically after adding more memory to the PC. The beeps are the computer's acknowledgment that its basic configuration has changed. The extra beeps are typically accompanied by a text message on the screen explaining that new hardware has been found (or something like that).

✔ Hard drives can get louder over time. That means that their bearings are giving out. Of course, the real question is *when* they will give out. A hard drive in one of my systems was loud for an hour after I turned the computer on, but then it got quiet. So the problem can be intermittent. See Part IV of this book for more disk drive information.

✔ Spinning parts in the computer can be affected by the weather. If it's an especially cold morning and the furnace hasn't quite heated up your office, the hard drives may peal an especially annoying squeak on startup. This squeak should go away when things heat up.

✔ A squealing monitor needs to be fixed by a professional. Or replaced. Or told that squealing doesn't work and that it has to find another, more polite way to ask you for something.

✔ You can replace a pinging fan yourself, if you're good with electronics. In some cases, however, replacing the fan involves replacing the entire power supply, which can be done by anyone who's handy with a screwdriver or who has ever set up a backyard barbecue. Even so, if the system is still under warranty, have the dealer or manufacturer fix it.

✔ Here's another good way to repair a noisy fan: Clean it! Unplug your computer and open its case. Then take a portable vacuum cleaner and suck out all the dirt, hair, and byte-bunnies that accumulate in all PCs. Ensure that you also clean the vents that the fan blows air through.

✔ Never open or try to repair a PC's power supply or the monitor. Despite whatever noises they make, these items cannot be fixed by mere mortals.

In the presence of unwelcome silence

A missing sound typically means a dead something-or-other inside your computer. Pee-yew! Take the thing in and get it fixed.

- ✔ Some computers don't beep when they first start up. Other computers may beep only if they're connected to speakers.

- ✔ One day, the sound stopped entirely in my old IBM PC. I heard no beep at startup and no music when I played my favorite game. The next time I opened the case, I discovered the problem. I was living in a rather decrepit apartment in El Cajon, California, and a mouse family (the rodent type) had moved into my computer and built a cozy nest atop the warm hard drive. The speaker apparently bothered them, so they *ate* the speaker's cardboard cone. I solved the problem by removing the nest, replacing the speaker, and moving to another apartment complex.

The Display Is Stuck in "Dumb" Mode

It's not dumb mode as much as it's the lowest possible resolution on a modern computer monitor: 640 x 480 pixels. Such low resolution renders everything on the display *very large,* and it doesn't offer much screen real estate to get any work done. Obviously, it's a problem that needs fixing.

- ✔ Dumb mode may also be caused by your computer entering Safe mode when it starts up. Not only does Windows alert you when Safe mode first starts, but you also see the words *Safe Mode* appear in the four corners of the screen.

- ✔ See Chapter 24 for more information on Safe mode.

- ✔ See Chapter 16 for more information on adjusting and fixing the PC's display.

- ✔ Yes, I am aware that even lower-resolution graphics are available (320 x 160, for example). The 640 x 480 resolution is the lowest mode supported by Windows. So there.

Annoying Icons in the Notification Area

One of the most vexing issues that vexes even the most vexless PC user centers around those ugly little booger icons in the *notification area,* shown in Figure 6-1. Whatever. It's littered with teensy icons collecting like dust bunnies under the sofa.

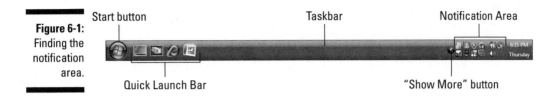

Figure 6-1:
Finding the
notification
area.

Start button · Taskbar · · · · · · · · · · · · · · · · · · Notification Area

Quick Launch Bar · "Show More" button

Although many people seem to tolerate the irritating icons, a few downright can't stand the boogers and want to stomp them out of existence. If that's you, heed the advice given in this section.

✔ The notification area is on the far right end of the taskbar, and the taskbar (typically) sits on the bottom of the screen.

✔ The icons in the notification area are hidden when they're not used. The chevron-thing button (refer to Figure 6-1) can be clicked to show all the icons.

✔ The *notification area* was once referred to as the *system tray.* You may still hear it called that.

"So what the heck are those icons, anyway?"

Each icon appearing in the notification area represents a program running in Windows — usually, a utility or some other "background" operation, or *process.* The icon offers you a way to check that program's progress or to get quick access to its settings or more information. And that sounds really nice.

In real life, however, the notification area has become an eclectic electronic junk yard, home to any old random icon to roost and rust. After seeing about ten or so icons there, I begin to think "What the heck is this?" It's from that thought that the urge to purge grows into an obliteration obsession.

Required icons for the notification area

What do you need to have in the notification area? Nothing. There's no requirement, and if you're crafty enough, you can eliminate *all* icons from that area. (A blank box remains, but that's it.)

Killing off teensy icons in the notification area

There are two ways to kill off icons you don't want to see in the notification area. The first is my preferred method, which works like this:

1. **Right-click the icon.**

2. **Look for a Remove command on the pop-up menu and choose it.**

   When there isn't any Remove command, continue:

3. **Choose the Options or Properties command, if available.**

4. **Scour through the dialog box that appears for an option or setting that removes the icon from the notification area.**

When those steps don't work, you can use Windows itself to help hide or remove the icons. Here's how that works:

1. **Right-click the mouse in the notification area.**

   Don't click an *icon* in the notification area — click in the notification area proper. If this step confuses you, just click the time display shown in the notification area.

2. **Choose Properties from the pop-up menu.**

   If you don't see the Properties command, you clicked an icon and not in the notification area proper.

   If you're successful, you see the Taskbar and Start Menu Properties dialog box, as shown in Figure 6-2.

   The Notification Area tab also lists what I call the four basic notification area icons: Clock, Volume, Network, and Power. The Clock and Volume icons are traditional, stuck in the notification area (then called the *system tray*) since Windows 95. Regardless, the Taskbar and Start Menu Properties dialog box is where you can turn those icons on or off.

3. **Click the Customize button.**

   The Customize Notification Icons dialog box appears, as shown in Figure 6-3. This box is where you can permanently hide any or all of the icons.

4. **To hide an icon, click to select it.**

   This step displays a drop-down list in the Behavior column, as shown in Figure 6-3 (to the right of the Java Update Available item).

5. **From the drop-down list, choose the option labeled Hide.**

6. **Repeat Steps 4 and 5 for all icons on the list that you want hidden.**

Figure 6-2:
The Taskbar
and Start
Menu
Properties
dialog box.

Figure 6-3:
Here's
where you
hide the
icons in
Windows
Vista.

7. **When you're done playing hide-and-seek with the icons, click the OK button.**

8. **Click OK again to close the Taskbar and Start Menu Properties dialog box.**

Note that even with everything hidden, the notification area doesn't vanish completely. The chevron-thing button (the Hide/Show arrow) on the left lip of the notification area still appears, which allows you to see the icons. But at least they're not "on stage" all the time.

Sleep Mode Poops Out, Hibernate Poops Out, We All Poop Out Now

Problems with Sleep mode (also known as Stand By) as well as Hibernation all stem from the same root: your computer's *power-management system*. That's the set of electronics that controls the computer's special low-power and power-saving modes of operation. For some reason, this hardware and software set causes many PC users grief beyond despair.

The PC can't recover from Sleep mode

Some computers go to sleep and never wake up. The problem was so bad about ten years ago that I recommended *not* using Sleep mode! But, since then, things have gotten better. Still, there are times when the computer just can't seem to wake up from Stand By mode. Rather than thump the computer on the head, there are a few things to try.

First, if your computer is a laptop, ensure that the battery light as well as the "moon" light are lit. These indicate that the computer has power and that it's still in Sleep mode, respectively. When either button is out, the laptop's battery has drained and, well, there's your problem! Plug the laptop into the wall, and you can use it again.

Second, determine whether this is a one-time event. Turn off the computer (refer to Chapter 2). When the computer comes on again, let it sit until Stand By mode comes back on. Then see whether the same thing happens and the computer cannot revive itself. If so, see the section "Fixing the power-management software," a little later in this chapter.

If the problem with Stand By is a one-time thing, what happened, most likely, is that some program kicked the bucket during the sleep process. The problem is with that lone program, not with Stand By mode itself or with your computer's power-management hardware. (And, it's tough to determine which program walked the green mile, so just let it be.)

Third, when all else fails, just avoid using Stand By mode or just use Stand By on the computer's monitor instead. Leave the system and its hard drives on, but after a given interval, have the computer shut off the monitor for you.

"Where is Hibernation?"

Not every PC has the Hibernation feature. Most modern PCs do, but in the switch from Windows XP to Windows Vista, the actual Hibernation option remains hidden; it doesn't appear on the Start menu's list of shutdown options. But that doesn't mean that Hibernation is absent as a system feature.

Adding Hibernation as a Power button option

You can change the function of the PC console's Power button to cause the computer to hibernate when the button is pressed. Here's how:

1. **From the Control Panel Home, choose Hardware and Sound or, from the Control Panel Classic view, open the Power icon.**

2. **Choose the link Change What the Power Buttons Do.**

   The link is found either beneath the Power Options heading or on the left side of the window. The System Settings window appears, as shown in Figure 6-4, listing options for the PC's Power and Sleep buttons.

3. **Use the menu buttons by each item to choose whether the given button puts the PC into Hibernation mode.**

   For example, to set the Sleep button to hibernate the PC, choose Hibernate from the button menu next to When I Press the Sleep Button.

4. **Click the Save Changes button when you're done.**

   (Optional) Close any open windows.

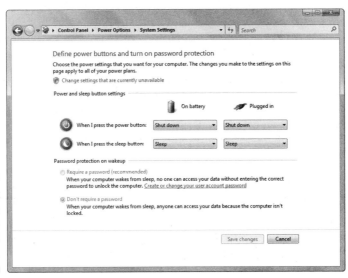

Figure 6-4:
Hibernate can be found lurking here.

You can also program the Start menu's software power button to put the PC into Hibernation mode. Those directions are a bit more involved, but I've written them carefully here:

1. **From the Control Panel Home, choose Hardware and Sound and then choose Power Options; from Control Panel Classic view, open the Power icon.**

2. **Click any link titled Change Plan Settings.**

3. **Click the link titled Change Advanced Power Settings.**

   The Power Options dialog box appears.

4. **Scroll through the list to find the Power Buttons and Lid item.**

5. **Open the Power Buttons and Lid item.**

   Click the plus sign (+) by the item heading. This expands that item.

6. **Open the Start Menu Power Button item.**

7. **Choose Hibernate as the option for when the power button on the start menu is clicked.**

   You may see two options there when the computer can also be run from battery power; choose for both.

8. **Click OK and close any open windows when you're done.**

The Start menu power button dwells on the bottom of the Start menu, next to the padlock icon.

Fixing the power-management software

Oddly enough, the power-management hardware in your computer isn't controlled from the Control Panel's Power Options icon. Nope, instead, you must use the Control Panel's Device Manager icon to help locate your computer's power-management hardware. When you find the hardware, you can reinstall the driver that controls things. This process is tough, but it's often the necessary step you must take to fix your PC's power-management troubles. Obey:

1. **Go visit the Control Panel.**

   You can get there from the Start button's menu.

2. **Open the Device Manager icon.**

3. **If prompted, enter the administrator's password or click the Continue button.**

   The Device Manager window appears, as shown in Figure 6-5.

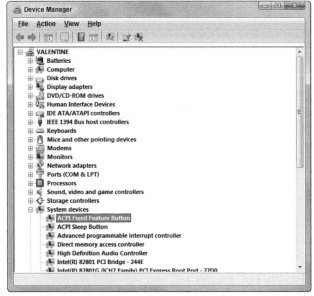

Figure 6-5:
The lovely
Device
Manager.

4. **Open the item named System Devices.**

   It's toward the bottom of the list.

5. **Look for a power-management or ACPI item.**

   This is the tricky part: Your PC's power-management system is uniquely named, so you have to search for it. In Figure 6-6 are two items prefixed by ACPI, which stands for Advanced Configuration and Power Interface, the industry standard for PC power management. You may not be so lucky, though you may find the word *power* or *power management* in your PC's Device Manager window.

6. **Open the power-management item to display its Properties dialog box.**

7. **Click the Driver tab in the Properties dialog box.**

8. **Click the Update Driver button.**

9. **Obey the wizard to select a new driver.**

   Follow the instructions on the screen. If you need to connect to the Internet to visit the Windows Update site, do so.

10. **When the process is complete, restart your computer as indicated or follow whatever directions are given by the wizard.**

    Close any windows or dialog boxes that you have left hanging open.

Reinstalling the software should fix your power-management issues. If not, my next-best advice is to visit your computer manufacturer's or dealer's Web site and look for any updates or new software there. Only when nothing new can be found would I consider phoning up tech support for a solution. When you need to do that, refer to Chapter 5 in this book beforehand.

Checking the battery

One keen aspect of power management, particularly on laptop PCs, is the battery. Power management software is responsible for helping you get the most from your laptop's battery and for recharging and monitoring duties.

The key to checking the battery is to look for the little battery icon in the notification area (refer to Figure 6-1). The tiny icon itself updates as your computer's battery is being used — but it's often too small to see. Pointing the mouse at the battery icon displays a pop-up window displaying more information; clicking the icon displays a larger, power-management window as well, as shown in Figure 6-6.

Figure 6-6:
The battery shows plenty of juice.

Another good way to check the battery is with your hand. It's normal for a battery in use to be warm, but when the battery is too hot to touch, there may be a problem. If so, turn off the laptop and remove the battery. Contact your laptop's manufacturer for assistance.

✔ Your laptop may sport a special laptop battery meter, perhaps even a special battery-monitor program. The meter or program might be accessed from a custom icon in the Control Panel or from the Start menu.

✔ Desktop PCs also show a battery meter when the PC is using a UPS or battery-backed-up power supply and that power supply is monitored by the computer.

Windows Cannot Open the File

Some files were not meant to be opened. They're data files or support programs for other things you do on your computer. There's nothing wrong with
poking around and trying to double-click every file you find. It's just that you
had better be prepared to reset if anything new and wacky happens to your
PC while you're poking around.

When you attempt to open an unknown file, you see the "I cannot open this
file" dialog box, as shown in Figure 6-7. What do you do in this situation?
Easy: Click the Cancel button.

Figure 6-7:
Windows
Vista is at a
loss.

Sure, you could have Windows venture out to the wilds of the Internet and
search for *whatever.* Windows may find a program to open the file, so if you're
curious, take a look, but my first advice is simply to click Cancel and give up.

✔ Most often, unknown file types arrive via e-mail. Typically, they're
PowerPoint presentations, Web archives, Acrobat (PDF) files, Photoshop
images, or other unique files. Please note: *Receiving a file that you cannot
open is not your problem.* It's the problem of the person who sent the
e-mail. Reply to the message and have the person resend the attachment
in a common PC file format. See the nearby sidebar, "Common file formats
your computer can read."

✔ You definitely don't want to select a program from a list (like the Section
option in the dialog box shown earlier, in Figure 6-6). If the file can't be
opened by your PC now, it can't be opened by you making a guess.

Common file formats your computer can read

Most of the time, I hear about file-opening problems because of strange e-mail attachments or files downloaded from the Internet. If you can't open a file, do what I do: Request that the person resend the file in a format your computer can read. Here are some of those common formats that just about any PC can read:

DOC: Generally, this is a "Document" file formation, though specifically most files ending with DOC are Microsoft Word files. Because Word is the most popular word processing program, many documents are saved and exchanged in this file format. (But note that Word 2007 requires that you specifically save new documents in the Word 97-2003 format; the Word 2007 native DOCX format isn't readable by any program other than Word 2007.)

GIF: This common graphics file format can be viewed by the Paint program or by Internet Explorer.

HTML: These documents are Web pages, which can be read by Internet Explorer. Just about any major application can save its documents in HTML format.

JPG: This is another common graphics file format.

PDF: This is the Adobe Acrobat file format. The P stands for Portable, which implies that you can read a PDF file on any computer. (DF is Document Format.) If your computer doesn't have the Adobe Acrobat Reader program, you can get it free at www.adobe.com/reader.

PNG: This one is another common graphics file format.

RTF: Using the rich text format for documents, any word processor can read these documents, which makes RTF even more common than HTML.

TXT: With plain-text documents, nothing gets simpler.

ZIP: Files in this compressed folder archive appear as Compressed Folders in Windows.

That Wicked File Is Read-Only

Read-only is one of a handful of file *attributes* that can be applied to a file. In this case, the read-only attribute tells Windows that the file can be opened, examined, printed, and copied, but cannot be changed in any way — look but don't touch, like the snake pit at the zoo or anything at Grandma's house.

Read-only files happen for two reasons. First, they're created that way. For example, any file on an optical disc (CD or DVD) is read-only. Second, you can change a file's read-only attribute at any time by using the file's Properties dialog box. That's also how you remove the read-only attribute from a file and restore it to normal.

The Microsoft Word read-only bug

Microsoft Word has a bug in it (although Microsoft doesn't call it a bug, I do). When you open a document created by another word processor, Word automatically makes that document read-only. It does this to ensure that you don't overwrite the original, non-Word document with a Word document. To overcome this bug, simply change the name of the document when you save it back to disk; use the File⇨Save As command and enter a new name as well as a new file type for saving the document.

Follow these steps:

1. **Right-click the file's icon.**

2. **Choose Properties from the pop-up menu.**

3. **Remove the check mark by the attribute labeled Read-Only.**

   Look near the bottom of the file's Properties dialog box, on the General tab.

4. **Click OK.**

   The file is restored to non-read-only status.

Keep in mind that the read-only status may be set on a file for a reason. It's one of the few ways you can protect a file in Windows.

You Can't Play That DVD, But . . .

Your computer can play movies using its DVD drive and movie-playing software, such as Windows Media Player or a similar program. But a problem that ticks people off is when the DVD is inserted and you're instructed that the video cannot be played unless you use special software.

My advice: Do not use your PC to play that particular movie. Use a standard DVD player attached to a TV instead.

To play the DVD on your computer, often you're asked to install special soft-ware. I do not recommend doing that under any circumstance. The software may claim that it's required in order to view the video. Beware! The software might do that, but it might also install unwanted spyware in your computer or restrictive software that prevents your PC from operating properly. Just don't take the risk.

✔ The term *codec* is use to describe software used to play video on a computer. In some cases, you need a specific codec to view a video. But my opinion is that all legitimate DVDs should be visible using Windows without modification.

✔ One item you're trying to avoid by not installing special DVD software is a program that restricts the media your PC can play. This software is designed to protect artists' copyrights, but often it ends up restricting your ability to fully use your computer.

Chapter 7

Gosh! This Is Embarrassing!

---

*N*o one has ever tried to paint computing, especially the Internet, as a bright, fun-filled meadow full of flowers, friendly, curious animals, and the soft warmth of children's laughter. No, the Internet is more like heavy, smog-choked traffic: noisy, contentious, and rude, and you're sitting in a hot car behind a smoke-spewing bus. Worse, as you go, you pick up various digital mementos, embarrassing or unwanted evidence that clings to you as you complete your journey. How *embarrassing!*

The stuff you gather from the Internet, as well as from your regular computer activities, is collected because the computer is programmed to indiscriminately remember just about everything you do. Remember that time you took a wrong turn in the hotel room and found yourself standing naked in the hallway? So does the computer. What this chapter does is show you where the computer remembers those things and how you can effectively eradicate the evidence.

Ghosts of Documents Past

For convenience, Windows makes it easy for you to recall things you've recently done. Specifically, you can find a list of recent files you've opened, which makes reopening those files easier. It also makes it easy for anyone else to see what you've been doing on your computer. Uh-oh!

There are two places where ghosts of documents past lurk: on the Start menu, in the Recent Items submenu; and in many programs, at the bottom of the File menu. The following sections describe how to deal with these remnants.

Removing documents from the File menu

For your convenience, many programs keep track of the past several files you opened or saved to disk. They lurk on the File menu, near the bottom. Yes, they can be removed, but the technique is specific to each program.

Generally speaking, try to find the program's Properties or Options command. It may be on the File, Tools, or other menu. Somewhere in the dialog box that appears is an option to set the number of recently opened files. By setting that value to 0, you clear the list. Then you can repeat the steps, if you want to use the list again, and set the number of recent files back to 4 or 16 or whatever it once was.

As an example, here's how to clear the recent file list in Microsoft Word 2007:

1. Click the Microsoft Office Button to display its menu.
2. Click the Word Options button, at the bottom of the Office Button menu.

   The Word Options window appears.
3. Choose Advanced from the left side of the window.
4. Scroll down to the Display heading.
5. Set the number by Show This Number of Recent Documents to 0.
6. Click OK.

   The recent document list vanishes.

If you want to use the list again, repeat these steps, but set the number of recent documents back to 17 (or whatever).

 ✔ The File menu is called the *Office Button* in Microsoft Office 2007 applications. Same deal.

 ✔ Yes, the names of files you've opened linger on the File menu long after the file itself has been deleted. The program lists only the filenames; it doesn't check to confirm that the file exists (or hasn't been renamed or moved).

Really, really removing unwanted files from a list

The method of removing unwanted files from a File menu as described in the preceding section has two drawbacks. The first is that it assumes that there's an option somewhere to clear the list. The second is that the *entire* list gets cleared. To truly pull the unwanted file from the computer's brain, you have to kick it up a notch and do some brain surgery. Follow these steps:

1. **(Optional) Set a system restore point.**

   I'd turn back to Chapter 4 for details on this useful tip.

2. **Press Win+R to open the Run dialog box.**

   Or, you can choose the Run command from the Start menu.

3. **Type** regedit **and click OK.**

4. **Type the administrator's password or click Continue, if prompted.**

   The Windows Registry Editor window appears. This program allows you to do brain surgery on Windows — no need to wash your hands or finish medical school.

5. **Press F3 to summon the Find dialog box.**

6. **Type the name of the file you're trying to pluck out.**

   For example, I'm typing nutjob on my computer because the offending file I want to remove is named just that.

7. **Click the Find Next button.**

   Wait until that text is found.

8. **Confirm that you're in the right spot.**

   The text you type may be common, so you need to confirm that you're looking in the right spot. To do so, look at the bottom of the window. The status bar gives the location where the Registry Editor has found your file. If the location makes sense, you can move on.

   For example, in Figure 7-1, the last part of the location contains the text Microsoft Office 12.0 Word File MRU. MRU is the key: it means Most Recently Used, and an MRU list is where Windows likes to keep files you've opened.

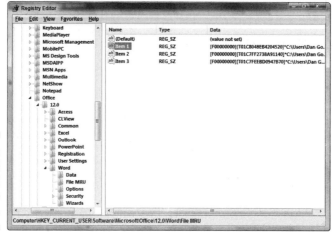

Figure 7-1:
A potential
file is found
in the
Registry.

9. **Upon confirming that you're in the right spot, proceed with Step 10. Otherwise, press F3 to keep looking for the proper bit of text.**

10. **Press the Delete key on the keyboard to remove the filename from the MRU list.**

11. **Click the Yes button to confirm.**

    Scary? No, not if you followed my advice.

12. **Close the Registry Editor.**

The filename no longer appears in the program's recently used list. If it does, you failed to find the proper entry in the Registry. Try again.

✔ In addition to seeing MRU, you may see other, similar names. For example, WordPad and Paint store their recent files in a Recent File List or Recent Items List.

✔ The Registry is *not* the place to experiment! Look, okay? Mess around with things? Best not.

Clearing the Recent Items submenu

The Recent Items submenu appears on the Start menu and lists all the files you have recently opened or viewed. Oops! To purge the list and cover your tracks, heed these steps:

1. **Right-click the Start button.**

2. **Choose Properties from the pop-up menu.**

The Taskbar and Start Menu dialog box wanders in, with the Start Menu tab up front and ready for action.

3. **Click to remove the check mark by Store and Display a List of Recently Opened Files.**

4. **Click OK.**

The Recent Items menu is gone.

And we all sing and dance a merry song of thanks.

Historically Speaking

Wherever you go on the Web, Internet Explorer (IE) makes a note of it, like some busybody neighbor or relative who must check up on you all the time. Internet Explorer notes which Web sites you visit and which pages you look at. At least it doesn't nag you about wearing a sweater. . . .

Supposedly, all this checking is done to make it easier to retrace your steps if you want to go back and visit someplace again. But it also serves as a trail of bread crumbs that just about anyone can follow to see what it is you look at on the Internet — obviously a potential source of embarrassment.

Clearing places from the history

To remove any Web site or specific Web page from the Internet Explorer History list, follow these steps:

1. **Click the Favorites button in Internet Explorer.**

2. **Choose History (if necessary).**

The history list appears on the left side of the browser window. Recently visited sites appear in time categories: 3 Weeks Ago, 2 Weeks Ago, Last Week, and Today.

3. **Open a time category.**

Within each category, you find a folder representing each Web site you visited. Within each folder are links to individual pages on the site.

4. **Right-click any item you want to delete.**

5. **Choose Delete from the pop-up menu.**

6. **Click Yes in the warning dialog box if you're asked to confirm.**

And, the offending entry is gone.

Alas, the entry still may appear on the Address drop-down list. If so, continue reading in the next section.

- ✔ The Ctrl+H key combination can also be used to show the History list.

- ✔ The number of days the history list keeps track of is initially set to 20. This value can be adjusted, as covered in the section "Disabling history altogether," just ahead in this chapter.

- ✔ Removing a History item isn't the same thing as removing an Internet cookie. For cookie information, see Chapter 18.

Clearing all the history

People who don't read history are doomed to repeat it. And, why not? Let's just go and make those same mistakes over and over. It builds character, or something like that.

When the entries on the History list appear to be overwhelming, consider zapping them all:

1. **Open the Control Panel.**

2. **From the Control Panel Home, choose Network and Internet, and then choose Internet Options; from the Control Panel Classic view, open the Internet Options icon.**

   The Internet Properties dialog box appears.

3. **Click the Delete button.**

   It's found in the Browsing History area. Clicking the button displays the Delete Browsing History dialog box, as shown in Figure 7-2.

Figure 7-2:
Delete lots
of Internet
things here.

4. **Click the Delete History button.**

5. **Click Yes to confirm.**

6. **Click the Close button to dismiss the Delete Browsing History dialog box.**

7. **Click the OK button to make the Internet Properties dialog box go away.**

For some reason, these steps do not completely erase your Internet history. No, the places you visited today aren't removed. You can manually remove those items per the directions in the preceding section.

Disabling history altogether

When the History list is a complete and utter bother, just get rid of it:

1. **Summon the Internet Properties dialog box.**

   Refer to Steps 1 and 2 in the preceding section.

2. **Click the Settings button in the Browsing History area.**

3. **Set the Days to Keep Pages in History option to 0.**

   This option is found at the bottom of the dialog box.

4. **Click OK.**

5. **Click OK again to close the Internet Properties dialog box.**

Although this technique eliminates history tracking for previous days, note that Internet Explorer still keeps track of the history *today*. So, if you have been somewhere today and you don't want anyone to know about it before midnight, you still have to manually delete the entries, as covered in the section "Clearing places from the history," earlier in this chapter.

Undoing the AutoComplete Nightmare

In Windows, the AutoComplete feature is one of those nifty utilities that makes typing long, complex things — like Web page addresses — easier. What Windows does is keep track of the places you have been and the addresses (and filenames) you have typed. When you start typing again, Windows automatically completes the address for you, by guessing what it is you want to type or by providing a drop-down list of alternative suggestions.

Suppose that late one night Phil's wife wants to visit Mary's Boutique on the Internet. She starts typing `Marysbo`, and suddenly the Address bar fills with `Mary's Bondage and Discipline Dungeon`. Oops! It's time she had a talk with Phil!

Yes, AutoComplete can also be a source of embarrassment. Happily, you have several ways to deal with it, as covered in this section.

Clearing AutoComplete

To remove unwanted items from the AutoComplete memory, you must bonk it on the head and cause some severe memory loss. It's okay; the computer will survive.

Refer to the steps in the earlier section "Clearing all the history" to summon the Delete Browsing History dialog box, as shown earlier, in Figure 7-2. In the dialog box, click the Delete Forms button. Click Yes to confirm. That zaps the AutoComplete history.

Turning off AutoComplete

When anything vexes you in Windows, the direct solution is usually to turn it off. Why not? Such features should be optional. On my computers, I find AutoComplete to be annoying; I'm startled when some other Web page spelling or suggestion comes up. No problem. AutoComplete can be turned off (or at least curtailed) by following these steps:

1. **Summon the Internet Properties dialog box.**

   Refer to Steps 1 and 2 in the section "Clearing all the history," earlier in this chapter; or, from within Internet Explorer, choose the Internet Options command from the bottom of the Tools button menu.

2. **Click the Content tab.**

3. **Click the Settings button in the AutoComplete area.**

   The AutoComplete Settings dialog box appears.

4. **To turn off AutoComplete, uncheck everything.**

   Click. Click. Click. Click.

5. **Click OK to banish the AutoComplete Settings dialog box.**

6. **Click OK to close the Internet Options dialog box.**

   Or, you can leave it open for the next section's directions.

These steps merely disable AutoComplete. To remove items from the AutoComplete list, keep reading in the next section.

Removing an AutoComplete item from the Registry

When all else fails, brain surgery seems to be the most likely course of action in a computer. For Windows, that means whipping out the Registry Editor and performing exploratory surgery. The thing to remove is AutoComplete text that continues to vex you despite other efforts to kill it. (And I recommend trying the methods in the preceding sections before you resort to something drastic, like using the Registry Editor.)

As with programs that remember recent documents (see the section "Ghosts of Documents Past," earlier in this chapter), AutoComplete stores the text it remembers in the Registry, in an MRU list. When all else fails, follow these steps to find the AutoComplete' MRU list in the Registry, where you may perform surgery to remove something embarrassing:

1. **(Optional) Set a system restore point.**

   Refer to Chapter 4 for more information on this useful tip.

2. **Start the Registry Editor.**

   In the Run dialog box, type **regedit**; refer to the section "Really, really removing unwanted files from a list," earlier in this chapter, for specific steps.

   Rather than tell you how to search for the text, I can point you to the exact location where AutoComplete stores its MRU:

   ```
   HKEY_CURRENT_USER\Software\Microsoft\Internet
        Explorer\TypedURLs
   ```

   Here's how to get there:

3. **Open the HKEY_CURRENT_USER folder.**

4. **Open the Software folder.**

5. **Open the Microsoft folder.**

6. **Open the Internet Explorer folder.**

7. **Open the TypedURLs folder.**

   You see the MRU list on the right side of the window. (Well, unless you cleared AutoComplete, in which case the list is empty. Duh.)

8. **Click to select an entry to delete.**

   For example, select that offensive Helping Thy Neighbor Web site.

   Select the "ab" icon to select an entry.

9. **Press the Delete key on your keyboard.**

10. **Click the Yes button to confirm.**

11. **Repeat Steps 7 through 9 to remove other entries.**

12. **Close the Registry Editor when you're done.**

    To be medical about it, you can shout "Closing!" just like they do on those doctor TV shows.

Avoid the temptation to monkey with the Registry beyond my simple words of advice offered in this book.

Images of Filth and Perversion

It happened to me just the other day. I was helping my son find a Web page related to his favorite musical group. Somehow, I typed the name wrong and — *blam!* — there on the screen was a porno page. We were both terribly embarrassed.

Beyond the shock of seeing something unwanted, you must also accept that such offensive images aren't removed by simply closing the Web page window. Nope, because the Internet sends an actual copy of the image to your computer, that copy is kept in storage until you remove it. The storage is a place called the *cache* (pronounced "cash"), and if you really want to purge your PC of such prurient pictures, please press on!

Finding the images

Everything that floats over the Internet transom to your computer is stored *in* your computer. The files — images, text, and others — are stored in the PC's storage system. The notion is that it's quicker for the PC to reload an image from memory than to transfer it from the Internet. Hence, the term *cache* is used to describe those files residing on your PC. But where are they, and what are they?

To look at your Internet cache, follow these steps:

1. **Open Internet Explorer.**

2. **From the Tools button menu, choose Internet Options.**

    The Internet Options dialog box appears. (You can also display this dialog box by using the Control Panel.)

3. **On the General tab, click the Settings button in the Browsing History area.**

    The Temporary Internet Files and History Settings dialog box appears.

4. Click the View files button.

A Windows Explorer window appears, listing the contents of the Internet cache. You see the files presented in Details view, looking like any folder on your PC's storage system — indeed, what you're viewing is exactly that.

You can view a file by opening its icon. You're warned: It can be a security risk to open random files that you downloaded from the Internet. But for image files, it's probably okay.

To remove a file, just delete it as you would any icon on your computer's storage system: Select the icon and press the Delete key.

Then again, you probably notice that you have *thousands* of image icons in the Temporary Internet Files folder. Viewing them all will be tedious. As a tip, if an offending image arrived (was stored on your computer) today, you can click one of the date/time column headings to sort the list and then find files downloaded today. But that will still be a might long list to cull through. And, do you really want to see that image again?

A better solution lies in the next section. But first, remember to close any open windows or dialog boxes.

Clearing the image cache

To pull a colon cleanse on your PC's potentially philthy picture pocket, heed these steps:

1. Summon the Delete Browsing History dialog box.

Refer to the steps from the earlier section "Clearing all the history"; the Delete Browsing History dialog box is shown earlier, in Figure 7-2.

2. Click the Delete Files button.

3. Click Yes to confirm.

4. Click Close, and then click OK to dismiss the various open dialog boxes.

The side effect of removing the entire cache is that the Internet may behave a bit more slowly the next time you make your Web page rounds. That's because images once pulled from storage now must be reloaded from the Internet. That takes time.

Dealing with nasty wallpaper!

When you right-click an image on the Internet, you see on the pop-up menu the option Set As Background (or something similar). It turns the image into the desktop background, or *wallpaper,* which you can see when you use Windows. Sometimes, this is an accident. It need not be a nasty image, but whatever image it is, you probably want it off the desktop. Here's how:

1. **Right-click the desktop.**
2. **Choose Personalize from the pop-up menu.**
3. **Choose Desktop Background in the Personalization window.**
4. **Select a new background.**

   Use the Picture Location menu button to choose a category, and then choose the type of background from the list that's displayed.

5. **Click OK, and close the Personalization window.**

Generally speaking, these steps should fix whatever unwanted desktop images you have.

Hiding Something on the Screen

I'm sure this never happens to you: You're looking at something diverse and interesting on the computer when someone else walks into the room. Do you panic? Do you freak out and yell at them? Or, do you quickly and stealthily hide the entire contents of the screen?

Hopefully, you know the trick to instantly hide everything on the screen: Press the Win+M key combination, where Win is the Windows key. Win+M automatically *minimizes* every open window and leaves only the desktop displayed.

✔ Alas, you have no Win+M key equivalent if your computer's keyboard lacks a Windows key.

✔ The mouse equivalent for this command is to right-click the taskbar and choose Show the Desktop from the pop-up menu. (Sometimes that's just too slow!)

✔ Oh, you can always switch off the monitor, though that tends to arouse suspicion.

Chapter 8

Startup Problems

· ·

In This Chapter

▶ Understanding how the computer starts

▶ Working out immediate startup trouble

▶ Dealing with a missing operating system

▶ Discovering various boot menus

▶ Using the Startup menu

▶ Avoiding Selective Startup

▶ Fixing missing-file messages

▶ Disabling those programs that start automatically

▶ Defending against unwanted startup programs

▶ Attempting to keep Windows from restarting automatically

· ·

S ome people rise bright and early in the morning, completely rested and refreshed. Those folks bounce out of bed and start their day with a big smile, boundless energy, and a positive outlook. Then there's the rest of us.

If you're one of the few who takes great efforts to pull yourself from the comforting arms of sleep, consider the plight of the poor PC. It takes a titanic amount of effort — yes, in the form of electricity — to get a computer up and working properly every time you start it. The fact that the computer starts at all should be considered miraculous. Indeed, those times that the miracle misfires, that's when you turn to this chapter to cover a smattering of issues that affect Mr. PC when he (unenthusiastically) starts his wary day.

Computer Genesis

In the beginning . . .

When you understand how the computer starts, you can better pinpoint various problems that can occur during the startup process. Although you really don't need to know this information, it helps to be familiar with what happens where and when, and how to be properly able to point the finger of blame.

Overall, remember that computer hardware is dumb. It needs software to tell it what to do. The problem, however, is that it's the hardware that starts up first. So, the hardware in a PC is geared toward immediately finding and desperately loading an operating system so that the computer can become a useful tool and not an impressive-looking but expensive office prop.

First: Within all your computer's hardware is software encoded on special chips, the ROM chips you might have read about in days of yore. Collectively, those chips are referred to as the computer's *chipset.* The software in the chipset tends to specific tasks, monitors things, and provides communications on a very low level. But before all that happens, the chipset performs a special diagnostic test, called the Power-On Self Test, or POST. This test ensures that all the basic input/output devices (monitor and keyboard, for example) are working.

> **If it goes right:** Various copyright text or manufacturer's graphics appear on the screen.

> **What can go wrong?** When the POST fails, the computer either beeps several times or, if the monitor is working, an error message is displayed. Note that any error you get at this stage is always a hardware error.

Second: When the chipset is working properly and has passed the diagnostic and found all the devices it was expecting, it attempts to find an operating system on one of the computer's storage devices. Depending on how your PC is set up, the hardware first searches for an operating system on the primary hard drive, the optical drive, or any external USB drives. (The order is determined by the PC's Setup program, which has been read in the previous step.)

> **If it goes right:** The operating system takes over and continues starting up the computer.

> **What can go wrong?** If an operating system isn't found on any disk, a `Missing Operating System` error is displayed. Nasty. Or, the text `Non-system disk` is displayed. (Not quite as nasty.)

Third: The operating system begins loading.

> **If it goes right:** You see the pretty Windows startup logo, or *splash screen.*

> **What can go wrong?** Anything at this point can go wrong because software is in charge of the system. For example, in Windows a problem can be detected and you're thrust into the dreaded Safe mode. Or, Windows may detect new hardware and attempt to install it. Or . . . just about anything!

Fourth: The operating system loads other startup programs, such as device drivers, startup applications, antivirus utilities, the Task Scheduler, plus other programs you specify.

If it goes right: Eventually, you're prompted to log in to Windows and start your merry Windows day.

What can go wrong? Lots and lots of things: You may find that you have missing devices or bad device drivers; an improperly uninstalled program can display various `missing file` or `missing DLL` error messages, and on and on. Some of these messages may appear after you log in, depending on which program generated them.

Fifth, and finally: You can start using your computer.

If it goes right: The merry works sing cheerful songs of loving praise to Chairman Bill.

What can go wrong? Everything.

Why bother knowing this stuff? Because a different solution exists for each step in the process. For example, a blank screen with a blinking cursor when you first turn on the computer means that even the chipset isn't working properly. That makes the solution relatively easy to find because you eliminate every other possibility.

- ✔ The chipset's instructions don't include loading the computer's operating system. Instead, a *boot loader* program is found on the PC's storage system, and the boot loader loads the operating system.

- ✔ On computers with multiple operating systems, the boot loader runs a program that lets you select which operating system to start.

- ✔ System Commander, Partition Magic, or even the Linux program LILO are all examples of boot loaders that let you select an operating system to start.

Immediate Trouble

Nothing beats a novel that gets into the action right away or a film that begins in the middle of things with a chase scene. (*Star Wars* comes to mind). The dramatic term is *in medias res,* which roughly translates into "We're starting this thing off in deep doo-doo."

When a computer gets into deep doo-doo right away, it's actually a good thing. No sense in waiting through a long, dreary process just to find out that something is wrong or missing. No, instant trouble is right there on the screen before you even have a chance to paw the PC mouse.

On the downside, instant trouble is often the unfortunate sign of impending expensive repair or replacement. Not always, but often.

"I see nothing — just a blinking cursor!"

When the computer first starts, text might be displayed on the screen. Some PCs display graphics, but often text is mixed in, such as in a copyright notice. The computer make and model number may be displayed. This is just for entertainment; internally, the computer is doing a memory check. (You may see the counter tick away on some computers.)

Depending on which hardware options are installed, you may see text regarding those options: hard drive, mouse, or video adapter, for example.

Eventually, the caboose on the text train is a prompt to press a certain key — usually, Delete or F1 — to enter the computer's Setup program. You have about a half a breath to decide about that, and then automatically the computer's operating system is loaded, takes off, and displays that colorful, graphic Windows logo. That's the way it's supposed to happen.

When all you see is a blinking prompt, it means one of the following things:

Problem: A motherboard failure has occurred. Something is wrong with the motherboard — an electronics fault, no power, or some other type of corruption.

Solution: Take the computer to the dealer and have them replace the motherboard. That can be expensive.

Problem: The computer is too hot. You can tell by feeling the case or checking to see whether the fans are spinning. A computer doesn't operate if its internal temperature is too hot.

Solution: Fix the fans. Some microprocessors have fans, and these can be replaced. Ensure that your dealer replaces only the microprocessor fan and not the entire microprocessor, which is expensive. (However, if the dealer replaces the fan and the microprocessor is damaged, the microprocessor needs to be replaced as well.)

Problem: The hard drive has no operating system. This problem happens on those systems that show logos and not startup text. Occasionally, you may even see a `Missing Operating System` error.

Solution: See the section "The dreaded Missing Operating System message," a couple of sections from here.

> ✔ Those computers that display a graphical startup message might have an option in the Setup program to display the diagnostic text instead. That's a good option to choose if you're experiencing startup trouble.

✔ Make a note of which key combination starts the computer's Setup program. Text on the screen informs you of which key or key combination to press to enter this program. On most PCs, it's the Del or Delete key, F1, F2, Alt+S, or F10. Whatever the key, make a note of it, for example, in the manual that came with the computer or on this book's Cheat Sheet.

✔ Sometimes, cables come loose, which may lead you to believe that you have a major component failure, but it's just not the case. If you're bold enough, unplug the PC's console and venture into its case. Check to ensure that all cables are properly connected and that all expansion cards are properly "seated" into their slots.

The nefarious Non-System Disk error message

The exact wording of the error message varies, but the cause is the same: In its efforts to find an operating system, the PC has encountered a disk without an operating system. The solution: Remove the disk and press the spacebar to continue booting from the hard drive.

✔ This error can also happen if you attempt to boot from a nonbootable CD. Same solution.

✔ If you get the CD error often, you can fix it on most PCs. See the section "The computer tries to find the operating system on the wrong drive," later in this chapter, for information on changing the boot order.

✔ If a hard drive produces this error, it means that the hard drive lacks an operating system. See the next section.

✔ This error message was extremely common in the days when all PCs first attempted to start by loading an operating system from Drive A, the floppy drive. Careless users would forget to remove the floppy disk from Drive A, and the error message would appear. For security reasons, computers no longer boot from floppy disks, though they can be foolishly reconfigured to do so in the PC Setup program.

The dreaded Missing Operating System message

The most terrifying error message I have ever seen is `Missing Operating System`. It's a hardware error message that comes from the chipset, though it can also be a boot loader message. Basically, it means that no operating system exists to load. Uh-oh.

There are many things you can do, however:

Boot from a bootable CD: For example, your computer may have come with a recovery disc, or you may have the original Windows disc. If so, try to start the computer with it. Again, this technique confirms that the computer is working fine; the problem may only be with the hard drive.

Use an emergency boot disc: This is something a third-party recovery utility may create, such as Norton Utilities. Disk partitioning software also comes with emergency startup discs in case something goes wrong with that software. Finally, some third-party backup programs have boot discs you can use so that you can restore your computer system from a set of backup disks.

Reinstall your computer system: The final step, which is most drastic and terrible, is to merely start over and attempt a full system recovery. Most PCs come with a recovery CD, which you can use to reinstall basic system software and return your computer to the same state it was in when you took it out of the box.

I wish that I had better news on this error message. Generally speaking, the only way your operating system (Windows) can disappear and go for a powder is if you have somehow messed with it. This situation can happen if you attempt to modify or change the hard drive's partition tables, boot sector, or master boot record or, well, if you just up and delete all of Windows.

- ✔ Another culprit? Computer viruses. The Monkey virus can delete information on a hard drive that tells Windows where to find files. When that information is gone, so is the hard drive.

- ✔ Hardware-wise, this problem may occur if the hard drive fails outright. However, that problem generates a BIOS error message on most systems when the hard drive fails to initialize.

- ✔ Does this stuff scare you? Then it's a good time to consider a backup strategy (see Chapter 26).

The computer tries to find the operating system on the wrong drive

Most of the time, your PC looks to load the operating system from the computer's main hard drive. It's tradition. But you can configure your PC to search other drives, such as the optical drive or even an external USB drive in addition to, or to the exclusion of, the main hard drive. It's that flexibility which saves your butt in the situation when the PC stubbornly tries to load Windows from the wrong startup device.

For example, you may have noticed that sometimes when you keep a disc in the optical drive and restart the PC, you see the message `Do you want to boot from the CD?` or `Press any key to boot the CD`. This option is valuable if anything happens to the hard drive, but it can be annoying.

To fix the program, run your PC's Setup program: Read the screen when the computer first starts. Take note of which key (or keys) to press to enter the Setup program.

In the Setup program, look for boot information. You may see an option there to change the boot order, by specifying which disk drives you want the PC to check for an operating system and in which order.

Be sure to save your selection if you make any changes.

- ✔ Not every PC's Setup program has boot options that let you change the order of which disk is checked for an operating system.
- ✔ If you have an emergency and you need to boot from a floppy or CD, you can rerun the Setup program and, once again, change the boot order. That way, you can use an emergency boot disc, if the need arises.

The Many Villages of Startup Menuland

Sometimes it's difficult to know what someone is talking about when they refer to "the menu that appears when the computer starts." That's because there can be up to *three* different menus — or more, depending on how the PC is configured.

Your PC's startup menus

How many menus can you see when the computer starts? Let me count the ways. . . .

PC Setup: The first menu you can encounter is the PC's Setup program, which must be summoned by pressing a key when the PC starts. (The specific key is displayed on the screen for an instant; blink and you'll miss it.) Pressing the right key — or doing the right dance or sacrificing the proper goat — displays a menu full of hardware options for your PC's basic configuration and startup settings. I call it the PC Setup menu.

Boot menu: This menu appears courtesy of the boot loader. The menu allows you to select an operating system to start, but only when more than one operating system is installed in the computer. Or, if you configured the Windows Recovery Console, the Boot menu also displays that option.

Windows Advanced Options menu: Also known as the Startup menu, this menu is used for troubleshooting your computer's startup woes. It's generated by Windows itself, so this is the last of the three startup menus available. You see it only if you know the trick.

Each menu affects the way your computer starts, and each has its purpose. The following sections mull over the details.

The PC's hardware setup menu

The hardware setup menu is what you see when you press the Del (or F1 or whichever) key when the computer starts. The menu is different for each type of chipset a manufacturer may put in a PC, but they all generally configure various parts of the computer hardware.

Your PC hardware setup menu may let you configure or set the following items:

- ✔ The date and time
- ✔ The hard drive setup
- ✔ The order in which the hardware scans for an operating system
- ✔ Printer port configuration
- ✔ Power management configuration
- ✔ Startup password protection
- ✔ Many other goodies

Setting or resetting these values is done by running the Setup program when the computer first starts. Generally speaking, as long as you don't upgrade your computer with a new hard drive or more memory, you most likely never have to mess with the Setup menu.

I do not recommend using the startup password. If you forget the password, it is impossible to use your computer.

The Windows boot menu

Your PC is more than capable of running multiple operating systems. In such a configuration, you see a boot menu appear as the computer starts. You can then select from a list which operating system you want. Windows helps by providing a dialog box where you can set various boot options. Here's how to get there:

1. **Open the Control Panel's System icon.**

   From the Control Panel Home, choose System and Maintenance, and then choose System. From the Control Panel Classic view, open the System icon.

2. **From the Tasks list on the left side of the System window, choose Advanced System Settings.**

3. **If prompted, enter the administrator's password or click the Continue button.**

   The System Properties dialog box shuffles forth.

4. **Click the Advanced tab.**

5. **Click the Settings button in the Startup and Recovery area.**

   The Startup and Recovery dialog box appears, as shown in Figure 8-1.

   The drop-down default operating system list displays the available operating systems on your computer. (At least, it displays the operating systems that Windows itself knows about.) This is where you choose which operating system you want to boot from automatically; for example, when you're away from your computer when it starts.

   The Time to Display List of Operating Systems option tells Windows how many seconds to display the list before the default operating system is automatically chosen.

6. **To disable the menu, click to remove the check mark by the option Time to Display List of Operating Systems.**

   This way, Windows always boots into the operating system you have selected.

Figure 8-1:
Controlling the boot menu in Windows Vista.

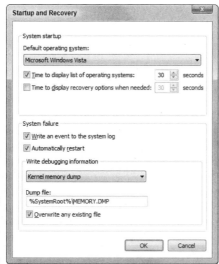

7. **Click OK when you're done making changes to this dialog box.**

   (Optional) Close any other open dialog boxes or windows.

Again, the list of operating systems appears only if you installed multiple versions of Windows on a PC and Windows itself is managing those operating systems.

✔ If you're using another system to control which operating system starts, such as System Commander or the Linux LILO program, you have to check its documentation for the various options and settings.

✔ Now would certainly be a good time for a fresh, hot, soft peanut butter cookie.

The Advanced Boot Options menu

The Advanced Boot Options menu appears after Windows first loads. But you must be quick! To see the Advanced Boot Options menu, press the F8 key immediately after you hear the computer beep or you see the menu to select an operating system or when you see the Starting Windows message on the screen. If you're paranoid, just keep tapping the F8 key until you see the Advanced Boot Options menu, a sample of which is shown in Figure 8-2.

```
Choose Advanced Options for: Microsoft Windows Vista
(Use the arrow keys to highlight your choice.)

      Safe Mode
      Safe Mode with Networking
      Safe Mode with Command Prompt

      Enable Boot Logging
      Enable low-resolution video (640x480)
      Last Known Good Configuration (advanced)
      Directory Services Restore Mode
      Debugging Mode
      Disable automatic restart on system failure
      Disable Driver Signature Enforcement

      Start Windows Normally


Description: Start Windows with its regular settings.
```

Figure 8-2: The Advanced Boot Options menu.

The menu displays the following items:

- ✔ **Safe Mode:** The computer is started, but Windows doesn't load any specific hardware drivers. Please see Chapter 24 for all the details and reasons why.

- ✔ **Safe Mode with Networking:** This option is the same as Safe mode but with networking abilities enabled so that you can use the network and, possibly, restore a network backup or download updated files from a server.

- ✔ **Safe Mode with Command Prompt:** The computer is started in text mode in Windows and uses only basic configuration files.

- ✔ **Enable Boot Logging:** A text file is created as the computer starts, listing which programs or processes start and whether they're successful. The file is named NTBTLOG.TXT, found in the Windows folder. You can use the file to pinpoint problems the computer may have when starting, though the information there is decipherable only by highly trained tech-support people or Vulcans.

- ✔ **Enable low-resolution video (640 × 480):** Select this option if you're having video troubles in Windows. The option looks similar to Safe mode, but unlike in Safe mode, the rest of the computer starts up normally. (Only the video driver is disabled.) That way, you can fix a video problem and still have the rest of your computer in working order.

- ✔ **Last Known Good Configuration (Advanced):** This option uses a type of System Restore "on the fly" to return the computer to a state where it last started properly. Choose this item when you're unable to start the computer to run System Restore after an upgrade. Alas, unlike a real System Restore, this option doesn't fix or uninstall bad drivers or missing files. (You need to run System Restore in Safe mode for that to happen.)

- ✔ **Directory Services Restore Mode:** You can happily avoid using this option (it's for Windows domain controllers).

- ✔ **Debugging Mode:** This option is used to check for problems on one computer using a second computer connected via a serial cable. Both this selection and the preceding one are advanced options most likely used by people in white lab coats and thick glasses who are best equipped to deal with such things.

- ✔ **Disable Automatic Restart on System Failure:** This option helps you avoid the endless-loop situation when Windows automatically restarts on a hardware failure. In such a situation, the computer forever starts up and restarts. Selecting this option ends the madness.

- ✔ **Disable Driver Signature Enforcement.** This option allows Windows to sally forth without warning you when an unsigned program attempts to run.

- ✔ **Start Windows Normally:** Just continue loading Windows as though you didn't press F8 to see the Startup menu.

  ✔ **Reboot:** Restart the computer.

  ✔ **Return to OS Choices Menu:** On computers that have multiple Windows operating systems (OSs) installed, this option returns you to the operating system selection menu (or the boot menu, as covered in the preceding section).

Make your choice based on your troubleshooting needs. Various sections elsewhere in this book recommend choices and options to take for this menu.

  ✔ On some computers, you can press and hold the Ctrl key rather than the F8 key.

  ✔ When you see the Please Select an Operating System to Start menu (the Boot menu), you have to press the F8 key again to get at the Startup menu.

  ✔ Any additional options not mentioned in the preceding list are generally advanced configuration items. Mess with such options only when directed to do so by a support technician.

  ✔ Believe it or not, the Advanced Boot Options menu doesn't appear, nor does the F8 key work, when you boot your computer into another operating system, such as Linux.

  ✔ If the computer starts in Safe mode no matter what, see Chapter 24 for more information.

  ✔ The Automatic Restart on System Failure problem has supposedly been licked by Microsoft. Reportedly, no option is available in Windows itself to turn on that feature, yet the menu option remains, most likely for old time's sake.

Mystery Startup Messages

Suppose that your computer starts as it normally does. However, along its tired journey, some oddball messages pop up. It's stuff you have never seen! Is Windows causing the message? Is the message something to be concerned about? And, most importantly, how do you get rid of the dumb message?

For some reason, Selective Startup is on

Selective Startup is a debugging tool set by the System Configuration utility (MSCONFIG). Here's how to turn it off:

1. **From the Start menu, choose the Run command.**

   The keyboard shortcut here is Win+R.

2. **In the Run dialog box, type** MSCONFIG **and click the OK button.**

3. **Type the administrator's password or click the Continue button, if prompted.**

   The System Configuration dialog box appears, as shown in Figure 8-3.

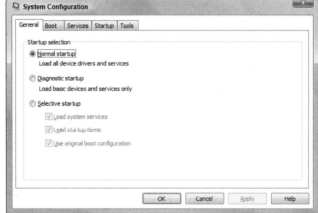

Figure 8-3:
The System
Configura-
tion utility
(MSCON-
FIG).

4. **Choose the option labeled Normal Startup.**

5. **Click the OK button.**

Windows may beg you to restart the computer after making this change.
Do so.

If this technique still doesn't work, check the Boot tab in the System
Configuration utility. Repeat Steps 1 and 2 in the preceding step list, and then
click the Boot tab, as shown in Figure 8-4. Ensure that the Safe Boot option
isn't checked. Indeed, ensure that *none* of the options is checked. Then click
the OK button.

See Chapter 24 for information on the System Configuration utility.

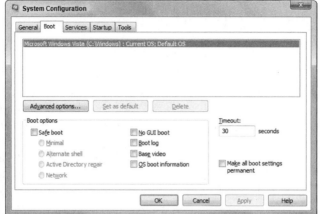

The missing-file mystery

One of the most annoying startup messages of all time is the one that alerts you to an absent file. It's the tattle-tale message. "Hey, Mr. Human! You know this file? Well, he's supposed to be here, but he's *gone!* He's probably out doing something naughty! Hurry! Do something, quick!" Trust me here: The missing file isn't your responsibility. But the message annoys you, so here's how I recommend that you get rid of the message and, potentially, fix the problem that caused the message:

1. **Write down as much as you can about the message.**

   If the missing file has a name, write it down. If another program is mentioned, write it down.

2. **Search for the file in question.**

   See Chapter 9 for information on finding files. You know the file's name; it was displayed in the warning dialog box. Now you need to check to see whether the file exists. If you can find it, note in which folder it lives.

3. **Start the System Configuration utility.**

   Refer to Steps 1 through 3 in the preceding section.

   Your job now is to try to find the program associated with the bum startup program. It may be started directly or run when another program starts.

   The name of the folder in which the missing file exists can be your clue to which program "owns" the file.

4. **Click the Startup tab.**

   Scroll through the list of programs and see whether you can find the "bad" one in there.

TECHNICAL STUFF

"What's a DLL file?"

The *DLL file* is one of the most regrettable mistakes made by the people who originally created Windows. The idea seemed worthwhile and wholesome: Much of computer programming involves the redundant rewriting of a few common routines. For example, most applications use the Open, Save, Print, and several other dialog boxes. Rather than re-create that programming code over and over, the wise programmers at Microsoft decided to save everyone time and bother. So, they created the Dynamically Linked Library (DLL) file concept.

A DLL file contains common routines to be used by all programs. For example, the COMMDLG.DLL file contains the programming needed to use the Open,

Save, Print, and other common dialog (COMMDLG) boxes. Other DLL files were created so that programmers could link into them and everyone could share all the same code and be happy and go on to live lives of religious and spiritual fulfillment.

Alas, the DLL solution became a problem in itself because just about everyone figured out how to make better DLL files. There were conflicts! There was competition! There was DLL hell! And eventually, the simple solution turned out to be a gigantic pain in the rear. I have heard a rumor that the next version of Windows will do away with DLL files. If so, there will be much rejoicing.

5. **If you find the bad program listed, remove the check mark.**

   By removing the check mark, you're preventing that single program from starting and the error message from being displayed. That fixes the message, but not the problem.

6. **Close the System Configuration utility when you're done.**

To fix the actual problem, consider the name of the folder you noted in Step 3. That folder may be the clue to which program is responsible for the missing file. If you can determine which program is trying to run the missing file, consider reinstalling that program to fix the problem.

When these steps fail to fix the problem, consider looking elsewhere. See the following section.

- ✔ Missing-file messages appear right after installing or uninstalling a program. If you just installed a program and you see the message, try installing the program again. If that doesn't work, phone the developer and have someone there fix the error.

- ✔ See the Microsoft Knowledge Base on the Internet for information regarding missing files for Windows. Visit http://support. microsoft.com/ and select your version of Windows. Search for the file's name; any information about the file appears in the search results along with information on how to fix any problems. (Also refer to Chapter 5.)

Stopping Things from Starting Automatically

Windows can stick programs in three places to start them automatically. The first two are covered in the preceding section; the System Configuration utility's Startup tab lists programs that Windows itself automatically starts for you. The Services tab also lists startup programs, but those don't tend to be a problem for the nongeek set.

For you, a mere mortal user, you have the Startup folder on the Start button's Programs menu: After clicking the Start button, choose All Programs and then click the Startup folder. The items you see are started automatically each time Windows starts. In Figure 8-5, you see only two items listed, but your system may have more or fewer or none.

The following sections describe ways to prevent a program in the Startup folder from starting.

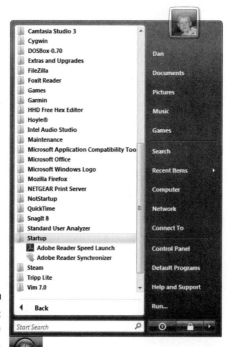

Figure 8-5:
The Startup folder.

Deleting a program from the Startup folder

To delete the program, and prevent it from automatically starting, right-click its entry on the Startup menu. Choose Delete from the pop-up menu, and the program is gone.

✔ Only a shortcut icon is deleted. The program isn't removed from the hard drive. (To remove a program, you must uninstall it.)

✔ If you make a mistake, press Ctrl+Z right away, and your deleted menu item is yanked back.

Creating a NotStartup folder

Better than deleting a Startup menu item is disabling the program from starting. You do that by moving the menu item from the Startup menu to a special menu you create, called NotStartup. Such a menu is shown earlier, in Figure 8-5 (above the Startup folder).

Here's how to create your own NotStartup folder:

1. **Right-click the Start button.**

2. **Choose the Open command from the pop-up menu.**

   By choosing Open, you can use a Windows Explorer window to edit the Start menu, which works just like editing folders and files.

3. **Open the Programs folder.**

   You see menu items (shortcut icons) and menus (folders), including the Startup folder.

4. **Choose New Folder from the toolbar's Organize button menu.**

   The new folder appears highlighted in the window.

5. **Type NotStartup as the folder's new name.**

   If this step doesn't work, reselect the New Folder icon by clicking it once with the mouse. Press the F2 key, and then you can rename the folder.

   The NotStartup folder is now a new menu on the main All Programs menu. You can pop up the Start button and look at the menu to confirm, if you like. Or, you can continue by moving those items you want disabled from the Startup folder to the NotStartup folder.

6. **Open the Startup folder.**

7. **Click to select the program that you don't want to run when the computer starts.**

If it's more than one program, press the Ctrl key as you click the mouse. Ctrl+clicking lets you select more than one icon.

8. **Press Ctrl+X to "cut" the files.**

   Cutting the files is the first step for moving them to another folder.

9. **Click the Back button to return to the `Programs` folder.**

   Or you can press the Backspace key on the keyboard.

10. **Open the `NotStartup` folder.**

11. **Press Ctrl+V to paste the files, moving them to the new folder.**

    The shortcut icons are moved — and disabled from starting up every time Windows starts.

12. **Close the window.**

The beauty of this technique is that you can easily reenable the programs by moving them from the `NotStartup` folder back to the `Startup` folder. Nothing is ever lost.

And now, the bad news: Windows uses more than one `Programs` folder. If you want to make this change for other accounts on your computer, you have to repeat the preceding steps. But, in Step 2, choose Open All Users rather than the Open command. Then repeat all steps as written. That operation builds the `NotStartup` folder for everyone to use.

Defending against unwanted startup programs

Perhaps the most virile tool to help you fend off unwanted startup programs — and I'm talking *nasty* programs you cannot get rid of — is to use the Windows Defender utility Software Explorer. Here's how to dig up that window:

1. **From the Start menu, choose All Programs➪Windows Defender.**

2. **Choose Tools from the toolbar.**

3. **Choose Software Explorer from the list of tools and settings.**

4. **From the Category menu button, choose Startup Programs, if necessary.**

   The Windows Defender window displays a scrolling list of startup programs, as shown in Figure 8-6. The programs are categorized by publisher. By each program is its classification: Permitted, Disabled, or Not Yet Classified.

Figure 8-6:
Processes
running
in your
computer.

To specifically disable a program from starting, such as some vicious program you accidentally downloaded from the Internet, locate the suspect program in the list, click to select it, and then click the Disable button. If that fixes the problem, repeat the steps in this section and click the Remove button to eliminate the program.

5. Close the Windows Defender window when you're done.

Just because a program is Not Yet Classified doesn't mean that it's evil. It usually means that the publisher doesn't yet have the proper certificate ensuring Windows that the product is legitimate. Especially with shareware software, you may never see a certificate that permanently permits the program to run.

✔ What type of program would be "suspect?" It depends. Refer to Chapter 24 for more information on using Windows Defender to detect nasty programs.

✔ You can also start Windows Defender from the Control Panel: From the Control Panel Home, choose Security and then Windows Defender.

✔ When you see a message telling you that Windows has blocked certain startup programs, it's the Windows Defender program that has done the blocking. This happens either because of spyware it has blocked or a program you personally have disabled.

The mystery of processes and services

Your computer runs things other than programs. Specifically, every day when the PC starts, it also starts services and processes.

- *Process* is the fancy-schmancy name given to any program that runs on your computer. This includes the programs you run yourself but also operating system programs that are started automatically.

- A *service* is specific task that controls or monitors some sort of activity in the computer. For example, a service monitors when you add a USB device to the PC. Other services carry out various network activities.

A single process can run multiple services. So, at the root of any service is a process or program that started the service. But because these processes and services are all running around inside your PC, they can potentially run amok. When that happens, you need to fix things.

To view the status of any process or service, you use a tool called the Task Manager. The Task Manager serves to monitor the software that's buzzing, bleeping, and boring your computer. To summon the Task Manager, press Ctrl+Shift+Esc. (This key combination is different from older versions of Windows, where the Task Manager appeared when you pressed Ctrl+Alt+Delete.)

Figure 8-7 shows the Processes tab in the Task Manager window. There are 48 processes, though only those belonging to the current user appear in the list. (To see the lot of them, click the Show Processes from All Users button.)

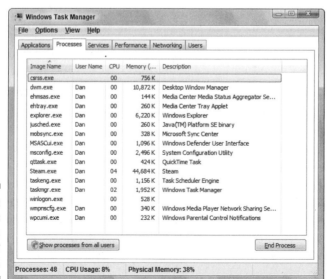

Figure 8-7:
Processes
running
in your
computer.

"My PC annoyingly phones the Internet every time it starts!"

Many programs have the urge to contact their developer's mother ship every time the computer starts. Some programs, such as antivirus utilities, may dial in to the Internet to obtain updates when your computer first starts. Other programs dial in to the Internet to complete the installation process. These operations are entirely normal, though to most folks it's kind of surprising to find the computer using the modem every time Windows starts.

Connecting to the Internet is a normal activity most of the time. It becomes an issue only when you have a dialup modem because you notice the modem's sounds as it connects to the Internet — seemingly by itself. (Broadband users don't notice this action because the connection is always on.) Again, all these things are normal. My only beef is that the program should be forthright about its intentions. A dialog box should appear and tell you, "This program needs to contact the Internet for important update information." Alas, few of these surprise programs do so.

The Services tab in the Task Manager window lists all services running in the computer. Many, many services are running, and the Description column in the list gives you an idea of what the service controls.

To kill a process, and end a program, you select the process on the Processes tab and then click the End Process button. This action isn't anything drastic; ending a process is the same as quitting a program. But sometimes you may see Not Responding by a specific process. In that case, often the only way to remove it is to click the End Process button.

To kill a service, you must stop the service. This is done by using the Administrative Tools icon in the Control Panel. The details are covered in Chapter 23.

Windows Has Magically Restarted!

Windows has the ability to shut itself down and restart, all on its own without asking your permission. Well, that's not honest. Windows *has* asked your permission — you probably just don't remember granting it.

The culprit here is the Windows Update program. It provides necessary and often vital updates to your computer. If you configured Windows Update as recommended, it automatically downloads and installs updates, and therein lies the rub: Some automatic updates require the computer to restart.

I don't recommend disabling Windows Update. But if the automatic restarts bother you, you can lower the settings. Here's how:

1. **Start Windows Update.**

   From the Start button menu, choose All Programs⇨Windows Update. Or, you can also open the Windows Update window from the Control Panel.

2. **From the list of tasks on the left, choose Change Settings.**

3. **Choose the option Download Updates but Let Me Choose Whether to Install Them.**

   I feel that this is the best option, next to having things done automatically.

4. **Click the OK button.**

5. **Enter the administrator's password or click the Continue button, if prompted.**

Of course, by setting the option to be prompted for updates, you find yourself besieged with pop-up balloons alerting you to the presence of new updates that need attention. So be it. Also, this is no guarantee that Windows won't disobey you and install an update and restart the PC; Microsoft has done such a thing in the past when it considers an update to be of a very high priority.

Obviously, automatically restarting Windows isn't an issue or even noticeable when you turn off your computer at the end of the day. Only when you leave the PC on all the time (or if you oddly schedule automatic updates in the middle of the day) do you notice that Windows has restarted overnight.

Chapter 9

Losing Things, Finding Things

There's an art to finding things. I find my stuff because I try to put it in the same place all the time. That works, but I still have moments of frantic searching when I misplace something. In those frenzies, I follow my mother's advice to "retrace your steps," and eventually I find the thing. Once, my grandmother lost her car keys and resorted to using something called "Kreskin's crystal" to help her psychically locate them. (It worked.) I'm sure other folks have other tricks for finding things, but I'll promise you that few will work inside your computer. That's why I wrote this chapter: to show you how to find things you have lost inside your PC.

Finding Files Lost and Lonely

In the top drawer of the Windows treasure chest is a wonderfully powerful file-finding command. It's fast. It's convenient. It's always correct. It's more reliable than Kreskin's crystal. It's the Search command.

Finding the Search command

It's not difficult to find the impressive Windows Search command. No, what's difficult is trying *not* to find it! There are Search text boxes just about everywhere: at the top right of each folder window, at the bottom of the Start menu, in the Windows Mail program, and on and on.

The Search command works simply: Type the text you're searching for. It can be part of a filename or a text tidbit inside a file or an e-mail message. Press the Enter key and you see results, similar to what's shown in Figure 9-1.

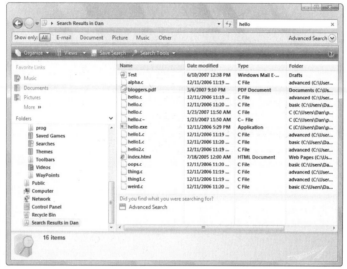

Figure 9-1:
The Search
Results
window.

From the Start menu, you can use the Start Search text box to search for things all over your computer. Just type the text and press Enter. Unlike searching elsewhere, when you use the Start menu, the results are displayed in the Start menu itself, as shown in Figure 9-2. You might also find a Search command directly on the Start menu, on the right side.

To move away from the confines of the Start menu, choose the link See All Results from the bottom of the list (refer to Figure 9-2) to see the Search Results window type of display (refer to Figure 9-1).

In the Search Results window, you can narrow your search by using the toolbar, as shown in Figure 9-3. For example, click the E-Mail button to see only those e-mail messages containing the text you searched for. Or, click the Document button to see documents either named with your search text or containing the search text.

Figure 9-2:
Search
results on
the Start
menu.

Figure 9-3:
The Search
Results
toolbar.

After you find your document, open it! You found it! Hurray!

Close the Search Results window when you're done.

- ✔ The Search text box in Internet Explorer limits its search to the Internet.

- ✔ If nothing is found, you see a message confirming your disappointment. See the later section "Finding nothing" for a nifty poem on the topic.

- ✔ Searching from the Start menu ensures that Windows searches for stuff all over the computer. See the later section "Limiting the search" for information on searching in only specific locations.

Useless information about indexed locations

There's some cheating going on to help make the Windows Search command superfast. Primarily, Windows creates a list of information about your files and those files' contents. The information is stored in a database of sorts, where an *index* is created. Like an index in a book, the index Windows creates is used to help the Search command quickly locate information on your computer.

Out of the box, Windows indexes only the files and folders in your personal area, the User Profile folder and its subfolders. This is why it's necessary to direct Windows to look elsewhere on the computer, and why such broader searches are slower.

You can expand the Search command's scope by using the Advance Search option and selecting

non-indexed locations (see the section "Using the Advanced Search Options"). You can also index those specific locations you plan to search more often, by using the Indexing Options icon in the Control Panel: Open the icon and click the Modify button to add a new location for Windows to index. Use the Show All Locations button to help locate folders and storage media to index.

You can also modify the Search command's behavior by opening the Folder Options icon in the Control Panel. In the Folder Options dialog box, click the Search tab to set or reset various search options or make other settings.

✔ When you want to open the folder containing a found file, right-click the file's icon in the Search Results window. From the pop-up menu, choose the command Open File Location.

✔ If you change your mind and don't want to search from the Start menu, click the X button on the right end of the Start Search text box. That restores the Start menu to normal.

Limiting the search

To limit the scope of your search, you need to be choosy about where you start the search. For example, to search only files in a specific folder (and any subfolders), open that folder window and type the search text in that folder window's Search text box.

To search through your contact list, use the Search text box found in the Contacts window. (The Contacts folder is found off your main account folder.)

To search only e-mail messages, use the Search text box in the Windows Mail program.

To search only drive E, open that drive's window and type the search text into the window's Search text box.

To search for song titles, use the Search text box found in Windows Media Player.

To limit your search to images, use the Search text box in the Windows Photo Gallery window. Of course, this advice assumes that you're using Windows Photo Gallery to manage the images stored on your PC.

When using the Search text box in the Windows Help system, your search is limited to only the information within the Help system.

Searching on the Internet, of course, limits the search to only those items on the Internet.

Using the Advanced Search options

For finding things quickly, the basic search works well. But sometimes you need more power, such as when you need to find a file on a specific date or when you want to take over the rest of Europe. To give yourself more control over the Search command and its results, you can use Advanced Search options.

The Advanced Search options appear when you click an Advanced Search link or the little Show Advanced Filters button by Advanced Search on the right side of the Search toolbar. Figure 9-4 shows the various Advanced Search options, many of which expand your search beyond what the Search command normally finds.

Figure 9-4:
Advanced
Search
options.

Location	⊞ Dan	Name	Specify name
Date	any	10/7/2007	Tags	Add a tag
Size (KB)	any		Authors	Add an author
☐ Include non-indexed, hidden, and system files (might be slow)			Search

For example, to search beyond indexed locations, choose a new location from the Location menu button. You can also (optionally) click to put a check mark by Include Non-Indexed, Hidden, and System Files (Might Be Slow) to expand a search.

To find files created on a specific date, use the Date button. For example, to find a file created today, choose Date Created and then choose Is, and then select today's date from the third button. To find files created within the past week, choose Date Created, and then choose Is After, and then click the Date button to choose a date on the pop-up calendar that's one week earlier than today.

To find files of a specific size, use the buttons by Size (KB). For example, to find all files 1KB large, choose Equals from the button menu and then type **1** into the text box. (All sizes are in KB, or kilobytes). To find huge files on your PC, first set the Location to Everywhere, and then from the Size (KB) area, choose Is Greater Than and type **1000** to locate all files 1 megabyte or larger.

 To hide the Advanced Search options, click the Hide Advanced Filters button.

✔ The search is affected by the item chosen from the Location button menu. Remember to set that button first; otherwise, you limit your search to the locations listed.

✔ One *megabyte* (MB) is equal to 1000 kilobytes (KB). One *gigabyte* (GB) is 1 million KB, which would be written 1000000 in the Size (KB) text box. There's no such thing as a zillion kilobytes, though apparently scientists in Russia are working on it.

✔ When the search results come up disappointing, maybe the file just wasn't saved to disk. That happens. You can try modifying the dates to search: Specify a date earlier than yesterday, for example, or try a different size or location, and then try again.

✔ Files you download from the Internet must be *saved* to disk. Choose the Save button, not the Open button, when you're downloading files.

"Wow! This Search command is awesome! Is there anything it cannot find?"

The Search command is good for locating files anywhere on your computer system, in any disk drive — except that the Search command *does not* look in the following places:

✔ The Recycle Bin

✔ Files stored in Compressed Folders or Zip file archives

✔ Text contained in a graphics image

Generally speaking, remember that Search looks only in the locations you specify. For example, Search doesn't find files in other users' folders on your PC, nor does it look in non-indexed locations. See the earlier sidebar "Useless information about indexed locations" as well as the earlier section "Using the Advanced Search options" for more information.

✔ Refer to Chapter 4 for more information on finding files in the Recycle Bin.

✔ To search text images, you must *tag* the images. Using an image-editing or -viewing program, such as Windows Photo Gallery, you can add descriptive text to any image. The text becomes a tag, which is used by the Search command to help you locate the image.

Using the Search command to find a program

Here's a handy trick that those hoity-toity Windows users are fond of: You can use the Start Search text box on the Start menu to quickly find and run a program. In fact, some of those nerds, er, *advanced* users don't even bother with the All Programs menu! Here's what they do:

1. **Pop up the Start button menu.**
2. **Type the first part of the program name into the Start Search text box.**
3. **Choose the program from the list that appears.**

For example, to run the WordPad utility quickly, type **WordPad** into the Start Search box. Eventually, WordPad appears in the results list on the left side of the Start menu. Choosing WordPad runs the program.

Saving a search

Windows lets you save a search, which may seem like an odd thing to do. I mean, why not just stop losing things in the first place? But that type of search isn't really the reason for saving a search.

First, when you find yourself performing the same type of search over and over, you can save it. Second, and more importantly, when you need to use various advanced options or settings, you might want to save the search to avoid reentering all that information in the future.

As an example, I created a search that looks on the hard drive for files larger than 5MB. The reason is that such huge files had better have a good reason to exist and, if they don't, I delete them or archive them to a DVD-R. Because such files tend to crop up, I saved the search, to save myself time when I'm doing a disk cleaning operation.

 To save a search, click the Save Search button in the Search Results window. A Save As dialog box appears, complete with a terse yet descriptive filename. You can change the name, if you like, or just click the Save button to save the file.

- ✔ Saved searches dwell in the Searches folder, which can be found just off your main account folder, the User Profile folder. (Also see the next section.)
- ✔ I highly recommend using the Searches folder when you save a search.

Using a saved search

Windows comes with a slew of specific searches, all designed and saved in the Searches folder, which can be found right under your main account folder. Because each search is predefined, all the settings are made for you. That way, you can quickly summon a search — with fresh results — any time you like.

For example, to quickly locate recently created or changed files, open the Search folder icon labeled Recently Changed. Almost instantly, a Search Results folder appears, listing the files found.

Also see the preceding section on creating your own saved searches.

Finding nothing

It's quite a major pain

When Windows does maintain

The text you list

Does not exist

Your efforts were in vain.

A message mighty terse:

"No items match your search"

No files were found

Lying around

How could this thing get worse?

So do keep up your chin

There is a way to win

Just take a chance

With options advanced

And try that search again

When at last you uncover

There is no file to discover

Not on the list

It don't exist

Give up or just start over.

Shortcuts to Nowhere

Computers and trust make the best attempt to go hand in hand. In fact, I'm sure the computer would rather blame *you* for its troubles than accept responsibility. Admittedly, computer users do some dumb things. But the computer also vacates its senses from time to time. A case in point is the shortcut icon, which occasionally loses its final destination and becomes a shortcut to nowhere.

Fortunately Windows is forgiving. When you try to open a shortcut icon that goes nowhere, you see the Missing Shortcut dialog box. You can do the following things:

- Choose the missing file from a list of suggestions.
- Use the Browse button to try to locate the missing file.
- Restore a deleted file from the Recycle Bin.
- Give up.

If you choose to give up, delete the shortcut icon so that you don't make the same mistake again.

Forgotten Passwords

The best way to remember your passwords is to *write them down!* The galactically wrong thing to do is write them down on a sticky note titled Passwords and paste that note to the side of your monitor. That's silly.

What's a good password?

The best password is cryptic, containing a mixture of letters and numbers, and also something that you can easily remember. The experts suggest creating a password composed of two common yet unrelated words that are connected by a number. For example:

```
Smart9dodo
hillarious1funeraL
annoying5Wealth
delicioUs77fungus
```

Good passwords are longer than six characters, and often longer than eight. Mixing in letters, numbers, and especially the occasional uppercase letter produces the best password.

Isn't this crazy? No! Security is important. As you start doing more online, you appreciate the added value of having a hard-to-crack password. The only better thing you can do is to frequently change your good password. The experts recommend doing so at least four times a year.

It's better to write down all the passwords and put them in your office's fire safe or between the covers of *The Elected Official's Guide to Ethics in Government* or some other book that no one else reads.

Another fine place to hide passwords is in your daybook or on a calendar. Jotting down a password on a page or a date looks innocent and random, but only you make the connection between that bit of text and your password. This is known as "hiding in plain sight" by the cloak-and-dagger bunch.

Yet, suggest as I might to help, there may be times when you just downright forget a password. It's missing! Where did it go! Think back to before the tequila binge last weekend. Then mull over this section.

Missing Internet passwords

Because you're most likely automatically logged in to the Internet, chances are that when you really need to know your password, such as when you're setting up a new e-mail program, you won't remember it.

I keep all records from my Internet service provider in a locked file cabinet. When I forget what my original Internet password is, I just open the file cabinet and look it up. Unless you have planned ahead like that, the only other solution is to phone your ISP and request the password. Someone there may tell you the password over the phone, or they may e-mail it to you. (Of the two, I prefer to hear the password spelled out over the phone.)

Immediately after getting the lost password, use your ISP's configuration Web page to change your password to something else. Try as they might, ISPs may not hire the most trustworthy people. Therefore, you should immediately change your password after it has been recovered.

Missing Web page passwords

More and more Web sites have passwords used to protect your account and verify your identity. It's not recommended that you use the same dang doodle password for all those Web sites (though many folks do). When you use multiple passwords, it's easy to forget them. Another flaw is that you can configure your Web browser to automatically type your password, which means that, after a while, you forget it.

Most Web sites have a feature where your password is mailed to you if you forget it. Take whatever steps necessary to have the Web page send you the forgotten password. Then wait, and in a few minutes or so, the password should arrive in your e-mail inbox.

Web sites may also employ a password hint. The hint is text you type that, hopefully, reminds you of your password. For example, if your password is the number and street of the house you grew up in, the hint may be "Address of first house." That's a good hint because it reminds *you* of the password but doesn't let others know what that address could be.

Using password recovery in Windows

The saying goes that if you forget your password in Windows, you're screwed. Microsoft can't help you. I can't help you. Gurus on the Internet can't help you. Some even laugh at you. I have heard rumors of password-cracking programs, but my guess is that those things are really nasty programs in disguise. What's a human to do?

First, you can add a hint to your password prompt in Windows. Follow these steps:

1. **Pop up the Start menu.**

2. **Click your account's icon at the top right of the menu.**

   By clicking your picture, you summon the User Accounts window in the Control Panel, where you can make changes to your account.

3. **Click the item titled Change My Password.**

   You use the next screen to enter a new password and also enter the password hint.

4. **Type your current password.**

5. **Type a new password, or just retype the current password, which you must do twice per the directions in the window.**

6. **Type a password hint.**

The password hint should help clue you in to what the password is, if you forget it.

Don't make the password hint the same as the password! That's like taping your house key to the front door — or leaving it in the lock!

7. Click the Change Password button.

To see the password hint, you need to be at the Windows login screen, where you type the password to log in. When you mistype the password, Windows first scolds you; but then when it displays the login screen again, your password hint appears below the password text box.

For even more protection against losing a password, you can create a Password Reset disk. Follow Steps 1 and 2 from the preceding step list to open the User Account information window. From the left, click the link titled Create a Password Reset Disk. Follow the directions on the screen to use the Forgotten Password Reset Wizard.

The Password Reset disk isn't a disk; it's a file, and it can be stored on any removable storage device.

To use the Password Reset disk, simply try to log in to Windows *without* typing your password. When you do, you're asked whether you want to use the Password Reset disk. Just follow the instructions to do so.

Chapter 10

Sounds Like Trouble

. . . .

. . . .

*I*t saved five dollars a machine. The TRS-80, Radio Shack's pioneer micro-computer of the late 1970s, didn't have a speaker. After all, computers didn't need to make sound, right? Five bucks is five bucks! But *foresight* wasn't big with the bean counters at Radio Shack. They didn't anticipate, for example, that their first run of microcomputers (what PCs were called before IBM bellied up to the bar) would sell out in less than a month. So how could they possibly know that in the first decade of the 21st century, computers and sound would be inseparable?

Today computers and sound are so close in relation that they could never get married. (Not outside Kentucky, anyway.) First, computers could beep. Then they could play silly, tinny songs. Then came CDs, and then MP3 audio files, and then portable music players, and, finally, the perfection of the digital jukebox. Beyond that, computers make noise, they talk, they sing. Sometimes you just want them to shut up! But when the silence they make is unex-pected, you can turn to the information in this chapter to get your PC to bleep again.

✔ As with most immediate boo-boos, try restarting Windows to see whether that gets the sound back.

✔ Don't forget the System Restore command! When you hear (or don't hear) sound trouble, immediately attempt a System Restore to go back to a louder time.

✔ If your problem is with playing a specific audio file, consider that the file may be corrupted — or you may not have the proper software to play that file.

Checking the Hardware

The sound trail starts at either side of your head, with your ears. Not to make light of excess cerumen buildup, but do ensure that your ears are clear of debris. That's the first step. Next, check your PC's speakers, that patch of ground where your computer becomes a stereo system.

✔ Refer to Chapter 8 for information on beeps (or no beep) that you may hear when the computer first starts.

✔ For solutions to problems with playing a music CD, see the section in Chapter 15 about CD-ROM catastrophes.

Are the speakers connected?

To be properly plugged, your PC's speakers must connect to the computer, to each other, maybe into a subwoofer and, optionally, to a power supply. Use the diagram in Figure 10-1 to help you check things.

From the computer, the sound goes out the speaker jack, which may also be labeled Line Out or Phones (as in headphones). This is where the speakers plug in, though newer speakers may use the USB port instead.

On the back of the speaker, the wire goes into an input jack, though most speakers have this wire permanently attached.

Another wire goes from one speaker to the other. In Figure 10-1, the Left Out wire goes to the input jack on the left speaker.

Finally, speakers need power, so a power cable goes from the main speaker (the one on the right in Figure 10-1) to a power source.

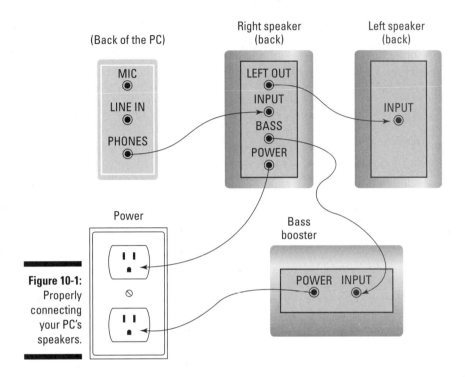

Figure 10-1:
Properly
connecting
your PC's
speakers.

If you have a subwoofer, the nightmare gets worse: Sound must go from the speakers to the subwoofer, and the subwoofer must be powered as well.

✔ Your PC may sport a special expansion card with additional speaker jacks on it, such as a video output card or even a special sound card. If so, plug your speakers into that card and not into the regular sound jacks.

✔ When the speakers have a USB connection *and* a standard audio (mini-din) connector, try using one or the other to see whether that helps.

✔ Make sure that everything is plugged in snugly!

✔ Subwoofers are also called bass boosters or, not very often, underwater dogs.

✔ As you're facing the monitor, the "right" speaker is the one that sits on the right side of the monitor. The "left" speaker is the one sitting on the left side. This arrangement can be confusing because when you work on the speakers, you're often working behind your computer, where left and right are reversed.

✔ The speaker jack is typically coded lime green on modern PCs.

✔ Figure 10-1 shows the right speaker as the main one, though the left speaker may be the main one on some models.

✔ In some situations, the subwoofer is the main speaker, and it connects directly to the PC. Then the left and right speakers connect to the subwoofer.

✔ Yeah, it's nuts.

✔ I hate to mention it, but you can often "test" the speakers by touching the input plug — the one that plugs into the computer — to the computer's case. If the speakers are okay, you hear a slight hum when you touch the plug, which is the sound of the speakers picking up the computer's electric field. I'm sure that audiophiles would cringe at the thought, but it works.

Any knobs on the speakers?

Some speakers have volume control knobs. Are they up? How about a power knob? Is the speaker on? Is the subwoofer turned on?

Some newer speakers have a sound-control wire attached to them. The control allows you to set the speaker's volume or mute the speakers without having to get up out of your chair. Yeah! More laziness! Be sure to check that wire as well as any volume-control or mute button on the wires attached to your headsets.

Where's the remote?

Some PC speaker systems have a remote control, joining the armada of remote controls you already have (TV, VCR, DVD, surround sound, cable, and so on). Is the remote control muting the sound?

Are the speakers getting power?

Yes, this is a speaker-connection issue, but note that some speakers use batteries as their source of power. Be sure to check the batteries.

Or, to hell with batteries! Go get a power converter for your speakers. It should have a little power plug that the converter can plug into. Listed somewhere on the speaker are its power requirements, which you should note and then go to the electronics store to buy the proper converter.

Are the speakers getting enough oomph?

If the speakers make noise, but only feebly, check the volume control, which is covered later in this chapter.

If the volume is all the way up, however, what's most likely happening is that the sound is unamplified. Check your PC's rump to see whether it has another hole for the speakers to plug into.

If none of these steps works, try running the speakers through a subwoofer.

If nothing seems to help, get a new set of speakers.

Checking the Software

So the speakers work, huh? Maybe it's the computer itself to blame? Check to see whether Windows has muted the situation. As usual, there are several places to check.

Volume control

The volume control in the notification area is your first stop on the software sound tour. Clicking the volume control icon displays a pop-up window. Figure 10-2 shows how to play with the icon's pop-up to test sound on your PC.

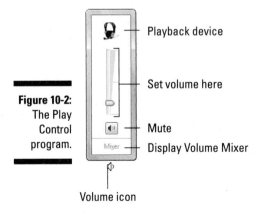

Figure 10-2:
The Play
Control
program.

Playback device

Set volume here

Mute

Display Volume Mixer

Volume icon

Check the sound level in the pop-up volume control (refer to Figure 10-2). Ensure that the Mute button isn't pressed. Confirm that the proper playback device is selected; in Figure 10-2, the headphones are used for playback, which may explain why no sound is coming from the speakers.

Playback device

Windows Vista lets you select which playback device sound seeps into from your computer system. To view or change the playback device, heed these steps:

1. **Right-click the volume icon in the notification area.**

2. **Choose Playback Devices from the pop-up menu.**

   The Sound dialog box appears, with the Playback device tab showing all installed (or recognized) sound-spewing gizmos on the PC, as shown in Figure 10-3.

3. **To choose another playback device, follow these steps:**

   a. Choose the proper playback device from the list.

   b. Click the Set Default button.

   c. Click OK to close the Sound dialog box.

   d. Check the sound.

   e. If you hear noise, you're done.

Figure 10-3:
The Playback tab in the Sound dialog box.

4. **To work with the selected playback device, click to select the device and click the Properties button.**

   The device's Properties dialog box appears.

5. **Click the Levels tab.**

6. **Ensure that the levels are not set to zero, and that the Mute button isn't chosen.**

   The mute button sports a red "no" symbol on it when the device is muted.

7. **Click the Balance button to ensure that either the left or right speaker isn't being muted.**

   There's a Test button in the device Properties dialog box, on the Advanced tab. Use the button to help test the speakers.

8. **Close the various dialog boxes when you're done poking around.**

Volume mixer

The final software goodie you can check quickly is the volume mixer. To see it, choose Mixer from the volume control's pop-up menu (refer to Figure 10-2). The Volume Mixer window is shown in Figure 10-4.

So? Is anything muted? Mute button pressed? Volume slider all the way down? If so, fix it! Close the window when you're done.

Note that unlike older versions of the volume mixer, the Windows Vista mixer is rather limited in the different types of volumes you can adjust. Also, no two computers can support the same list of volume devices.

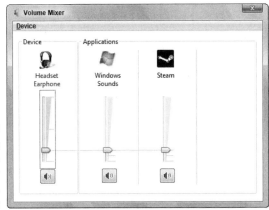

Figure 10-4:
The Volume
Mixer
window.

Device Manager

How about a look under the hood? The final software place to find any reason for silence is Device Manager. Here's what you do:

1. **Open the Control Panel.**

2. **In the Control Panel Home, choose System and Maintenance and then scroll down to click Device Manager; from the Control Panel Classic view, open the Device Manager icon.**

3. **Enter the administrator's password or click the Continue button, if prompted.**

4. **Open the item titled Sound, Video, and Game Controllers.**

   Opening that item displays a list of sound-generating hardware installed in your PC. If anything is run amok, it will be noted, as covered in Chapter 3 and shown in Figure 3-2. Refer to Chapter 3 to see what to do in that situation.

   If the Device Manager seas are rather calm, you might want to poke around.

5. **Open the item for your computer's sound card.**

   This is the tricky part: The name isn't that obvious, but it's similar (if not the same) to the Playback devices listed in the Sound dialog box (refer to Figure 10-3).

   When you're successful, you see a Properties dialog box for your computer's sound system.

6. **Click the Driver tab.**

7. **Ensure that the device isn't disabled; if so, click the Enable button and you're done; go to Step 9.**

8. **Click the Update Driver button and follow the directions on the screen.**

   Windows checks the software that controls the sound hardware, and goes out to the Internet (if necessary) to find a newer or better device driver.

9. **Close all open windows when you're done troubleshooting.**

Hopefully, that fixes the problem. If not, consider visiting the hardware developer's Web page or contact your computer dealer.

Holy smokes! That was loud!

When the computer unexpectedly grows thunderous on you, check the usual suspects: the volume control in the system tray/notification area, the volume knobs on the speakers, and even the master volume control.

Then check the program you're running. Some games make their own sounds, which means that the sound setting must be made in that game independently of Windows. See the game's options or settings to see whether you can reset the sound level to something your neighbors would be more comfortable with.

Chapter 11

The Mystery of System Resources (and Memory Leaks)

Computers are technical beasts. They always have been. Remember those photos of the nerdy-looking scientists back in the 1950s? They'd stand by those behemoth, vacuum-tube, room-size computers, wearing white lab coats and holding clipboards. They were the *system engineers*. Their job was to keep the PC running. That's still your job, contemporary advertising and marketing drivel to the contrary.

Your role as a computer owner implies that you should monitor a little bit of the system for the system's sake. Particularly in the case of troubleshooting, it helps to know, for example, what a *system resource* is and how to monitor performance. It also helps to understand the concept of a *memory leak* and how putting a pan under the PC won't assist with plugging the leak. This chapter tells you how to play the role of your PC's system engineer without getting a degree at MIT, donning a white lab coat, or cradling a clipboard.

The Terror of System Resources

No one cares about system resources until they're depleted. That's just human nature. It's why cars have gas gauges and oil lamps. Computers work the same way: You're alerted when system resources get low. But unlike your car, there is no twist-top on the PC into which you can pour a quart of new resources. Then again, it helps more to know about resources than to know which twist-top to unscrew.

System resources are simply the way the computer allocates its hardware — primarily memory, long-term storage, CPU or processor power, and networking. Within each category are additional resources: Memory is reserved for system activities, programs, and graphics; storage is managed and organized; the CPU divides its time between your programs and system activities; and the network is sending and receiving information as well as monitoring activity. All those things combined are system resources, so now you can speak knowledgeably about the subject among your friends and at town hall meetings.

Normally, you don't need to care about system resources. Windows manages things much better today than it did years ago. But occasionally a system resource error crops up, specifically when resources get low (meaning lots of memory is being used). The quick solution is to simply close a few programs and try again. Or, restarting Windows often flushes out all the resources and lets you run the program.

Monitoring resources

The Reliability and Performance Monitor window is used to check up on resources and see how much of them are left and how much Windows is using. Here's how to check on your PC's resources by using the Reliability and Performance Monitor window:

1. **Conjure forth the Run dialog box.**

2. **Type** perfmon **into the box and click OK.**

3. **Type the administrator's password or click the Continue button, if prompted.**

   The Reliability and Performance Monitor window appears on the screen, looking something like Figure 11-1. You see six bars in the window; the Resource Overview bar is open in Figure 11-1. To show or hide a bar's information, use the arrow button on the bar's far right end.

   In Figure 11-1, and most likely on your screen, the Resource Overview bar is open, displaying nifty-looking animated graphs describing your computer's use of the four basic resources: CPU, Disk, Network, and Memory. What can you do here? Nothing but watch. It's like TV. Cable TV. Up in the digital channel range.

   The bottommost bar is titled Learn More. It contains links for various items in the window as well as for help on how to best use the Reliability and Performance Monitor window.

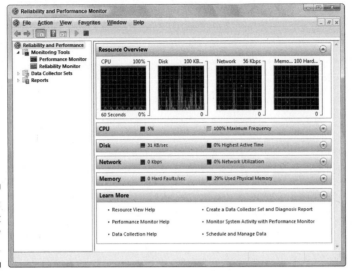

Figure 11-1:
Ooo! Look at
the pretty
graphs.

4. **Open other bars in the Reliability and Performance Monitor window to view the exciting and trivial information they display.**

   Woo! We're having fun now!

5. **Close the Reliability and Performance window when you've had enough.**

   Or, just keep it open for the next section, if you're disobeying my advice and reading this book from front to back.

Yes, it might seem like the Reliability and Performance Monitor window is the in-flight meal of the Windows troubleshooting restaurant, but it does have its purpose. When you know what to look for, spotting problems and pinpointing solutions are easier using a tool like the Reliability and Performance Monitor window.

For example, if running a particular program causes all resources to suddenly dwindle, you know that there's a great demand for resources in that program. Starting the program with the Reliability and Performance Monitor window open graphically details the problem. Ditto for programs that slow down the computer, or for just monitoring the computer's speed status in general.

Another place to monitor performance is in the Task Manager window. Press Ctrl+Shift+Esc to bring forth the Task Manager. Click the Performance tab to see a summary of the system's CPU and memory usage. There's also a handy button there to quickly jump to the Reliability and Performance Monitor window, though the button is titled Resource Monitor.

Perusing performance

A place in Windows where you can specifically monitor performance is the Performance Monitor, which was named *after* they decided what it would do. The Performance Monitor is part of the Reliability and Performance Monitor window, which is covered in the preceding section.

Follow Steps 1 through 3 from the preceding section to summon the Reliability and Performance Monitor window. When you see the screen, open Monitoring Tools on the left side of the window, and then choose Performance Monitor. Figure 11-2 shows what the Performance Monitor thing looks like.

 You can add more graphs to the Performance Monitor by clicking the Add button on the toolbar (it's a green plus sign) and then using the Add Counters dialog box to choose an item to add. Which items are good to choose? Golly, that depends on which part of your PC seems to be suffering from poor performance.

For example, if the PC is slow, use the Add Counters dialog box to add processor time (under Processor) or add available megabytes (under Memory). The usage monitor shows you whether processor or memory resources are dwindling over time or whether you're just having a slow day.

Close the Reliability and Performance Monitor window when you're done playing.

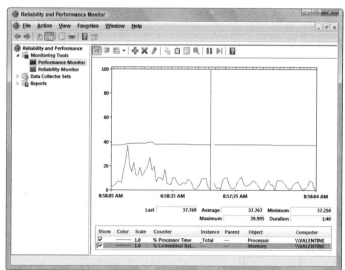

Figure 11-2:
The PC's performance is being monitored.

"Omigosh! My performance meter just suddenly and randomly spiked!"

Yeah, it does that. You can sit there and watch your PC's performance graph do *nothing,* and then suddenly it peaks and is *very* active. But then it returns back to where it was.

No, nothing is wrong. This behavior is entirely normal for a computer (and cats). That's because a typical Windows computer has dozens of processes running at one time. A performance spike simply means that one of those programs went about doing its task and occupied the PC's microprocessor for a wee amount of time. That goes on all the time. It doesn't mean that your computer has a virus or a worm; it's just standard operation.

Checking reliability

Reliability is a quality that's taken for granted with a computer and with pretty much any other modern device used in our culture. For me, reliability in a PC means that it works. Simple. But there's more to it than that, which can be seen by examining the Reliability Monitor, as revealed in Figure 11-3.

Whether the Reliability Monitor really shows you how reliable Window is isn't the question. What it does provide is more of a status update to the activities going on in Windows that *could* cause you problems.

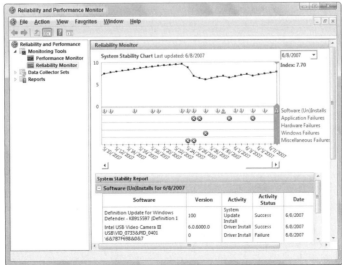

Figure 11-3: This window looks really cool.

In Figure 11-3 you see several incidents, flagged by red X circles. These indicate various times that the system has failed. Details about the failure can be found using the expandable bars at the bottom of the window.

Click to select a specific date to read more about any potential failures. Although you can't really do anything specific after the fact, the information does tell you which program or hardware is causing the problem. When problems are consistent, you can then look for software or hardware updates to address the issue.

Close the window when you're done.

✔ The biggest benefit in the Reliability Monitor is helping you determine differences between software and hardware errors. See Chapter 3.

✔ Also see Chapter 23 for information on reviewing the event logs.

Leaky Memory

One thing the various performance monitors, meters, charts, and gauges can help you fix is a memory leak. Unlike a gas leak, there's no need to evacuate the building, and unlike a plumbing leak, nothing in the computer will get wet.

A memory leak is a common and nasty problem. No, it's not your fault. *Memory leaks* are caused by programming errors or bugs. What happens is that a program continues to consume more and more of the computer's resources. Gradually or rapidly, the PC's performance suffers as the system clogs and bogs, and then the computer just poops out.

Memory leaks are easily spotted using the Performance Monitor (refer to Figure 11-2, in the section "Perusing performance," earlier in this chapter.) Use the plus button (+) on the toolbar to add memory monitoring to the graph; I recommend using the item labeled % Committed Bytes to the list — and perhaps even unchecking other items in the graph so that you can monitor memory consumption over time.

You don't need to keep a constant eyeball on the Performance Monitor, but check it as you start and quit different programs. The memory used should come *and* go. For example, in Figure 11-2 you see a small bump in the top line, which indicates when I started another program and then quit that program. Had the bump been a new plateau, it might indicate a memory leak.

The cure for the memory leak is to rewrite the program, which isn't your job. All you can do is attempt to track down which program is causing the leak. By killing off the leaky program, you can free memory and resources and restore your PC's performance.

✔ *Leak* is perhaps the wrong term. A better description is *hole,* or a place where memory is poured in and never returns.

✔ Memory leaks are also caused by dead programs in memory. The leak doesn't grow in size, but the memory used is never recovered. To check for dead programs, view a memory usage monitor and verify that the memory used by a program is released when the program has quit.

✔ When you're unable to kill off a leaky program, your next (and potentially only) choice is simply not to run the program. Attempt to contact the developer to alert them to the situation, but that's all you can do.

How to Improve Performance

Having lots of resources available to your PC is the key to top performance. But even then, keep in mind that your computer system will never have 100 percent free resources. That's because Windows must use *some* resources to do those things it does. In fact, the only way to have 100 percent free resources is not to even turn on the computer! But that's not my best advice.

Adding memory

Resources equal memory! Adding more memory to your computer fixes many low-resource problems.

✔ A great place to purchase memory online is `www.crucial.com`. It's not the cheapest, but the memory is high quality, the Web site is excellent, and the support is outstanding. I recommend the site and use it myself.

✔ Windows Vista claims it needs 1GB of memory to do well. Seriously, all my Vista PCs have at least 2GB of memory installed; 4GB is even better.

Removing fonts

Sure, you can have 10 zillion fonts installed, but fonts definitely drain resources, and too many of them slow things down. The solution: Install only those fonts you regularly use.

For the rest of the fonts, keep them on an optical disc or on an external hard drive or network drive. Wherever you store them, create an Excess Fonts folder. Just move into that folder the fonts you seldom use; move them as you would cut and paste any file.

✔ Windows comes with a core set of fonts; don't move them. You can't really tell which fonts are those that Windows came with, other than by checking the date or just knowing the common font names you see over and over again in Windows. Nothing bad happens if you move the fonts, but you have to move them back if you enjoy using them in Windows.

✔ You can get to the Fonts folder from the Control Panel; open the Fonts icon.

✔ Also avoid moving the following fonts, which are often used by Web pages:

- *Arial*

- *Comic Sans MS*

- *Tahoma*

- *Times New Roman*

- *Trebuchet*

- *Verdana*

Disabling services

Background programs — such as antivirus utilities, disk optimizers, animated icons, Windows Sidebar, and other items — consume resources. If resources are low, consider disabling or halting such programs.

✔ Refer to the section in Chapter 8 about stopping programs from automatically starting for more information on disabling programs.

✔ Also refer to the appendix to find information about running processes and which ones you need or can do away with.

Uninstalling what you don't use

If you're like me, you occasionally download and install programs from the Internet just to see what they do. If so, great. But be mindful to uninstall the program if you don't use it. See Chapter 22 for more information on uninstalling programs.

Chapter 12

The Slow PC

*I*t puzzles me that people hang on to their computers for such a long time. Generally speaking, the typical PC has a lifespan of about four years. (Once upon a time, it was two years, so be thankful for four!) After four years, a computer not only begins to wear out, but by that time the new technology is also so much better and less expensive that it makes sense to upgrade simply to keep your productivity up. Still, people hang on to their PCs, perhaps because they don't know better, but I suspect that there's some emotional attachment involved as well.

Whenever you get a new PC, you're certain to notice one key thing: It's faster than your old one. Yes, that's because the new system uses faster technology. But more importantly, PCs get slow over time, as you use them. There's no specific reason; it just happens. The tips and suggestions in this chapter can help you deal with a sluggish PC.

Slow Is Relative

Computers aren't designed to be slow. In fact, if you were to peer into a tiny window and observe the microprocessor, you would discover that it spends most of its time doing *nothing*. It waits. That's because most things the computer does aren't that speed intensive.

When you word-process, the computer spends electronic epochs waiting for you to type the next letter — even if you're a fast typist. And, no matter how fast your Internet connection, the computer is literally twiddling its thumbs while waiting for the next byte of data to stroll in.

There are intensive operations, of course: Any time you manipulate graphics, you're making the computer do some real work. Windows spends a surprising amount of processor time displaying fonts. And, some mathematical calculations cause the microprocessor to fire all its burners. Even then, for the most part, the computer sits and hums.

- ✔ Refer to Chapter 17 for information on improving slow Internet connections.

- ✔ Speed apparently isn't a true issue when it comes to computer performance. Developers could make software go even faster than it does now, but there's little demand for it. Also, increasing program speed would mean that the programs would take longer to develop, so as long as people don't mind waiting, developers have no incentive to make things faster.

Why things can get slow

Your computer can slow down for a number of reasons, almost too many to mention. Slothfulness boils down to one of these guilty subjects:

Malfunctioning hardware: The hard drive may be on its last legs, in which case it has to read and reread information because of errors. That adds overhead. Or, you may have two conflicting types of RAM installed, in which case the slower type sets the speed.

Corrupted programs: Most sudden slowness is caused by some corrupt program, which may be tainted on the disk or somehow besmirched in memory. In any event, the program's response time dwindles, which affects overall PC speed.

Malware: Nasty programs — viruses, Trojan horses, worms, spyware, and their ilk — can also slow things down, by either corrupting existing files or consuming resources in memory or on the hard drive. In some cases, the malicious software (that is, *malware*) is designed to slow down your computer as its purpose in life!

Age: In a way, computers can be like people; as we age, we accumulate the detritus of life. Our joints weaken; a computer's soldering joints weaken. We absorb the toxins of our environment; a computer absorbs dust bunnies and grit. Software-wise, a computer collects useless files, and file fragments accumulate on disk. It's a natural thing, but as with humans, you can fight the aging process in a PC.

The solutions for a sluggish PC depend on the source of the sluggishness: Malfunctioning hardware can be replaced. Corrupted programs can be reinstalled or updated. Malware can be removed using tools such as Windows

Defender. For an old computer, you can practice regular system maintenance, as well as unplug the case, open it up, and use a small vacuum to clean up the dust.

- ✓ Often, recovering speed is simply as easy as restarting Windows. Refer to Chapter 2.

- ✓ Please be patient! Yes, restarting Windows probably fixes the situation. But give the slow computer its due. Obey the rules! Shut down like you normally do, even if it seems to take longer. Give the computer a chance before you impatiently punch the power switch or defiantly unplug the sucker.

- ✓ Corrupt programs may be spotted by their memory leaks. Refer to Chapter 11.

- ✓ Some third-party utilities, such as Norton, have various disk diagnosing programs that can indicate pending hard drive doom.

- ✓ Also check with the Microsoft Knowledge Base on the Web to see whether the slowness can be attributed to any known flaws in Windows or other Microsoft products: http://support.microsoft.com/.

- ✓ Little-known fact: A hard drive can misread data on a disk up to three times before it reports an error. The operating system itself can tolerate as many as five errors of this type before it reports a problem with the drive.

Any way to speed things up?

The old joke went that you could double your computer's speed by plugging it into a 240-volt socket. I actually got e-mail from a man who believed this statement to be true and wanted to know where he could get a power adapter. Of course, following through would have resulted in a blown-up power supply.

Computers do some things fast and some things slow. Aside from getting a newer computer, you can do only a handful of legitimate things to improve overall performance:

- ✓ Eliminate what you don't need. Uninstall programs you don't use.

- ✓ Review your startup programs, as covered in Chapter 8. Ensure that utilities you don't need are disabled and not using RAM or disk space.

- ✓ Install more RAM. Computers can always use more RAM.

- ✓ Check for malware, as covered in Chapter 24.

- ✓ Keep an eye out for memory leaks, which are discussed in Chapter 11.

- ✓ Defragment (especially good for older drives), which you can read about in Chapter 25.

In your applications, try to avoid using lots of fonts or pasting images into a word processor until the text editing is done. Word processors, such as Microsoft Word, bog down when you add graphics into the mix. Write your text first and then add images.

For image editing, consider using a draft mode, such as Adobe Illustrator's Outline view. And. when things get really thick, try not running several demanding applications at the same time. That conserves resources and gives more power to the programs that demand it.

Above all, try to avoid software fixes that claim to speed up your computer. Although some of them may subtly tweak resources and give you better performance, most of the ones I have encountered are shams. These programs seldom perform as promised and usually end up turning your PC into a billboard for endless advertisements or porn.

- ✔ I don't recommend upgrading the microprocessor as a solution to a slow PC. Older PCs that could theoretically benefit from a newer CPU are typically not compatible with the new microprocessors. And, the replacement CPUs you can get often don't give you the same bang for the buck as a better upgrade, such as more RAM or a second hard drive.

- ✔ Also refer to Chapter 11, on system resources. Low resources can also cause a system to run slowly.

- ✔ Internally, the computer uses only 5 or 12 volts to run things, so doubling the input voltage from 120 to 240 volts — even if you could — wouldn't improve your speed situation.

Some Slow Q&A

Anyone who has used a PC for any length of time has encountered the slow PC. After initial disbelief, you probably act like I do and seriously wonder whether a black hole is nearby and slowing down the entire space-time continuum.

Do you slam your keyboard into the desktop? I have tried it. Doesn't work.

And yes, a few times I just flipped off the power to the UPS because the computer was taking geological time to restart. I know. Naughty me, but sometimes the stupid device wears my patience paper-thin.

Q: It's suddenly slow, and it wasn't like that yesterday!

Sudden slow is good. Sudden slow means that some program has twisted itself into a confusing garden of electronic salad. A simple reset fixes this problem.

Try checking the Task Manager's Processes tab to see whether you can find the process hog and kill it off. Obey these directions:

1. **Press Ctrl+Shift+Esc to summon the Task Manager window.**

2. **Click the Processes tab (if necessary) to see the list of processes.**

   Both the programs that you're running and the programs being run by Windows are displayed, as shown in Figure 12-1.

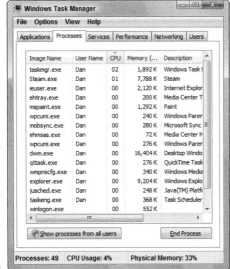

Figure 12-1: Processes running, as divulged by the Task Manager window.

3. **Click the CPU column heading to sort the programs running by the amount of CPU time they use.**

   You may have to click the CPU heading twice to sort the list from busiest to idle tasks; busy tasks have numbers by them; idle tasks show 0.

4. **Scour the top of the list for any task that's consuming vast quantities of CPU time.**

   If necessary, click the Show Processes from All Users button to see the full slate of processes. (Enter the administrator's password or click the Continue button if prompted.)

5. **When you find the process that's gobbling up CPU time, click to select it; otherwise, go to Step 8.**

6. **Click the End Process button.**

7. **Click the End Process button that appears in the confirmation dialog box.**

8. **Close the Task Manager window.**

If the computer instantly speeds up, you found your program. If not, your problem isn't a software problem.

9. **Restart Windows.**

Just in case the process you shut down is a vital one, I highly recommend restarting Windows after you mess with the Task Manager.

Q: Something seems to be wrong with my USB connections.

I have noticed that some USB devices may fly south and attempt to take other USB devices with them. For example, the scanner may be on the fritz, so the USB keyboard no longer responds quickly. Consider disconnecting (from the computer) the USB devices that you're not using and see whether that improves the situation.

Q: The computer is *always* slow.

Remember that speed is relative. Or, as it was put to me long ago by a friend with a much better computer: You never know how crappy your system is until you sit down at a better one.

- ✔ Buy more RAM!

- ✔ Consider running fewer programs.

- ✔ Also consider using a thorough disk drive analysis utility, such as Norton Utilities, to see whether the hard drive is becoming too error prone. If so, replace the hard drive.

Q: The computer gets slower the longer I leave it on.

This is definitely a sign of a memory leak. The best way to track this one down is as follows:

- ✔ **First, don't run any software.** Just let the computer sit and stew. Note whether it's getting slow. If so, it's Windows itself that's slow, or perhaps one of the supersecret startup programs (refer to Chapter 8) or malware is causing the problem.

- ✔ **Second, run your programs one at a time.** Pause. Note whether that particular program is causing the computer to slow down. If not, restart the computer and run your next program. Run them one at a time to search for the culprit.

When you find the program that's slowing down the computer, check with the developer to see whether it has any information about causes or fixes. Refer to Chapter 5 for more information on tech support.

Q: The computer has gotten slower and slower in recent weeks.

This problem is most likely caused by a nasty program infiltrating your computer, such as a virus or a worm or some spyware — all commonly referred to as *malware*. These programs consume resources and run without your knowledge, so it isn't readily obvious what's to blame for the slowdown. See Chapter 24 for information on tools to fight malware.

Another problem may be hardware oriented. A full hard drive can slow down a computer. To check the hard drive's capacity, follow these steps:

1. **Open the Computer window.**

   This step is easy when you see the Computer icon on the desktop. If not, choose Computer from the Start button menu. Or, you can press Win+E on the keyboard and choose Computer from the list of folders or the Address bar.

2. **Right-click the hard drive you want to examine.**

3. **Choose Tiles from the toolbar's View button menu.**

   In Tiles view you can see a small thermometer graph beside the various storage media that are active on your PC. (Unmounted media, such as empty memory card slots, don't show a thermometer graph.) Better still is the famous disk pie chart.

4. **Right-click any disk icon.**

5. **Choose Properties from the shortcut menu.**

   The storage media's Properties dialog box appears. On the General tab you find the pie chart, as shown in Figure 12-2. When the free portion of the pie becomes the kind of sliver that Aunt Kathy (who is always on a "diet") would eat, then you need to clean up the hard drive to help improve performance: Click the Disk Cleanup button, right there by the pie chart.

6. **Close the Properties dialog box as well as the My Computer window.**

Refer to Chapter 25 for more information on what you can do to help remedy a full hard drive.

Slowness can also just be a sign of "tired RAM" or an older computer in general. It's time to buy a new one.

Q: The computer's clock is slower than normal time.

Yes. Computers make lousy clocks. The clock in your typical PC is off anywhere from several seconds to a few minutes at the end of each day, depending on what you do with the computer. This is normal.

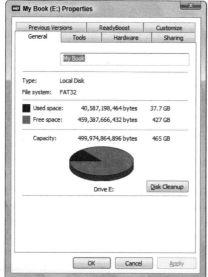

Figure 12-2:
The famous
disk pie.

In Windows, you can configure the computer to automatically set the time. Follow these steps:

1. **Right-click the date-and-time display in the notification area.**

2. **From the pop-up menu, choose Adjust Date/Time.**

    The Date and Time dialog box appears.

3. **Click the Internet Time tab.**

4. **Click the Change Settings button.**

5. **If prompted, enter the administrator's password or click the Continue button.**

6. **Click to place a check mark by the item Synchronize with an Internet Time Server.**

7. **For extra measure, click the Update Now button.**

8. **Click OK, and then close the Date and Time dialog box.**

Some network routers may run a time server that sets your computer's clock. Check with the router's manual to see how to set up such a time server.

Chapter 13

Keyboard, Mouse, and Monitor Dilemmas

··

In This Chapter

▶ Knowing whether to blame the peripheral or the PC

▶ Controlling the keyboard

▶ Dealing with Sticky Keys

▶ Fixing mouse troubles

▶ Dealing with monitor troubles (hardware only)

▶ Cleaning stuff

··

*A*t its core, your PC is just as complex and confusing as the old vacuum-tube monster computers from the industrial revolution. The features that make your PC truly useful are its handy input and output devices: the keyboard, monitor, and mouse. You would have known this had you gone to computer camp as a child. Oh, I remember those days: sitting 'round with my nerdy friends, singing songs about input and output, all while staring at the crackling, sputtering campfire screen saver. Those were the days.

Without a keyboard, mouse, or monitor, your computer would have to communicate with you via its flashing lights or beeping speaker. You (the human) would have to flip rows of switches or actually rewrite the thing to get work done. Not fun. Therefore, all three of these devices — keyboard, mouse, and monitor — have similar troubleshooting issues, problems, and resolutions: Hence, this combined chapter.

> ✔ This book assumes that you are human or, if visiting from elsewhere, that you're currently assuming human form.
>
> ✔ In 1978, a divider was installed beneath the table to prevent the world chess champion Anatoly Karpov and the challenger Viktor Korchnoi from kicking each other during the match.

Which Is the Guilty Party?

When it comes to the keyboard, mouse, or monitor, a common question pops up: Is the device itself or the computer to blame? For example, is your mouse itself wacky, or is it the mouse port or the motherboard or the mouse software? The easy way to find out is to *swap it out.*

First, turn off the computer.

Second, remove the device that's causing trouble — the keyboard or mouse or monitor. Set it aside.

Third, install a working replacement device. It can be a keyboard, mouse, or monitor from another computer or a friend's computer. Ensure that you know the device is working properly.

Fourth, turn on the computer and see whether the device works. If the swapped-in component works just fine, you have solved your problem: Replace the keyboard, mouse, or monitor with something that works.

✔ Keyboards and mice are relatively inexpensive to replace.

✔ Before replacing, see other sections in this chapter for some potential solutions to keyboard and mouse problems.

✔ Never try to fix a monitor yourself, even if you have the proper footwear. Monitors and PC power supplies are two things you should never disassemble or otherwise mess with.

✔ There's no need to turn off the computer if your mouse or keyboard (or even the monitor) is a USB device. You can plug or unplug any USB device without damaging the computer.

✔ Never plug a mouse or keyboard into the standard mouse or keyboard port when the PC is on. Doing so can damage the keyboard, mouse, or computer.

✔ You can plug a monitor in or out from a working computer. I have done it a few times. But I feel better about turning the thing off whenever I attach or detach any hardware.

Keyboard Kraziness

Keyboards don't have the run-amok potential of other computer peripherals. I think that the reason they stay so well behaved is that they know how cheap replacement models are. So, unless your hands weigh 75 pounds each, your computer's keyboard will most likely outlive just about anything else on the computer.

✔ A simple reset should cure most keyboard strangeness, such as one key producing another key's character.

✔ Also see "The language problem," later in this chapter.

✔ Keyboard-mapping and macro programs are available, such as QuicKeys, from CE Software, Inc. (www.cesoft.com/). You can use these programs to customize keyboard behavior as well as assign lots of text or complex commands to simple key combinations.

✔ For more information about PC keyboards, see my excellent book *PCs For Dummies* (Wiley Publishing, Inc.), which is not only informative but also a gripping read.

The keyboard's Control Panel home

The first place to look for keyboard adjustment and behavior control is the Control Panel. From the Control Panel Home, choose Hardware and Sound, and then Keyboard; from Control Panel Classic view, open the Keyboard icon. The Keyboard Properties dialog box, shown in Figure 13-1, is where you adjust things such as the keyboard's repeat delay and repeat rate.

Figure 13-1: The official keyboard-messing location.

✔ The *repeat delay* is how long you have to hold down a key before its character is repeated.

✔ The *repeat rate* is how quickly the character is repeated.

According to Figure 13-1, pressing and holding down the *P* key after a medium-long delay quickly prints a bunch of *p*'s: ppppppppppppppppppppppppp. (Supposedly, that's how kitty cats do it.)

The language problem

You can configure your keyboard to mimic the behavior of foreign language keyboards. For example, in France, they have keys on the keyboard for the ç and Ç keys. In the United Kingdom, Shift+3 produces the £ character rather than #. And many foreign language keyboard layouts have "dead keys," which are used for diacritical marks, such as ü or á, or are just not used for anything.

All this foreign language nonsense is controlled through the Control Panel's Regional and Language Options dialog box. When you suspect that your keyboard is misbehaving in a strange, foreign manner, check its language. Follow directions hither:

1a. **From the Control Panel Home, click the Change Display Language link from beneath the Clock, Language, and Region heading; go to Step 3.**

1b. **From Control Panel Classic view, open the Regional and Language Options icon.**

2. **Click the Keyboards and Languages tab.**

3. **Click the Change Keyboards button.**

   The Text Services and Input Languages dialog box appears. Choose the keyboard language. It might already say `English - (United States) - US`, which is the type you want to use in the United States. If another language is showing, you should choose English to return proper keyboard function.

4. **Click OK to close the various dialog boxes and windows after you have made your choices.**

Many folks who use several keyboard layouts also employ something called the Language bar in Windows. The Language bar is an icon or a window that allows you to choose between one or more input languages, essentially to change the keyboard layout on the fly.

For example, the Language bar may show up as a tiny pair of letters on the taskbar, such as EN for English. To choose a new input language and change the keyboard's function, you click the EN (or other two-letter) icon and select a new language from the pop-up menu.

The Language bar appears when two or more languages are activated in Windows. Use the Text Services and Input Languages dialog box to choose a new language, and then use the Language Bar tab in that same dialog box to control the Language bar.

The bane of Sticky Keys

Sticky Keys aren't caused by sticky fingers. Nope, this is a different type of sticky. Specifically, Sticky Keys in Windows is an accessibility feature designed to *help* disadvantaged people use their computer.

What typically happens in an unwanted way is this: You hear a sound. The program you're using suddenly stops. A Sticky Keys dialog box appears, as shown in Figure 13-2. Click No and the dialog box scampers off, but that doesn't stop the same thing from happening again. To disable Sticky Keys, follow these steps:

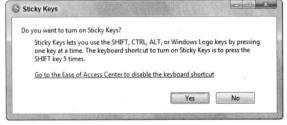

Figure 13-2:
Sticky Keys
rears an
unwanted
head.

Sticky Keys

Do you want to turn on Sticky Keys?

Sticky Keys lets you use the SHIFT, CTRL, ALT, or Windows Logo keys by pressing one key at a time. The keyboard shortcut to turn on Sticky Keys is to press the SHIFT key 5 times.

Go to the Ease of Access Center to disable the keyboard shortcut

Yes   No

1. **Open the Control Panel.**

2a. **From the Control Panel Home, choose Ease of Access and then click the link beneath Ease of Access Center titled Change How Your Keyboard Works; go to Step 4.**

2b. **From Control Panel Classic view, open the Ease of Access icon.**

3. **Choose the link by the keyboard icon (scroll down), Make the Keyboard Easier to Use.**

4. **Choose the link titled Set Up Sticky Keys.**

5. **To disable the warning, remove the check mark by the item Turn On Sticky Keys When Shift Is Pressed Five Times.**

   Yep, that's what did it: You idly or rapidly tapped the Shift key five times in a row. That sets off Sticky Keys on most Windows Vista computers.

6. **While you're in the Set Up Sticky Keys window, remove all the check marks you can find.**

   Unless you're experiencing difficultly while using the computer, you probably don't want to mess with any of the features on the page.

7. **Click the Save button.**

8. **Close the window.**

You're now free to whack, slap, punch, poke, press, and tap either Shift key at your whim.

- ✓ Sticky keys caused by sticky fingers can be cured. First, don't eat sticky stuff and then type, and keep little kids (who are naturally attracted to sticky things) away from the computer. Second, consider getting a keyboard cover if you can't keep away from the baklava while computing or if you spill drinks into the keyboard. Finally, you *can* wash your computer keyboard. See the next bullet.

- ✓ Yes, you can clean your keyboard. Refer to the later section in this chapter, "Yes, you can clean your keyboard."

That bleepin' keyboard!

There are a number of reasons why pressing a key on the keyboard causes the computer to beep at you:

Reason 1: You can't type at this time! Whatever program you're using doesn't want you to type or expects you to be pressing another key.

Reason 2: You're typing too fast. This isn't as bad a problem as it once was, yet it's still possible in some programs to out-type the PC's capacity for input. When that happens, you get beep-beep-beep. Wait until the computer has digested all your input before continuing.

Reason 3: You have an annoying keyboard beep feature turned on. In real life, computers are quiet. But on TV and in the movies, they make noise when you type and when text appears on the screen. If that's happening on your PC, a program is making the noise. Turn the program off.

Reason 4: The computer needs to be restarted.

Though many windows can be open at once, only the top, or *active,* window accepts keyboard input. Even though you may be looking at another window, the computer is paying attention only to the top window.

The Internet/Media/Whatever buttons don't work

The standard PC keyboard sports 105 keys. Any extra keys aren't really part of the PC, but rather are bonus buttons placed there by the PC or keyboard manufacturer. Those nonstandard keys — Volume Control, Play, Eject, Home Page, E-Mail, and others — aren't controlled by Windows, but by special driver software supplied by the keyboard manufacturer.

When the special keys no longer work, you need to update or reinstall the special keyboard drive. It's on a disc that came with the keyboard, or else you can download new drivers from the manufacturer's Web page.

The F-keys don't work!

F-keys, or Function keys, are a standard part of any PC keyboard. Some keyboards, however, have a separate set of functions assigned to the keyboard. The functions are either controlled by special software (see the preceding section) or by pressing a special F or Fn key on the keyboard.

For example, the Microsoft Wireless Multimedia Keyboard has an F-lock key, which is used to shift between standard function key functions and the special label functions on the keyboard (Copy, Paste, and Open, for example.) Ensure that the F-lock or similar key is turned on, to get the function keys to behave normally.

Mouse Mayhem

I once wrote "You need a mouse to use Windows." Well, you kinda do. I have discovered that many things done with a mouse — especially with regard to clicking menus and buttons — can be done faster with keyboard shortcuts, the so-called *accelerator keys*. But that's another story. If the mouse doesn't work, I would bet that you would rather keep using the mouse as opposed to training yourself how to use keyboard shortcuts, whether they're faster or not.

Give me mouse control!

Most common mouse options (speed, pointer appearance, and special effects, for example) are set from the Mouse Properties dialog box. To see it, from the Control Panel Home, find and click the Mouse link; from Control Panel Classic view, open the Mouse icon. A typical Mouse Properties dialog box is shown in Figure 13-3.

A weird thing about the Mouse Properties dialog box is that it's not consistent from PC to PC. Depending on which type or brand of mouse is installed, your computer may sport special, custom options in the Mouse Properties dialog box you see. This requires a wee bit of poking around to find some options and settings that may not be in the same location for everyone.

Figure 13-3:
One type of
Mouse
Properties
dialog box.

🖛 If you have trouble seeing the mouse, select a new mouse pointer from the Mouse Properties dialog box. The Pointers tab is the place to look.

🖛 The mouse can be made left-handed, if you like. Refer to either the Buttons or General tab for the details.

🖛 For more mouse configuration information, refer to that most excellent book, *PCs For Dummies*.

Common mouse maladies and cures

Most mouse mishaps can be cured with a simple restart of Windows. Why does the mouse go nuts? I don't know — probably bad cheese. But whenever my mouse pointer is missing or the mouse freezes or just acts plain weird, restarting Windows solves the problem.

If you have a USB mouse, unplugging the USB connection and plugging it in again sometimes wakes the mouse right back up.

If restarting doesn't work, check the Device Manager, which displays any conflicts and offers some fixes or suggestions. Refer to Chapter 3 for information on opening the Device Manager window. After it's open, look under the category titled Mice and Other Pointing Devices. Beneath that item is an entry for every mouse or pointing device installed on your computer. (Yes, you can have more than one.)

Start by checking to see whether the mouse is nonfunctioning (flagged by a warning triangle). If so, the problem could be hardware or software, so more checking is necessary.

Open the mouse item by double-clicking it. In the Properties dialog box that's displayed, review the Device Status area. The fault and cure might be listed.

Next stop is the Driver tab. Click the Update Driver button to see whether new software can fix the problem. Heed the wizard's instructions to properly reinstall or update the mouse driver.

If all else fails, you may need a new mouse. First, swap out the possibly defective mouse with one you know that works. If the second mouse works, toss out the first mouse and buy a new one (or just don't return the one you borrowed).

✔ In my travels, rarely have I had to install any specific mouse device drivers. It's really Windows itself that controls the mouse. The only reason to reinstall or update a mouse driver would be to use any special, nonstandard features on the mouse, such as extra buttons or "Internet" buttons.

✔ Oh, and those wacky nonstandard mice — including the infamous 3D flying mouse — they need their own software to do their tricks.

✔ Mouse pointer jumping around? Hard to control? See "Cleaning the mouse," later in this chapter.

✔ Your laptop's mouse is typically a touchpad. Yes, you can install an external mouse on your laptop, in which case it sports *two* pointing devices.

✔ You can find software for the various breeds of the Microsoft mouse at the Microsoft download center, at `www.microsoft.com/downloads/`.

✔ Logitech mouse support is on the Web at `www.logitech.com/`.

Your mouse is getting slow
Your mouse is getting slow
Hi-ho, the derry-o
Your mouse is getting slow

Mice get slow when they're dirty. Consider cleaning your mouse, as discussed later in this chapter. A more common cause is simply age. Old mice slow down. They get crappy. They break. Kaput.

If the mouse is older than about four years (sometimes not even that old) and it's getting frustratingly slow, replace it. Buy a new mouse. That fixes the problem.

Beyond fixing the slow mouse problem, nothing is more satisfying than repeatedly pounding the mouse into the table with an aggressive fist.

Monitor Madness

Monitors are possibly the most peaceful of computer peripherals. Unless, of course, you're watching a science fiction TV show from the 1960s. In that case, the monitor is most likely the thing that explodes whenever the computer becomes confused. But that's mere fiction! Ha-ha.

Monitors don't explode. They implode. And, that's only the CRT (cathode ray tube) type of monitor. In fact, most of the monitor woes you can have are from CRT monitors, not from the newer LCD monitors, as witnessed by this small assortment of monitor hardware problems:

- **Connections get loose.** If the image is missing or appears in all one color or "weak," check the monitor cable. Ensure that one end is snugly plugged into the monitor and that the other end is snugly plugged into the PC.

- **The monitor buzzes or hums.** All CRT monitors buzz and hum naturally. Loud humming can be a problem, however. If the humming distracts you from doing your work, repair or replace the monitor.

- **The image is distorted.** CRT monitors are sensitive to interference from other electronic devices. Strong magnetic fields can distort the image on a CRT monitor. If the monitor is exposed for long periods, the magnets damage the monitor permanently. To fix this problem, move the monitor away from whatever is causing the interference. (This isn't an issue for LCD monitors.)

- **The image gets fuzzy.** CRT monitors lose their crispness over time. The sure sign of an old monitor is a fuzzy image. If the image doesn't improve the longer the monitor stays on, retire the monitor and get another.

Another way to fix a fuzzy, flickering, or generally frazzled CRT monitor is to adjust the refresh rate. You can use the buttons on the front of the monitor or change the screen's resolution or number of colors.

The monitor is only half of your PC's graphical equation. The other half is the graphics adapter or hardware inside the PC's console. If the monitor checks out okay but the image is still ga-ga, suspect the graphics adapter. You can tell by trying out another monitor on your computer. (*Remember:* Swap out to test!) If the other monitor is ga-ga, you know that the graphics adapter hardware needs replacing. You may want to have a technician or your dealer swap you in a newer, better graphics adapter.

A Time to Clean

Another thing that the keyboard, mouse, and monitor have in common is that they're easy to clean. And — boy! — is that ever necessary. I have been using the same keyboard for almost 14 years now. Although the robust sucker has lasted me through five different computers, it's just filthy! Time to clean:

- ✔ The best way to keep your stuff clean is *not to eat in front of your computer.* I know that's a hard admonishment to keep. (I'm typing this with one hand as I dig into a bowl of peanuts with the other.)
- ✔ Also, if you sneeze, cover your mouth and nose so that nothing ends up on the screen. I'm certain that your mother would agree with that one.
- ✔ Smoking? Bad for the computer. And you.
- ✔ Keep cats away from computers. Computer mice attract cat hair, and it eventually screws up the mice. Cat hair also loves to stick to the monitor.

Yes, you can clean your keyboard

They're hard to find, but when you see one of those tiny keyboard vacuum cleaners, get it! It deftly sucks the dirt, crud, hair, and potato chip chunks from the inner crevices of your keyboard.

One good way to clean the keyboard: Flip it over and give it a good, vigorous "You've been naughty" shake. Have a whisk broom and dustpan handy to dispose of the results of this action.

Another good way to clean between the keys of your keyboard is with a blast of air. No, don't let Uncle Cliff use his air compressor. Instead, go to an office supply store and get a can of compressed air. A few shots help blow all that *stuff* out of the keyboard. And, yes, you have to clean up the *stuff* as well.

To clean the key caps, use an old toothbrush — or if you're angry with your spouse, use their toothbrush — and some household cleaner, like 409 or Fantastik. It you can stand the smell, ammonia is perhaps the best key cap cleaner. Put the cleaner on the toothbrush and then brush away at the key caps. Don't use much liquid because it drips into the keyboard's guts.

Finally, in a last desperate step, you can give your keyboard a bath. For example, if you spill orange soda pop into the keyboard — and I'm not saying that I did — try to save matters by bathing the keyboard. First, turn off the computer. Second, unplug the keyboard. Third, immerse it in some warm, soapy water. Let it sit for a spell. Then remove the keyboard and let it drain upside down. Keep it out overnight so that it's utterly dry when you reconnect it. If it doesn't work, that's okay; at least you gave it your best shot. Buy a new keyboard.

Cleaning the mouse

Mice pick up crud from your desktop or mouse pad and, boy, does that really gum up the works!

For a mechanical mouse, remove the ball from its belly to clean it. A cover twists off so that you can remove the ball. Rub the ball with a damp cloth, though the real filth is on the rollers that detect the ball's movement.

To carefully clean the rollers, get an X-Acto knife and a pair of tweezers. Carefully scrape the gunk away from the rollers by using the X-Acto knife. The gunk generally comes off in large chunks, which you can then extract using the tweezers. Replace the ball when you're done cleaning.

Optical mice get dirty too! To clean them, use a pair of tweezers to pull out the hair and gunk in the optical mouse's "eyehole." In fact, any time an optical mouse gets weird on you, flip it over and clean the eyehole. Chances are that a strand of hair is wreaking havoc with the LED sensor.

✔ While you're at it, clean your mousepad too. Use a stiff brush to clean the cloth pads. Or, heck, just toss out the old pad and get a new one.

✔ If cleaning doesn't help, get a new mouse. That's what the wizard did when Mickey tried to clean up.

Cleaning your monitor

The only part of the monitor worthy of cleanliness is the screen — the part where information is displayed. Sure, you could clean the monitor's housing, but rarely have I seen that done, nor is it even necessary (unless you opt to clean off that daisy-like effect of all those yellow sticky notes).

For a CRT monitor, spray some window cleaner on a soft cloth. Wipe the cloth on the monitor.

For an LCD monitor, buy and use special cleaning solution and static free towelettes. *Never* put ammonia or alcohol on an LCD monitor!

- ✔ Never spray cleaning solution directly on the screen.

- ✔ It helps to have a nice, bright yet plain image on the screen while you clean. I open up the Paint program and fill the screen with a nice, white palette so that I can see all the gunk on the monitor.

- ✔ For cleaning LCD monitors, I recommend Klear Screen, from Meridrew Enterprises (www.klearscreen.com).

- ✔ On the other hand, dust disappears unless you turn off the monitor. If you're just doing a good dust job, turn off the monitor and you see all that "pixel dust."

Chapter 14

Printer Problems

● ●

In This Chapter

▶ Getting to know printer trouble

▶ Using Print Preview

▶ Finding key printing spots in Windows

▶ Fixing various printer maladies

▶ Printing on the edge of the page

▶ Adjusting colors

▶ Stopping a print job

▶ Taking care of general printer maintenance

● ●

I suppose that deep within the printer's core, it secretly despises the computer. There's an envy there that's palpable. That's because the computer gets all the attention. The computer has a keyboard, and the printer has a tiny row of input buttons. The computer has a monitor, and the printer may have a multiline display, perhaps even just a single LED. Yet the printer is responsible for that hard copy, for that final result that makes all the toil worth it. I'll bet no one pats their PC printer on the head after printing out a swell job. No one!

Yes, printers have problems. And the problems are more than just emotional ones. Who out there still thinks of a printer jam as a type of sweet preserve? Case in point: this entire chapter on printer troubleshooting. It's necessary, emotionally and electronically.

Don't Blame the Printer

The printer is really a separate computer, a device customized just to print, yet it has many of the same computer components as your desktop PC: a CPU, memory, input, output — the whole nine yards. Therefore, dealing with a printer is like dealing with a second computer. So the first thing to determine is whether the problem is with the printer itself or with some software on your PC. There's an easy way to tell.

When every program has the same printer problem, it's a printer problem, with either the printer hardware or the printer software (the *printer driver*). If only one program can't print, the problem is most likely with that particular piece of software. Contact that software developer — ignore its vain attempts to shuttle you off to the printer manufacturer — and get the problem solved.

Your best friend, Print Preview

When the printer acts up or the hard copy looks strange, don't be too quick to blame the printer! First check the Print Preview command (File⇨Print Preview) to ensure that the printer isn't just blindly obeying orders.

How does the document look in Print Preview? How are the colors? The margins? The fonts?

If the screw-up is visible in the Print Preview window, blame yourself or the application. If Print Preview looks like you intended, blame the printer driver or the printer itself. Read on!

- ✔ *Hard copy* is another term for the stuff that comes out of the printer — printed information as opposed to information on the screen.
- ✔ Not every program has a Print Preview command.
- ✔ Graphics applications in particular seem to lack a Print Preview command. That's because the graphics image you see on the screen is supposed to be identical to the one that's printed.

Controlling the printer from your application

The printer, like all hardware, is dumb all by itself. It needs your carefully guided instructions to tell it what and how to print. That's the job of the Print dialog box, but also the Page Setup dialog box in most applications.

Figure 14-1 shows the Page Setup dialog box for the WordPad application in Windows.

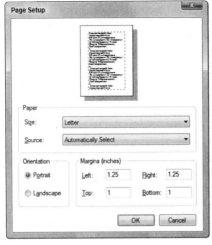

Figure 14-1:
Various
printer
options in
the Page
Setup
dialog box.

The Page Setup dialog box in other applications contains similar commands, though often more of them and perhaps organized a bit differently. Typically, you can set the following items in the Page Setup dialog box:

✔ **Margins:** These define the area where printing takes place. Most printers require a minimum margin, either ½ or ¼ inch, inset from the edge of the paper. The margin on one edge of the printer may be larger; see the section "The edge of the page won't print," later in this chapter.

✔ **Paper size:** Most often, you print on letter-size paper, but you can tell both the application and the printer that you're printing on another paper size, such as legal or envelope, using the Page Setup dialog box.

✔ **Paper source:** Some printers have different trays for different paper sizes. Or, if the paper is manually fed into the printer, that's where you set that option.

✔ **Orientation:** You have only two choices: normal, which is called *Portrait* orientation, or longways, which is called *Landscape* orientation.

✔ **Layout options:** These settings can include options for binding, centering the page, scaling the image (larger or smaller), headers, footers, and multiple pages per sheet. Not every Page Setup dialog box offers these features.

Some applications lack a Page Setup dialog box. In that case, the application may offer some printer control in the Print dialog box itself, as shown in Figure 14-2.

What happens when you Ctrl+P

Several things happen when you print a document on your computer. First, you summon a print command, Ctrl+P in nearly all Windows programs, and make settings in a Print dialog box. Clicking the Print or OK button sets everything in motion.

The application itself doesn't print the program. (It did in the old days, which is why computers were so difficult to use back then.) On your PC, the operating system handles all the printing. So the program communicates to Windows what needs to be printed and how. Windows passes off that information to a specific piece of software called the printer driver.

The *printer driver* is a part of the operating system, installed when you first set up Windows. The driver's job is to control the printer, by telling it what to print. So, although some things — document content, margins, colors, and styles, for example — are controlled

by your application, it's the printer driver common to all of Windows that's really in charge of the printing job.

As the printer driver takes over, a wee little "printer guy" icon shows up in the notification area (on the right end of the taskbar).

The printer driver's job is to talk directly with the printer and send it the proper instructions that tell it to print what you want. Hopefully, if all goes well, your stuff gets put down on paper and you become O So Very Happy with the results.

After the document is printed, the printer driver goes back to sleep and the wee printer-guy icon disappears from the notification area.

Problems? They can occur anywhere along the line. Having a general idea of how the process works, however, can help you pinpoint who or what is to blame.

Figure 14-2:
Options in
the Print
dialog box.

Yes, you find additional printing options here:

✔ **Select a printer:** Windows affords you the luxury of using one of any number of printers, either directly connected to your PC or accessed through the network. It's in the Print dialog box that you choose which printer you want to print on.

✔ **Configure the printer:** The Print dialog box is a part of Windows, but it typically contains extra tabs or an Advanced, Properties, or Preferences button (refer to Figure 14-2) that lets you set custom printing options, such as graphics resolution, color settings, printer language, and other, often trivial, settings.

✔ **Choose the pages to print:** Normally, you print all the pages, though the Print dialog box lets you select a single page, individual pages, or a range of pages to print.

✔ **Select the number of copies:** You can also print multiple copies of the same document. When I create my annual Christmas letter, I specify several dozen copies to print, one for everyone on the list.

✔ **Collation and other options:** Each Print dialog box is different, with different options and settings depending on the printer or application. An option common to many of them is *Collate,* which prints multiple copies, either one page at a time (seven Page 1s followed by seven Page 2s) or in sets (Pages 1 through 5 and then another set of Pages 1 through 5). Another option is printing in reverse order, which is nice when pages spew forth from the printer faceup.

The Page Setup and Print dialog boxes are two places you can use to configure your printer from your application.

After you click the Print button in the Print dialog box, control passes to the printer driver. Any problems from that point on are blamed on the driver itself or on the printer, as covered in the rest of this chapter.

✔ Setting the page margins isn't the same thing as setting paragraph margins inside a word processor. Refer to your word processor's Help system for more margin information, or just read the best book on Microsoft Word ever written, my own *Word For Dummies* (Wiley Publishing, Inc.).

✔ Yes, many applications mix and swap options between the Print and Page Setup dialog boxes. In some programs, you select paper orientation in the Page Setup dialog box; in other programs, you do that in the Print dialog box.

✔ Selecting a printer other than the *default,* or main, printer may affect the outside margins on a page. If so, you have to print again, by returning to the Page Setup dialog box to fix your margins. Check Print Preview to be sure.

✔ Acquaint yourself with some of your printer's more esoteric options. If additional tabs are in the Print dialog box or if you see a Properties or Preferences button there, click it to peruse those extra options.

- ✔ Be especially observant of the location where you can turn color printing on or off for a color printer. For example, in Figure 14-2 you would need to first choose a color printer and then click the Properties button to set color options.

- ✔ Some applications may also have a Document Setup or Page Setup command on the File menu. You can find additional page-configuration items in that dialog box.

- ✔ In Office 2007, the Page Setup dialog box is accessed by choosing the Page Layout tab and then clicking the Dialog Box Launcher in the lower-right corner of the Page Setup group.

- ✔ Which dialog box has priority? The Print dialog box does. Any changes you make there directly affect the printer. Often times, however, some coordination is required between the Page Setup and Print dialog boxes. For example, if you're printing in Landscape mode, you need to tell both the application (via the Page Setup dialog box) and the printer (via the Print dialog box) to print in that mode and on that paper.

TIP

Fabulous envelope-printing tips

The best way to print an envelope is to use a program designed to print envelopes! After all, a specialist knows more about his specialty than the jack-of-all-trades. For example, the Envelope printing tool in Microsoft Word is a great way to print envelopes. But, printing an envelope on the fly in a program like WordPad takes skill and, well, knowledge of the following pointers:

- ✔ An envelope is merely a specialized type of paper. Specifically, in the US, envelopes are known as number 10 or Envelope #10. If you choose that type of "paper" in the Page Setup dialog box, your document automatically formats itself to envelope dimensions.

- ✔ Use the Print Preview command to see how the envelope paper is oriented on the page. You want to ensure that this orientation matches how the envelope is fed into your printer.

- ✔ Use the program's margin settings (the paragraph margins, not the page margins) to set the locations for the address and return address.

- ✔ Use Print Preview again to determine that you have placed the address and return address in the proper position and orientation.

- ✔ Pay special attention to how the printer eats envelopes: unlike plain paper, there's an upside and a topside to an envelope.

- ✔ Print a test envelope first. Better still, mark which end of the envelope went into the printer first and which side of the envelope was "up." That way, you can confirm that the envelope was inserted in the proper orientation.

Where the Printer Stuff Lurks in Windows

To properly futz with a printer in Windows, you need to know where these printer things are and what they do:

- ✔ The Printers window
- ✔ Your printer's window
- ✔ The little printer guy

Each one has something to do with printing, as described in this section.

Finding the Printers window

The Printers window is where Windows stores information about all the printers, faxes, and other text-spewing devices available to your computer. This window is the spot where you can add new printers, remove existing printers, or configure which printer is the main, or *default*.

To open the Printers window, follow these steps:

1. **Open the Control Panel.**

2a. **From the Control Panel Home, click the Printers link beneath Hardware and Sound.**

2b. **From Control Panel Classic view, open the Printers icon.**

   Either way you get there, you see the Printers window, looking similar to the one shown in Figure 14-3.

Figure 14-3:
The Printers and Faxes folder.

You can do several things in the Printers and Faxes folder as far as trouble-shooting is concerned:

- ✔ **Open your printer's Properties dialog box by right-clicking your printer's icon and choosing Properties from the pop-up menu.** This method is good for adjusting and tweaking the printer. You can also print a test page from the dialog box.

- ✔ **Instantly halt printing by right-clicking your printer icon and choosing Pause Printing from the pop-up menu.** See the section "Halting a printer run amok," later in this chapter, for more information.

- ✔ **Delete and reinstall a printer by clicking to select an icon and then choosing the toolbar button labeled Delete This Printer.** That command removes the printer. You can then use the item labeled Add a Printer Task to reinstall that same printer. Often times, this technique fixes printer driver problems.

- ✔ **Choose which printer you want to use as your main, or default, printer.** Just click the printer to select it and choose File⇨Set As Default Printer from the menu. The default printer has a white-on-black check mark by its icon, as shown in Figure 14-3.

Close the Printers window when you're done messing around.

- ✔ When you select a printer, the toolbar grows a few more buttons, some of them useful. When you don't see the extra buttons, remember to select a printer first.

- ✔ Don't see a printer you want? Then you need to add the printer. Refer to my book *PCs For Dummies* (Wiley Publishing, Inc.) for directions.

Seeing your printer's own window

When you print, you can open your printer's icon in the Printers window to view the progress of the documents being printed. The documents appear there, in the order you printed them, marching off to the printer one by one while you move on to do something else.

Most of the time the printer window is blank; modern printers are quite peppy. When trouble looms, however, you see documents listed in the printer's window — the *printing queue*. You can use the window to change the order of the documents or to cancel or pause printing, as discussed elsewhere in this chapter.

The items waiting to be printed are print *jobs*.

Locating the little printer guy

 You never really need to keep an eye on the Printers folder while you print. Whenever something is printing (or, to be technical, whenever the printer driver is sending information to the printer), a teensy printer icon appears in the notification area on the taskbar. You can double-click that icon to instantly open your printer's window and review the documents waiting to be printed.

The little printer guy goes away when the last byte of data has been sent to the printer.

And Then, the Printer Goes Wacky

Printers are dutiful little creatures, handily going about their work without care or notice . . . until they screw up. Then the printer can become the most hated piece of office equipment in the building. Vile creatures. Cruel and unkind. And, stubborn? I don't care how fancy the display is on your printer, when it's acting stupid, it has nothing useful to say.

General troubleshooting advice

The first thing to try when the printer goes haywire is the printer trouble-shooter. This is the Microsoft Q&A way to help track down most printer problems. Follow these steps:

 1. **Summon the Help command.**

   Choose Help and Support from the Start menu, or click the tiny question-mark Help button in the Printers window.

2. **Type** printer troubleshooter **into the Help window's Search text box.**

3. **In the results displayed, choose the item titled Troubleshoot Printer Problems.**

   The Windows Help and Support window dons its troubleshooter apron and displays the Troubleshoot Printer Problems menu of solutions, as shown in Figure 14-4.

4. **Work the troubleshooter.**

   Choose an item from the list that best describes your problem, such as The Printer Is Out of Paper. Clicking a link displays more information, and perhaps even a set of steps to follow or links to other helpful locations in Windows.

Figure 14-4:
The printer trouble-shooter.

5. **Close the Windows Help and Support window when you're done.**

If the troubleshooter doesn't help (either the proper answer cannot be found or the troubleshooter is acting all snotty), you can try these techniques:

✔ Check to see whether your printer came with any self-diagnostic software or utilities or its own troubleshooter-like program.

✔ Consider reinstalling the printer driver software. The easiest way to do that is to delete your printer from the Printers folder and then add it again.

✔ You may want to check with your printer manufacturer's Web page to see whether it has any updated printer drivers. Refer to Chapter 5 for more information on finding those Web pages.

Things to check when the printer isn't printing

Ah, the usual suspects: Check all the cables. One cable must plug between your computer and the printer — both ends must be snug. The other cable plugs between your printer and the wall socket. Snug. Snug. Snug.

"'PC Load Letter'? What the @#$% does that mean?"

The quote (in the heading) is from the popular movie *Office Space,* uttered by a frustrated employee who is doing battle with a Hewlett-Packard laser printer. The error message isn't used any more, though you may see it displayed if you have an older-model HP Deskjet printer. It means that the paper cartridge (PC) must be stocked with the proper (letter size) paper and placed into the printer for printing to continue.

Now if only someone will tell that to Michael. . . .

USB printers cannot be run from USB power! Most printers that I've seen must also be plugged into a power source.

Is the printer turned on?

Is the printer *selected?* Some printers have the ability to be powered up but deselected or taken offline. You typically push a Select or On-line button to ensure that the printer isn't ignoring the computer. (This option is on high-end printers, mostly.)

Ensure that you have chosen the proper printer from the list in the Print dialog box. I once sent three copies of a document to a printer in another office before I figured out that I had the wrong printer selected and *that* was the reason nothing was printing on my own printer.

Also check the printer's display or panel for errors. Some low-end printers simply blink their lights if they have a paper jam or low-ink problem.

The computer network must be up and running for you to print on a network printer. Sometimes, you may need to turn your computer off and then on again for it to "find" the network printer. You also need to check the computer's firewall software to ensure that network printing is allowed. (You may need assistance from your network manager to help set that up.)

The edge of the page won't print

Printing happens in a given area on every page, no matter how large the page. Generally speaking, the outside half inch of any page cannot be printed on. That's to account for the mechanism that feeds the paper through the printer.

On some printers you can print to the edges of the paper.

One most printers, one edge of the page is the feeding edge, which must either go into the printing mechanism first or last, and that edge of the page has the largest unprintable margin on it. For example, on my inkjet printer, the bottom half-inch of the page cannot be printed on because that's the edge that enters the printing mechanism first.

Can you fix this problem? No! But remember to account for it when you go to print documents that sport wide margins.

Word won't print a page border

The secret to get Word to print a page board is to measure the board from the *text,* not from the edge of the page. This is covered properly in any of my books on Word, such as *Word 2007 For Dummies,* (Wiley Publishing, Inc.), and given five stars by various famous Las Vegas pastry chefs.

There are lines or blanks or rivers of white on the page

Long story short: It's ink! Either you're short of ink or the printing heads are clogged. The solution is to clean the inkjet's printer nozzles. This isn't something you do with Mr. Clean and a scrub brush. Instead, you need to look in the printer's manual, or sometimes just under the lid or cover, to find the instructions for cleaning the nozzles or printer heads.

Do not remove the ink cartridges and attempt to manually clean them yourself. The result is a terrible mess, plus the expense of having to purchase new ink cartridges.

The "weird text atop the page" problem

Printers that print strange text across the top of the first page, or ugly text on every page, have a driver problem. Most likely, the wrong printer driver was installed when the printer was set up, such as 401B when you really need a 401A — like that.

The easiest way to change or update printer drivers is to reinstall the printer. Delete your printer from the Printers window, and then click the Add a Printer button to reinstall it. Also consider checking with the printer manufacturer's Web site to see whether it has updated printer files or even a printer setup utility you can download and use.

- When the problem is a network printer connected to a specific computer, you must update the driver on that computer, not on your own computer.

- If the weird text appears only when you print from one application, it's the application's doing and not the printer driver's.

- Use the Print Preview command to ensure that it's not the application itself that's producing the weird characters.

- When the characters at the top of the page appear to have their heads cut off, your page's top margin is set too high; use the Page Setup dialog box to increase the top margin.

The color is all wrong

Adjusting the color of printer output is an obsession with some people. But this type of error doesn't involve the subtleties between PMS 133 and PMS 140. If the color is wrong, such as too green or not enough red, your printer is probably low on one type of ink.

- Sadly, unless you have a printer with separate ink cartridges, you have to replace the entire three-color ink cartridge when only one color gets low. I know: It's a rip-off. But the printer was cheap, wasn't it?

- PMS is an acronym for the Pantone matching system, a set of numbers matched to specific colors. PMS is used by graphics professionals to ensure that their printed results are exactly the color they want and to justify the high markup they charge.

- You can try checking the Print dialog box for an Advanced, Properties, or Preferences button to see whether you find controls there for manipulating the color. Yet most of the time a discolored image is the sign of low ink.

A black-and-white image prints in dark blue

Some color printers come with a three-color ink cartridge and then a single black ink cartridge. Their controls can also switch so that you can use only the black cartridge, which is the case if you're printing a black-and-white or grayscale image. Simply tell the Print dialog box that you want to use only the black ink.

Halting a printer run amok

I have done this tons of times: You print and then . . . you realize that you want to take it back and stop printing at once! Here's what you do:

1. **Open the Printers window from the Control Panel.**

   Specific directions are provided earlier in this chapter.

2. **Right-click your printer's icon.**

3. **Choose the Pause Printing command.**

   This step gives you a break so that you can stop panicking.

4. **If necessary, reset your printer (if it has such a feature) or take your printer offline (if it has that feature as well).**

5. **Open the printer's icon in the Printers window.**

   Remember that printing has been *paused,* not cancelled.

6. **From the queue in the printer's window, choose the document you want to stop printing.**

7. **Choose Document⇔Cancel from the menu.**

   If nothing seems to happen or the document remains, repeat Step 7. You might also try choosing Printer⇔Cancel All Documents just to zap the entire queue.

8. **Close the various open windows when you're done.**

You may need to eject a page, depending on your printer model. Most printers have a page eject button right up front, or the page eject command is accessed through a difficult-to-use menu system.

Sometimes you might even need to turn the printer off and then on again. If so, turn it off, pause a few seconds, and then turn it on again.

Some new printers now come with Print Job Cancel buttons on them, or on a menu you can access from the printer's control console. Consider yourself blessed if your printer sports such a feature. Press that button or access the menu to cancel printing, which should be your first (and only) step.

Printer Maintenance Chores

Printers run relatively maintenance free, which is amazing considering how many moving parts are inside. The only regular maintenance you need to perform on the printer is the routine changing of the ink cartridges or toner. Oh, and the printer does enjoy a little love every so often.

If you have a nice inkjet printer, which means that you paid more than $300 for it, I recommend buying brand-name or approved replacement ink cartridges. The reason is that these high-end printers rely on the high-end cartridges to help keep the inkjet nozzles clean.

If you have a cheaper printer, you can save some money by using those ink cartridge refilling syringes that are advertised on TV and sold in office supply stores. They work just fine and aren't really that messy, but the ink is of a lower quality, so you don't want to use them in a high-end inkjet printer.

For laser printers, you can get a few extra sheets out of the thing by "rocking" the toner cartridge when the first Toner Low warning comes. Simply remove the toner from the machine and rock it from left to right gently in your hands. This technique somehow redistributes the toxic "inkstuff" so that you can print a while longer before you have to shell out beaucoup bucks for another toner cartridge.

A new toner cartridge can also instantly fix those smudgy-smeary pages that are produced when the toner cartridge is of an older age.

As far as jams go, simply clear them as best you can. Printer jams happen because the paper is damaged, too thin, or too thick. If the paper is too old, it may contain moisture that can make a laser printer grunt.

In my travels, I have discovered few printers that can print on paper stock heavier than 25 pounds. One printer could do it, but it was a laser printer where the paper passed in a straight line from the front to the back of the printer. Other printers, where the paper scrolls up and down and back and forth, cannot handle thick paper stock, which jams and causes you undue delay and stress.

And we could all use a little less stress.

Chapter 15

Mishaps in the Storage System

*T*hey named the command Save for a reason. The word implies safety, a reprise from peril. And it's a much better term than Transfer, which was the original command to save stuff in old Microsoft applications, back when Bill Gates was worth only tens of millions of dollars. Your PC's storage system safely stores not only your own stuff but also all your programs and the operating system. Storage is a key part of the computer, and therefore it's near panic-inducing terror that strikes at your soul when something goes amiss with the storage system: disk disaster, media card mayhem, or DVD death. Turn to this chapter to help ease your pain.

✔ Your PC's storage system includes disk drives as well as media cards and memory cards. It's all the same storage system, though the disk drives are your PC's primary storage gizmo and the source of most troubleshooting needs.

✔ Refer to Part IV of this book, which deals with preventive maintenance, backup, and other storage system tools.

"My Storage Device Is Missing!"

You may not have seen it scamper off, but suddenly you notice that one of your PC's storage devices is missing. You may see a Drive Not Available error, or you may just notice that the drive letter isn't showing up on a menu or in the Computer window. Whoops! How did the thing escape? That depends on the type of drive.

- ✓ **Hard drive:** Your first option, as usual, is to restart the computer to see whether the missing hard drive can be found. That generally fixes the problem. If not, turn off the computer and open up the console to see whether the device is properly connected. Or, if that makes you uneasy, consider having your dealer do it.

- ✓ **Media cards:** Like other removable media, the "drive" may show up in the Computer window and on various lists, but the drive itself is useless without the media inside. Check to ensure that the media is present and properly inserted.

- ✓ **External drives:** First, ensure that the device is properly connected and getting power. I have noted that some external USB or IEEE 1340 (FireWire) drives must be attached directly to the computer console for them to work, or, at minimum, attached to a powered hub (a hub that's plugged in for extra power). Check to see whether the drive is turned on.

- ✓ **Network drives:** Obviously, the network must be connected and working properly for shared network drives to appear. Further, the computer or server sharing the drives must be on, alert, and willing to cooperate with other computers on the network.

Sometimes, the media's icon may be hidden in the My Computer window; choose List from the toolbar's Views button menu to change the way the drives are displayed. That reveals any icons hiding behind other icons.

Smells Like Hard Drive Trouble

Securely spinning in the bosom of your beloved PC, the hard drive is expected to last anywhere from four to five years. After that time, the hard drive begins to hear the electronics gods call it home. Older hard drives have problems with increasing errors, and they get slower. That's expected. Anything wrong before that is not only unexpected but also unwelcome.

Hard drive failure warning signs

Most of the time, hard drives let you know well before they die. Supposedly, some hard drives send you e-mail, though I have no solid evidence of it. Mostly, the hard drive goes through its death throes for a short period, complaining about this or that. Then it dies. There's good news and bad news regarding this process.

The several signs of impending hard drive doom may occur in this order, in any order, or all at once, or only one may occur. Heed the warning signs:

Hard drive technobabble you don't have to read

The terms *hard drive* and *hard disk* are fairly interchangeable, though I'm sure that nerds at cocktail parties would argue the differences down to the tiniest micron, which isn't anyone's idea of a swell evening.

The *hard drive* is a chunk of electronics about the size of a thick paperback book, like something Stephen King would write. Laptop computers use a smaller hard drive, about the size of a Stephen King book when you edit out the useless parts. As a unit, the hard drive contains several spinning disks, all stacked on the same spindle and all of which store data on both sides. That whole thing is a hard drive.

A hard drive is also known as a *physical drive*. Most PCs can have two or more physical drives installed internally and as many external physical drives as you can afford.

The operating system sees only *logical* drives. A typical hard drive can be viewed by the operating system as a single logical drive, but the single drive can be *partitioned* into two or more logical drives. So the one physical drive inside your computer could be two logical drives: C and D.

You can find lots of technical folderol having to do with disk drives, partitioning, and such, but my point is that when a single physical hard drive goes bad, it can bring down one or more of the logical drives as well. Conversely, a corrupt file on a logical drive may not affect any other logical drives on the same physical drive.

So, the terms hard drive and hard disk aren't really important, although it helps to know that a physical hard drive can be divided into logical hard drives.

First sign: An increasing number of errors and *bad sectors* occur. As you run your programs, you may see access or read errors or the infamous Blue Screen of Death. Or, when you run various disk utilities, errors may be reported. At first, they're fixed — which is great. But as time rolls on, the number and frequency of errors increase.

Second sign: Drive performance suffers. Disk access becomes sluggish. Defragmenting the drive doesn't help.

Third sign: The drive becomes louder and louder. I caught one recent and rather sudden drive failure because I noticed a clicking sound as the drive was accessing data. The clicking got louder over the next hour, and immediately I backed up the entire drive. Good thing too because the next morning, the hard drive was dead.

Other sounds include an increasing whistling or grinding noise that may diminish over time, but still is a sign that the drive may be on its last leg. Or spindle.

- ✔ The monitor, too, can make a loud, annoying noise when it's starting to go berserk. Refer to Chapter 13 for information on how to tell whether it's the monitor, the hard drive, or just tinnitus.

- ✔ See Chapter 25 for more information on Check Disk.

- ✔ Hard drives also tend to die when you turn on the computer, so if you suspect trouble — keep reading at the next section.

What to do when you suspect trouble

Whenever you suspect trouble, *immediately* back up your data. If you have a backup program, run it at once! Refer to Chapter 26 for directions on doing a full backup. Now is the time.

Hands down, you have to replace the defective drive. You're buying, at minimum, a second hard drive for your computer. If possible, try to get an internal hard drive. Have your dealer set it up as the main hard drive, and have that person reconfigure the existing hard drive as the second hard drive. Then you can copy information from the old hard drive to the new hard drive and eventually dispense with the old one.

- ✔ It helps to get a second, larger hard drive in any computer. The cost isn't that much.

- ✔ Yes, you can add a second hard drive yourself. It's not that difficult, but it does require opening the computer's case, which contains all those scary electronic and pointy things. Also, you need to ensure that your PC's console has room inside for a second hard drive. Your dealer will know for certain.

Dead drives ≠ Dead data

Just because the hard drive has gone to the hereafter doesn't mean that your data is doomed as well. Sometimes the information on the hard drive is still intact. That's why it's best to copy that stuff from the failing hard drive while you have the chance. If the hard drive goes, however, it's still possible to recover your data.

Electronic exorcists exist in most major cities, specializing in disk disaster data resurrection. Most of these places can take an old hard drive and, as long as you didn't blast the thing with a shotgun, fully recover all the data and either place it on a DVD, an electronic tape, or a new hard drive.

Although this service sounds wonderful, data recovery is *very* expensive. It's primarily used in large companies or the government or other situations where the files are critical and no other backup exists. If your stuff is precious to you, *back up your hard drive,* as covered in Chapter 26. Save the data recovery job for those who can afford it.

Optical Disc Disaster!

Doubtless, your PC has an optical drive. If you're an old-timer, you probably still call it a CD-ROM drive. *Hello!* This is the 21st century. By now, all optical drives are dual CD/DVD drives — plus, they can create discs. Your optical drive is important for backup, software installation, and ripping CDs and DVDs so that you can turn your thousand-dollar computer into a cheap stereo or TV. Whatever — like anything else in the computer, the optical drive can go kaput at the most ugly of times.

The all-purpose, do-or-die, tried-and-true optical drive troubleshooter

When the optical drive doesn't read a disc, play music, or do anything, you can follow these steps to effectively troubleshoot the drive:

1. **Push the eject button on the drive.**

   What should happen: The tray slides out or the disc spits out (depending on the type of drive). This action confirms that the drive is getting power.

   If nothing happens: The drive is dead. There are two things you can do: First, you can (if you know your screws and nuts) turn off the computer and check the drive connections to see whether they're loose. If they're all snug, choose the second option: Replace the drive with one that works.

   If you can't eject a disc, use the "beauty mark" hole on the front of the drive. Stick a straightened paper clip into the hole. Push gently. This action ejects the disc — even when the computer is off or the drive totally lacks power.

2. **Insert a music disc.**

   The computer is smart enough to know that you play music discs when they're inserted. Some optical drives even have a headphone jack and volume control. You use them to hear whether the music CD is playing.

   What should happen: You hear the music play over the headphones. This means that the drive is working and what's missing is the connection between the drive and the motherboard.

   If nothing happens: The drive is dead or the connections are loose. You can check the connections, and that may fix the problem. If not, replace the drive.

Know your CD/DVD drive letter

If you're going to be working with your optical drive, and especially if you end up phoning tech support, you need to know which drive letter it uses. This PC puzzle is one that many users haven't yet solved.

In most documentation, the optical drive letter is referred to as Drive D. That's because Drive D is the CD-ROM or DVD drive in about 70 percent of the computers sold. Drive C is always the primary hard drive. Drive D, the next letter, belongs to the optical. But that's not always the case.

If you have a hard drive D, the optical drive letter may be E.

If you're a clever user and have reassigned your optical drive letter, or when you're using an external optical drive, it could be any letter of the alphabet, up to Z! On two of my computers, the CD-ROM drive is drive letter R.

So, how can you tell? Open the Computer window; either open the Computer icon on the desktop or choose Computer from the Start menu. In the Computer window, choose the Details command from the toolbar's Views button menu. In the Details presentation, you see your computer's disk drives organized as shown in the nearby figure. Look in the Type column for any CD drive entries. That's your PC's optical drive. Note which letter it is, such as D in this figure.

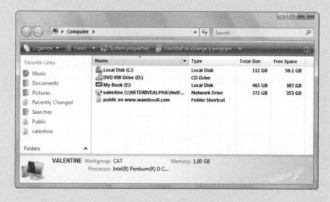

3. **Insert a cleaning disc.**

   Go to Radio Shack or Wal-Mart or wherever and pick up an optical-drive-cleaning disc. This disc buffs out the laser lens and possibly fixes a drive that skips or reads data intermittently.

   What should happen: The drive suddenly works again.

   If nothing happens: It's time to get a new drive.

   Don't use a cleaning kit on a recordable optical drive. Those drives have self-cleaning laser heads, and using a cleaning disc on them can damage the drive.

Yes, optical drives die. Remember that anything with moving parts is more likely to die than something fully electronic. The good news is that replacing an optical drive is easy, and the new drives are not that expensive — more good news.

The R/RW disc won't record

An optical drive that cannot record may have a hardware problem and need replacing. But first ensure that you're using a recordable drive. The drive says Recordable or has the CD-R/RW, DVD±R/RW logo on it somewhere.

If the disc still doesn't record, try burning another disc. Recordable optical discs go bad. When they do, toss them out and try again with another disc.

Turning AutoPlay on or off

Windows comes configured to automatically play any disc you stick into the optical drive. This means that music CDs should play automatically and that the Autoplay programs on most data discs run a Setup or Install program when the disc is inserted.

You can turn the AutoPlay feature on or off, or you can control how the disc is treated when Windows recognizes which types of files it contains. Here's how to do that:

1. **Open the Control Panel.**

2. **From the Control Panel Home, choose the link Play CDs or Other Media Automatically from beneath the Hardware and Sound heading; from Control Panel Classic view, open the AutoPlay icon.**

   The AutoPlay window appears, as depicted in Figure 15-1.

3. **Locate the type of disc you are inserting into the drive.**

   For example, Audio CD or Software and Games or Blank DVD.

4. **To disable any activity when that type of disc is inserted, choose the command Take No Action from the button menu by the disc type.**

   For example, to have the computer *not* play a music CD, use the button by Audio CD to choose the Take No Action item.

5. **Repeat Steps 3 and 4 for each type of disc you plan on bullying.**

6. **Click the Save button to force Windows to obey your choices.**

7. **Close the Control Panel window.**

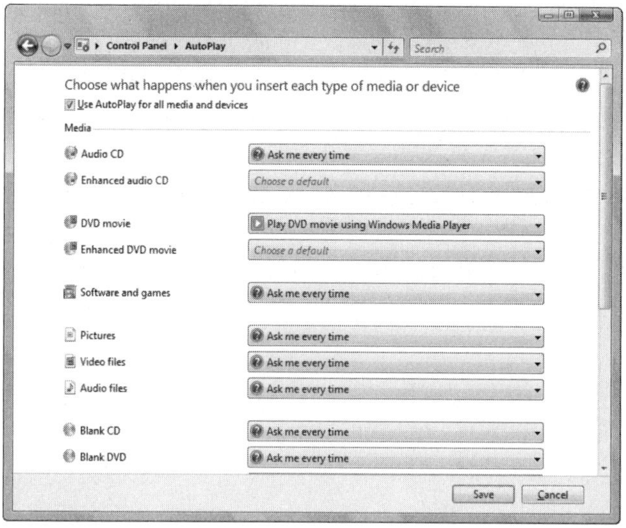

Figure 15-1:
Controlling
AutoPlay
for your
PC's optical
drive.

You can change your mind at any time by repeating these steps to choose what you want to happen when you insert any optical disc.

✔ By choosing an action from the AutoPlay window, you remove the appearance of the AutoPlay dialog box each time you insert a disc (or add a media card) to your PC.

✔ These steps apply to any and all optical drives on your PC. There's no need to make separate selections for each optical drive, if your computer has more than one.

Recordable optical drive stuff

A recordable optical drive presents other problems in addition to that of the normal optical drive. That's because, as its name implies, this type of drive can *write* discs. That throws into the mix a whole bunch of things that can go wrong.

Here are some thoughts:

✔ I don't recommend using RW (re-recordable) discs any more. First, they're more expensive than the non-re-recordable discs. Second, they don't always reliably erase, and the number of times they can be reused is limited. Third, using them seems to be more time consuming. Therefore, I recommend that you simply buy and use non-RW discs instead.

- ✔ My advice is to "burn" data to a CD-R disc using the Mastered format. See my book *PCs For Dummies* (Wiley Publishing, Inc.) for the details, as well as exciting new ways to prepare asparagus.

- ✔ Recordable optical discs fail, just like other types of discs. If the disc cannot be written to, throw it out.

- ✔ The optical drive may appear to be dead, but most likely the disc is full. Try replacing the disc and see whether it still works.

- ✔ I lied: There's nothing about asparagus in *PCs For Dummies*.

Chapter 16

Correcting Graphics Disgrace

. . . .

In This Chapter

▶ Understanding graphics resolution

▶ Using the dots per inch (DPI) measurement

▶ Knowing about image size versus resolution

▶ Changing the monitor's resolution

▶ Viewing large images

▶ Setting graphics resolutions for e-mail

▶ Setting image resolutions in a digital camera

▶ Changing an image's size or resolution

▶ Understanding graphics file formats

▶ Using JPG compression

▶ Converting between graphics file formats

. . . .

O, shame! The powerful computer is slowly consuming the gentle, patient art of photography. Although the camera companies continue to strive toward making things easier, computer users' graphical efforts are often met with disgrace and shame. Grandma bemoans, "It took me 40 minutes to download your baby's picture, and all I can see on the screen is one big eye!" Then, to make matters worse, she adds, "I thought you were supposed to be some sort of computer genius!"

The problems surrounding graphics images, scanning, and digital photography aren't centered as much on computer problems as they are on misunderstanding. Graphics is a big arena. There are plenty of places where things can go wrong, and problems can crop up. This chapter helps smooth those rough edges and offers soothing words of advice for grappling with graphics.

Unraveling Resolution

Most of the basic graphics questions and problems orbit the mysterious planet of *resolution*. To understand why an image appears too large on the monitor or prints too tiny on paper, you need to understand resolution.

This section helps break down the concept of resolution, as well as other graphical terminology, into easy-to-see, byte-size chunks.

"What are pixels?"

All graphical images — whether on the screen, in a file, or printed — are composed of tiny dots. On the computer screen, these dots are called *pixels,* which is a contraction of *pic*ture *el*ements. A typical pixel is shown in Figure 16-1, enlarged for your viewing enjoyment.

Most of the talk about computer graphics deals with pixels: An image is formatted with so-many pixels across (horizontally) and so-many down (vertically). The monitor's resolution is set in pixels (refer to Chapters 6 and 13).

The printer, on the other hand, doesn't use pixels. Instead, the printer composes an image using tiny dots of colored or black ink. Like pixels, the dots are printed and arranged in a pattern that forms an image. The printer's *resolution* refers to the number of dots it can print in a linear inch.

Figure 16-1:
A single
pixel,
magnified.

Dots and pixels are really the same thing: an individual piece of an electronic photograph. The difference is only in the name; the same blue pixel on the monitor becomes a blue dot printed by a color printer. Or a black dot on a grayscale printer. Or a purple dot on a printer that's low on blue ink.

The mysterious depths of color

Each pixel on the screen is assigned a specific color or tone. Back in the old days of monochrome monitors, there were no colors: The pixel was on or off. When the pixel was on, it glowed white (or amber or green). When the pixel was off, it was black, as depicted in Figure 16-1. With color monitors, the pixel's color value is more diverse: It ranges from the basic 16 colors up to millions of colors.

Obviously, having a high color depth is good; more colors render images more realistically than a limited range of colors can. Images with fewer colors look flat and phony — like a cartoon.

Though a higher color depth is better, there's a premium to pay: Having more colors requires more video memory to store the pixels' information; plus, more microprocessor speed is required in order to manipulate that vast amount of information; plus, more hard drive space is required in order to store the image. That's why the system resource requirements are so great for graphics and photo-editing applications.

The number of dots per inch

An image's resolution comes into play when you set the number of pixels, or dots, per inch for an image. You see, this value varies. Unlike other measurements in computers (characters per kilobyte, speed in GHz, crashes per hour) the number of pixels that can be crammed into an inch isn't a constant thing.

The higher the resolution, the more pixels, or dots, per inch.

The lower the resolution, the fewer pixels, or dots, per inch.

Figures 16-2, 16-3, and 16-4 illustrate the same image taken at different *resolutions,* or numbers of dots per inch.

Figure 16-2:
A very low-resolution image.

Figure 16-3:
The same image as shown in Figure 16-2, at double that resolution.

Figure 16-4:
The same image again, at four times the resolution of the image shown in Figure 16-2.

In Figure 16-2, the resolution is low enough that you can see the pixels. (The stair-stepping phenomenon is called *aliasing.*) In Figure 16-3, the resolution is double that of Figure 16-2, and Figure 16-4 is doubled again.

- ✔ The more dots per inch, the higher the resolution and the more realistic the image appears.

- ✔ Higher-resolution images take up a tremendous amount of disk space. Those pixels cost memory!

- ✔ If you're editing an image by using photo-editing software, such as Adobe Photoshop Elements, you *want* a very high resolution. The more pixels that are available, the easier it is to work with the image.

- ✔ The fewer dots per inch, the lower the image's resolution and the less realistic it appears.

- ✔ Lower-resolution images have the advantage of taking up less disk space.

- ✔ More color depth can be used to compensate for lower resolution, which is how nondigital television sets work. But more color depth also makes the file size larger without necessarily increasing any detail in the image.

"Why does the image look so large on my monitor?"

When you use the term *resolution* to refer to a computer monitor, the values discussed are the number of pixels horizontally and vertically. For example, the monitor's resolution is 800 x 600 pixels or 1024 x 768 pixels. But those numbers mean nothing. The true resolution is the number of dots per inch. The typical PC monitor has a resolution of about 96 dots per inch (dpi).

Suppose that a graphics image uses 300 dots per inch as its resolution. That image appears *three times larger* on the PC's monitor when it's displayed at a 1-to-1 ratio, dots per pixel, as shown in Figure 16-5.

If the image's size is less than the monitor's "resolution" — 1024 x 768 pixels, for example — you can still see the whole thing on the screen. But most images with 300 dpi resolution have much larger dimensions than 1024 x 768 pixels. Therefore, the whole thing cannot show up on the monitor at one time.

Changing the monitor's resolution

Your monitor's resolution isn't stuck at 96 dpi. It can be adjusted up or down, depending on the monitor's and graphics adapter's abilities. Follow these steps to see whether you can change your monitor's resolution:

1. **Open the Control Panel.**

2a. **From the Control Panel Home, choose Appearance and Personalization and then choose Personalization.**

2b. **From Control Panel Classic view, open the Personalization icon.**

   The Personalization window appears.

3. **From the list of tasks on the left part of the window, choose Adjust Font Size (DPI).**

4. **If necessary, click the Continue button or type the administrator's password to continue.**

   The DPI Scaling dialog box appears.

Image appears "big" on monitor   Monitor set at 96 DPI

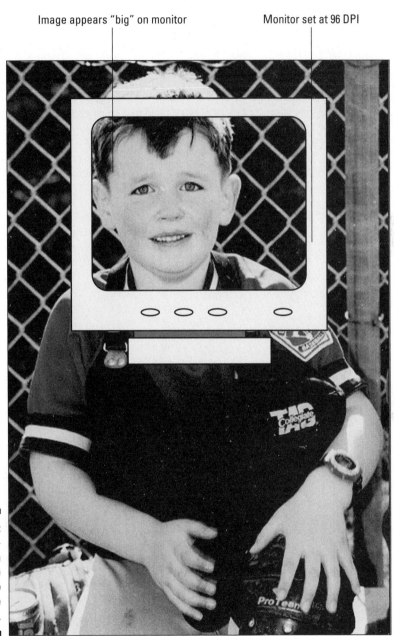

Figure 16-5:
A high-
resolution
image
shows up
big on the
screen.

5. **Click the Custom DPI button.**

   The Custom DPI Settings dialog box appears, as shown in Figure 16-6. In the figure, it's shown as Normal Size (96 DPI).

6. **You can also use the mouse to drag the ruler in the Custom DPI Settings dialog box to the left or right to set a new monitor resolution.**

7. **Click the various OK or Cancel buttons to back out of the open dialog boxes or windows.**

Note that the monitor's resolution isn't *exactly* one inch per one inch. For example, if you get to Step 5 in this set of steps, place a ruler on the monitor to see whether those tick marks in the Custom DPI Settings dialog box (refer to Figure 16-6) are *really* one inch wide. I would bet that they aren't! This is why some graphics mavens follow these steps to set their monitors' resolutions to exactly one inch per inch.

The Macintosh uses a monitor resolution of 72 dpi. This is one reason that graphics designers prefer that platform: One pixel on the Mac's monitor is equal in size to one typesetter's point.

Figure 16-6:
Set the PC
monitor's
resolution
here.

Custom DPI Setting

For a custom DPI setting, select a percentage from the list, or drag the ruler with your mouse.

Scale to this percentage of normal size: 100%

0   1   2   3

9 point Segoe UI at 96 pixels per inch.

☑ Use Windows XP style DPI scaling   OK   Cancel

Updating your graphics device driver

A low-resolution display, or what I refer to as dumb mode in Chapter 6, is often caused by Windows losing track of your PC's graphics device driver. How can the computer lose something like that? I don't know. But I do know that human beings are far more capable than computers and they often lose important items, like eyeglasses or car keys. Anyway.

Without a specific driver, Windows uses what's known as the *standard VGA* driver, which gives you either 640 by 480 or 800 by 600 boring and dumb pixels to play with — not enough.

Fortunately, although Windows has lost track of the video driver, the driver most likely still exists on your computer. The solution is to go to your graphics adapter's Properties dialog box and reinstall the existing driver software. You can do that in two ways.

First, the best way to recover a lost video driver is to use System Restore to reinstall the old video driver: Go back in time to when you remember the display working properly. It could be yesterday or last Friday or whenever you last used your computer. Refer to the Chapter 4 discussion on using System Restore.

Second, and whenever System Restore doesn't work, you can follow these steps to manually replace the computer's graphics device driver:

1. **Bring forth the Control Panel.**

   You can get there from the Start button menu.

2a. **From the Control Panel Home, choose Hardware and Sound and then choose Device Manager.**

2b. **From Control Panel Classic view, open the Device Manager icon.**

3. **If prompted, enter the administrator's password or click the Continue button.**

   The Device Manager window appears.

4. **Open the item named Display Adapters.**

5. **Open your display adapter by double-clicking on its name.**

   Opening the display adapter entry summons the adapter's Properties dialog box.

6. **Click the Driver tab in the Properties dialog box.**

7. **Click the Update Driver button.**

8. **Obey the wizard to select a new driver.**

   Follow the instructions on the screen. If you need to connect to the Internet to visit the Windows Update site, do so.

   The wizard attempts to locate a better driver for your graphics adapter. Chances are, for this particular problem, that Windows will find the driver already on your computer. If so, use that driver, and everything will be fine.

9. **When the process is complete, restart your computer as indicated or follow whatever directions are given by the wizard.**

10. **Close any windows or dialog boxes that you have left hanging open.**

11. **Take whatever steps are necessary to finish installing the driver.**

In some cases, Windows may not be able to find a better driver. If so, consider visiting the Web page for the graphics adapter or the computer manufacturer to see whether you can find and download a newer or better device driver.

- ✔ If your computer has two display adapters, it's a guessing game to determine which one is the one that requires a new driver. My advice: Update them both.

- ✔ If the display is still in dumb mode after you restart Windows, visit the Display Properties dialog box to see whether you can then increase the resolution (refer to Chapter 6).

How resolution affects image size

The image resolution and its physical size depend on the device used to either capture or display the image. This concept is strange to understand, so pay attention only if the subject perplexes you or you're in desperate need to win a bar bet.

Suppose that an image has physical dimensions of four inches by five inches. If that image is captured at 100 dpi, its resolution is 100 dpi. But the image's dimensions are 400 pixels x 500 pixels. That's because

> 4 inches x 100 dpi = 400 dots on the vertical

> 5 inches x 100 dpi = 500 dots on the horizontal

Got it? Don't worry if you don't. It's just math, and if there's one topic that frightens people more than computers do, it's spiders. But that's not important right now.

Consider that the same image (4 x 5 inches) is now captured at 300 dpi. Here's the math:

> 4 inches x 300 dpi = 1200 dots on the vertical

> 5 inches x 300 dpi = 1500 dots on the horizontal

Though the image still measures 4 x 5 in the real world, it now occupies 1200 x 1500 pixels inside the computer. Same image but more *information*. That's because the image was scanned at a higher resolution. But when the image is displayed on a monitor with 96 dpi resolution, where the screen shows only 1024 x 768 pixels, the image is *huge*.

The relationship between image size and resolution also comes into play when you print the image. Suppose that your printer has a resolution of 600 dpi. If you print the 1200 x 1500 image without adjusting its size, the image comes out at *half* its size, or 2 inches x 2½ inches when printed. That's because the printer's resolution is twice that of the image's resolution.

Confused? You bet! But read this section another time and you may, I hope, grasp the basic notion: An image exists at a given resolution, which is set when the image is first captured (either scanned, created, or snapped in a digital camera). The image's size is then dependent on the device used to display or print the image.

✔ The image's real size depends on the resolution of the device used to render the image.

✔ You can also set the printed size of an image in most graphics applications. But note that although you can print a lower-resolution image larger, the result might be a "blocky," or *aliased,* image.

✔ The best way to set the resolution is to know in advance where the image will end up. For e-mail, a resolution of 100 dpi, or roughly what the computer's monitor displays, is fine. For printing, try to match the printer's resolution. For photo editing, higher resolutions are best to ensure that enough pixels are present to properly edit the image.

"How can I see the whole image?"

Most graphics applications have a Zoom command or tool, which can be used to reduce or enlarge the image that's displayed. For example, an image taken at 300 dpi appears three times larger than normal on a 96 dpi monitor. If you use the Zoom tool to zoom out and reduce the image's visual size, you can see the entire image on your monitor.

Likewise, when an image is too small, you can use the Zoom tool to enlarge it. However, the computer cannot create pixels where none exists. So, zooming in on a low-resolution image results in the kind of pixel-laden image you see in Figure 16-2.

Setting Resolution

One of the decisions you must make when you create a graphics image is to set the resolution. What is the proper number of dots per inch for that image? The key here is to know where the image will end up. After all, there's no point in oversizing an image's resolution, and therefore making the image consume more memory, when you don't really need to.

At what resolution should an image be for e-mail?

Images captured for the Web or for e-mail need have no higher resolution than the computer's monitor does. Because PCs are set at 96 dpi, 96 dpi is a fine resolution, though most professionals choose 100 dpi simply because it's a round number.

Although 100 dpi is the perfect resolution for a monitor, and therefore for the Web and e-mail, you still need to gauge how large the image will appear. Generally, I prefer to set the image size so that the longest edge is between 300 and 400 pixels. That way, the image isn't too large even on the lowest-resolution monitor.

✔ If you set the image size so that it's larger than 600 or 800 pixels, the whole thing may not appear on some folks' monitors.

✔ Most digital cameras, and indeed some scanners, have a *Web* or *E-mail* setting, which is a rather low resolution, but one specifically designed for viewing the image on a monitor.

✔ If you need the image for purposes other than the Web or e-mail, create a copy of the original image and reduce the copy to a size and resolution best suited for the Web.

✔ Not every computer monitor is the same! In addition to size and resolution matters, not every monitor has the same color balance. What the image looks like on your monitor will be different on other monitors.

"At what resolution should an image be for photo editing or enlarging?"

For photo editing, you want lots and lots of those juicy pixels available, so the higher the resolution, the better.

For snapping digital pictures, set the camera to its highest available resolution, which is typically the *camera raw* format. At that resolution, the image sizes are huge (several megabytes), but that abundant and glorious information makes all the difference when you're photo editing, duplicating, enlarging, or printing the images.

"How can I change an image's resolution?"

Technically, you cannot change an image's resolution. Pixels are stuck like stars in the firmament. New ones cannot be plucked from the ether, just as a magician doesn't really pull coins out of the air. So, if you snap an image at 100 dpi, you cannot magically convert it to 800 dpi for output on a high-quality digital printer.

Or can you?

Photo-editing programs have commands for increasing resolution. But they cheat. They *approximate* pixel values. Some programs do this quite well; Photoshop is the master, by using complex algorithms and software sorcery to approximate and interpolate pixels where none existed. Keep in mind that the result is never as good as when the image was captured at the proper resolution in the first place.

"How can I resize an image?"

Changing an image's size is done in photo-editing or any type of graphics application. The key is to find the resizing command. For example, in Photoshop the command is Image➪Image Size. That command allows you to resize an image based on its horizontal and vertical pixel measurements. (It may also let you set the image's resolution.)

When you're changing an image's size, be sure to *constrain* the image. That is, when you resize the number of horizontal pixels, ensure that the vertical pixels are resized in a similar way so that the image doesn't appear stretched or skewed.

Figure 16-7 shows the Image Size dialog box from Photoshop Elements. See the linked chains to the right of the Width and Height areas? That means the values are linked, or constrained, so that when one is resized, the other dimension follows accordingly. The Constrain Proportions option (at the bottom of the dialog box) ensures that things remain together.

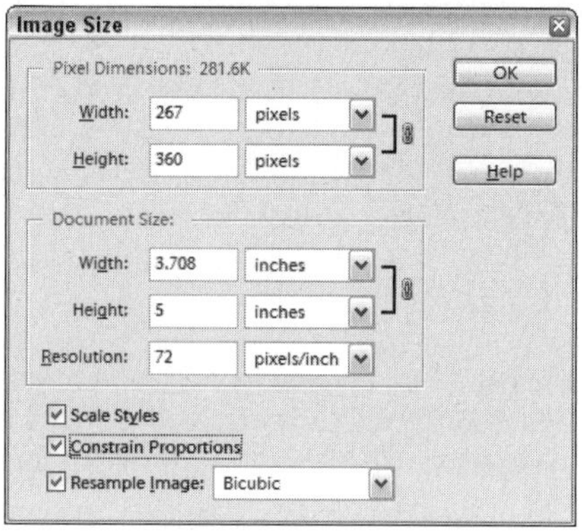

Figure 16-7:
Resizing an
image is
done here.

Graphics File Formats from Beyond

Beyond the confusion of image resolution exists the multiple mania of graphics file formats. You may think that one format would be enough, but there are literally *hundreds* of computer graphics file formats. These many formats document the different computer platforms as well as the gradual improvement of graphics technology over the years. The good news is that only a few of the graphics file formats are popular now, which narrows the choice and eases the confusion.

Graphics file format reference

Out of gazillions of graphics file formats, there are only six common ones you need to confuse yourself over:

TIFF: This is the most compatible, common graphics file format, though it's best suited for documents or sharing images between different applications. TIFF images are too large to use for sending e-mail photos. But, for long-term storage or archiving images, I highly recommend using TIFF.

JPG: The most common graphics file format, JPG (or JPEG) renders real-life images, like photographs, very well. Unlike TIFF, JPG files can be compressed so that they don't take up huge amounts of disk space. The smaller file size also makes JPG images the ideal format for the Internet.

GIF: This older file format is still popular on the Internet. GIF images aren't as good as JPG, however, because of a limited number of available colors. Therefore, you see graphical designs or art, but not photographs, rendered in the GIF format.

PNG: PNG is the graphics format of the future. Pronounced "ping," it's perhaps the most versatile graphics file format developed. Most applications now support PNG, so feel free to create, e-mail, and use PNG images, if you can.

BMP: This is the ancient Windows graphics file format, where BMP stands for *bitma*pped image. The file size for BMP images is obnoxiously large, which makes the BMP file type impractical for use in e-mail. Thump someone in the head if they e-mail you a BMP image.

Native: This format is whatever your photo-editing software uses to save its images. In Photoshop Elements, it's the Photoshop, or PSD, file format. Generally speaking, this is the best file format to save images you edit using image-editing software.

- ✔ For the Internet, use the JPG file format.
- ✔ JPG is pronounced "jay-peg." Note that the files can also end with the JPEG extension.
- ✔ GIF is pronounced "gif" with a hard *g,* as in "give." Some folks say "jiff" instead, but to me Jif will always be the pea-nuttiest peanut butter.

The JPG compression stuff

JPG graphics files achieve their small size thanks to built-in compression. When the image is saved to disk, a dialog box appears, such as the one shown in Figure 16-8, from Photoshop Elements. The dialog box prompts you to set the compression, either 1 (or Low) for lots of compression or 10 (or High) for no or little compression.

Figure 16-8: Setting a JPG image's compression.

The low compression values yield smaller file sizes, which is good. But the image tends to get very fuzzy and ill-defined at tight compression values.

The higher values ironically indicate little compression. That means that the file size is larger, but the image quality is better.

I have never been in a situation where I have had to use compression values less than 5. I don't like the way the images look at those settings, so I save images at 6 or higher. For images where I want lots of detail I use 8, 9, or 10 values. For other images, values of 6 or 7 are just fine.

JPG graphics use what's called a *lossy* compression routine. That is, every time a JPG image is saved to disk, some of the image information is lost. The more you open and resave JPG images to disk, the worse the image looks over time. If you just open and view an image, this isn't a problem. If you plan to edit or reuse an image, save it in the TIFF file format instead.

"What's the best graphics file format for e-mail?"

JPG. Or PNG.

"How can I convert my image from [whatever] format to [whatever] format?"

Some wonderful graphics conversion programs are available, and I could recommend a few, but why bother? Windows itself comes with the Paint program, which can be used to convert between many of the common PC graphics file formats. It's not the swiftest way to convert a graphics image, but it works:

1. Start the Paint program in Windows.

The program can be found on the Start button menu: Choose All Programs➪Accessories➪Paint.

2. Choose File➪Open.

3. Use the Open dialog box to locate the file you want to convert.

From the drop-down list labeled Files of Type, choose the All Pictures Files option. It directs Paint to display any picture file it can open.

4. **When you find the file to convert, click the Open button to open its image inside the Paint program.**

   There it is.

5. **Chose File⇨Save As.**

6. **Use the Save As dialog box to find a proper location for the file.**

   I offer specific instructions for using the Save As dialog box in my book *PCs For Dummies* (Wiley Publishing, Inc.), a book I not only wrote but also have read.

7. **Choose the graphics file type from the Save As Type drop-down list.**

   There, you find JPEG, GIF, TIFF, and PNG as options. For e-mail, you want to choose JPEG.

8. **Click the Save button to save the file.**

Now you can use your e-mail program to send the picture. Don't forget where you saved it!

Chapter 17

Internet Connection Mayhem

· ·

· ·

*I*t truly is a miracle that your computer manages to use the Internet at all. First, there's the connection. Then comes the transfer of information. And finally, there's the way the computer deals with that information. It's very complex — not merely Rubik's cube complex, but more like your-brain-is-about-to-explode complex. I hear that the manual that describes how Internet connections really work is too thick for a human to read. The post office won't even ship the thing without applying the extra Dangerous Knowledge fee.

Good news for you: You don't have to understand one bit about how the Internet manages information. Nope! That's because I've done it for you. I survived. Sure, I had to have them implant a third eye, but cosmetically, it enhances my face. And the government paid for it. So enjoy this chapter, which offers words soothing and solutions simple for Internet connection worries and woes.

A Sampling of the Zillions of Potential Problems with a Dialup Connection

It's supposed to work like this: You start an Internet program, and your computer automatically connects to the Internet and dishes up whatever data it is you're requesting: a Web page, some e-mail, a file — whatever.

This section, presented in a somewhat logical order, describes the things that can go wrong, or may go wrong, with the Internet connection. Please note that these issues deal with dialup Internet connections only. You know dialup: It puts the *dumb* into modem.

Automatic-connection dilemmas

People automatically complain about two things in connecting to the Internet: They want it to happen, or they want it not to happen.

For example, if you enjoy automatic connection, whenever you start an Internet application (such as Internet Explorer), the connection box just pops up and the modem dials in to the Internet. That's automatic connection in action.

On the other hand, some people prefer to have the Connect dialog box pop up and then to have to click the Dial button to manually connect to the Internet.

Either way is possible, controlled from the Internet Properties dialog box, shown in Figure 17-1. Here's how to dig that up:

1. **Open the Control Panel's Internet Properties dialog box.**

   From the Control Panel Home, choose Network and Internet, and then Internet Options; from Control Panel Classic view, open the Internet Options icon.

2. **Click the Connections tab.**

3. **Choose the option labeled Never Dial a Connection.**

4. **Click OK.**

   You can close the Control Panel window too, if needed.

Figure 17-1:
The Internet
Properties /
Connections
dialog box.

The Never Dial a Connection option isn't stupid; it doesn't mean to *never* dial a connection. In fact, it should be relabeled Never *Automatically* Dial a Connection. That way, you have to manually connect to the Internet, which is why you would choose such a setting. Control!

Here's a description of each of the connection choices listed in the Internet Properties/Connections dialog box:

> **Never Dial a Connection:** Windows doesn't automatically connect to the Internet. You must manually dial in by using the Connect dialog box. You do this by opening the Internet Connection icon in the Network Connections window. Or, the Connect dialog box may appear whenever any program attempts to connect to the Internet.

> **Dial Whenever a Network Connection Is Not Present:** This option is the one that most people with traditional modems should select. It tells Windows to connect to the Internet whenever you open an Internet program.

> **Always Dial My Default Connection:** Don't bother with this option.

Most people get into trouble in the Internet Properties/Connections dialog box when they choose Always Dial My Default Connection rather than Dial Whenever a Network Connection *Is Not* Present. The Default Connection thing is handy only when you set up several ISPs and you tire of choosing between them when you're prompted to dial.

You can still connect to the Internet if you choose the Never Dial a Connection option. Rather than start any old Internet program, such as Internet Explorer, Windows Mail, or Paul's Pervasive Porno Peeper, you simply use the Connect To command found on the Start button menu. Here's how that operation works:

1. **Choose the Connect To command from the Start menu.**

   The Connect to a Network window pops into view, as shown in Figure 17-2. Dialup connections are shown with the dialup network icon on the right. Wireless networks might also be visible, though possibly sporting another icon as well as other types of network connections, which, I assume, shall also sport their own unique icons.

2. **Choose your ISP's connection icon.**

3. **Click the Connect button.**

4. **(Optional) Enter your username and password, or bother if prompted for that information; then click the Dial button.**

   Whether or not you're prompted depends on whether you provided that information when you first set up the connection. (I recommend *not* providing that information for laptop computers that can get lost or stolen.)

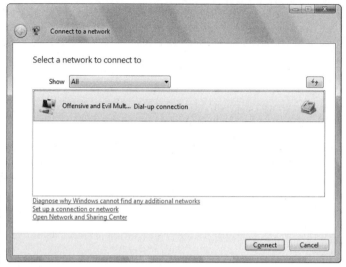

Figure 17-2:
The Network
Connections
window.

5. **Wait for the modem to connect.**

   After some annoying screaming from the modem over the computer's speaker, you're connected to your ISP and the Internet.

Note that some national online services, such as AOL, may require you to connect to the Internet by using their own icons and their own methods. If so, follow those instructions and not what's written here.

The PC dials in to the Internet at seemingly random times

In many instances, your computer attempts for some reason to dial in to the Internet. It seems random because you may not be doing anything directly related to the Internet at the time. Or, it may happen when you start the computer. Is the computer possessed? Call the digital exorcist!

Obviously, *something* in your computer is trying to connect. What it could be is anyone's guess. Usually the culprit is a computer program trying to contact its digital mother ship on the Internet. Prime suspects include antivirus programs and Windows, both of which rely heavily on regular updates. Microsoft Office may want to dial into the Internet when you ask for help or use the Reference feature. Also, any new software you install might want to contact the Internet to "register" itself.

The way I deal with the problem is to turn off the automatic-connection feature, as described in the preceding section. That way, when I see the Connect
dialog box, I click the Cancel button and the computer stops dialing into the
Internet.

Losing the Connection

Dialup Internet connections drop for a plethora of reasons — anything from
squirrels on the line (I kid you not) to someone else in the house picking up
the phone extension. The dialup connection is a delicate thing, and just
about anything short of wishful thinking can bring it down.

- Do you suspect that your phone lines are to blame? If so, you can have
  your phone company test the wires all the way up to your house for
  reliability. The wires inside your house, however, must be tested by an
  electrician. See whether your ISP can recommend an electrician familiar
  with digital communications.

- By the way, the phone company can do nothing to improve slow service.
  It only guarantees a certain speed over its phone wires — nothing faster.
  (You have to see what the speed is for your area, which depends on the
  age of the equipment and, well, how lazy or cheap your particular phone
  company is.)

- Sometimes the connection works better at night. Radio interference
  from the sun can wreak havoc with communications.

- Often, phone line interference portends an interstellar attack from the
  winged bat people of Venus.

- At two times during the year, satellite modems get interference from
  the sun: during the fall and vernal equinoxes. It typically happens about
  noon or so, when the satellite passes between the earth and the sun.

- Call waiting can sure knock a dialup connection off the Internet. See the
  following section.

- A dialup connection can drop because of inactivity. See the section
  "Adjusting the Connection Timeouts," later in this chapter.

- Sometimes, your ISP may drop the connection, especially during a
  busy time of day. AOL doesn't admit to it, but that doesn't mean it never
  happens.

- The modem may drop the connection because of the heat. In this type
  of situation, you can connect for only about 20 to 30 minutes before
  getting disconnected. For an internal modem, ensure that your PC's fan
  is working. For external modems, ensure that it's located in a well-
  ventilated place.

Disabling the Annoying Call Waiting

Your computer's dialup modem can be taught to automatically switch off the call waiting feature so that you don't get accidentally disconnected by it when you're on the Internet. You do that by heeding these steps:

1. **Summon the Phone and Modem Options dialog box.**

   From the Control Panel Home, choose Hardware and Sound, and then choose Phone and Modem Options; from Control Panel Classic view, open the Phone and Modem Options icon.

2. **Click the Dialing Rules tab, if necessary.**

3. **If locations are entered, select your current location and click the Edit button. Otherwise, click the New button to create a new location.**

   The location feature is best used on PC laptops, where the computer's location can change from place to place. On a desktop system, you need only enter the computer's permanent location.

   After creating the location, click the Edit button to proceed to the next step.

4. **Put a check mark by the item labeled To Disable Call Waiting, Dial.**

   It's near the bottom of the dialog box, shown in Figure 17-3.

Figure 17-3:
Disable call
waiting
here.

5. **From the drop-down list, select the proper dialing sequence for your area to disable call waiting.**

   This information can be found near the front of your area's phone book.

6. **Click OK to close the Edit Location dialog box.**

7. **Click OK to close the Phone and Modem Options dialog box.**

   You can, optionally, close the Control Panel window as well.

After you make these adjustments, Windows automatically disables call waiting for each call the modem makes.

✔ For more information on using a PC laptop, get my book *Laptops For Dummies* (Wiley Publishing, Inc.).

✔ If you would rather keep call waiting on but have the computer not disconnect and instead notify you, you can check out the following Web pages for specialized software:

```
www.buzzme.com
www.callwave.com
www.catchacall.com
```

✔ The AOL service also has a feature, AOL Call Alert, that notifies you of a pending call while you're dialed into AOL.

Humble Words of Advice for When Your Broadband Connection Goes Bonkers

Broadband modems — those of the cable, DSL, and satellite varieties — are more like remote network connections than modems. Therefore, any problems they have are most likely to be network-related problems rather than the typical problems that plague dialup users.

The first thing to check when you suspect a problem with your broadband modem is the modem's lights. You see a power light, a network light, and maybe a few other lights just for show. The one that's most important is the connection light, which may be the one that blinks as data is sent and received. When that light goes out, it means that the network connection is down. Phone your broadband provider and ask whether it's experiencing problems. Someone there will let you know immediately (hopefully) or help you troubleshoot potential problems on your end of the line.

The final thing you can do when everyone else says "Nope — nothin' wrong here!" is to disconnect your broadband modem. Wait a while (about a minute). Then reconnect the thing. In many cases, that fixes the problem.

- Broadband modems are fairly robust and reliable. If your broadband connection has been up and running for a few weeks, chances are that it will perform flawlessly for a long time.

- When the broadband modem is inside the computer, such as on some satellite modems, you have to turn off the computer, wait, and then turn it on again to restart the modem.

- Yes, it's okay to leave the broadband modem on all the time. In fact, many ISPs and broadband providers want you to keep the modem on.

- Merely turning a broadband modem off and on again may not be enough. Sometimes you must turn off your computer *and* any router or network switch. Turn on the modem first, and then the router or switch, and, finally, the computer to restore full operation properly.

- Broadband modems go down during power outages. Consider plugging the broadband modem into a UPS, or *u*ninterruptible *p*ower *s*upply. That way, the modem stays on during brief power outages. (Sometimes it takes a while for the broadband connection to reestablish after a power outage, but not if you're using a UPS.)

Adjusting the Connection Timeouts

To ensure that you don't waste precious Internet connect-time, Windows has built in a connection timeout system to disconnect your dialup modem after a period of inactivity. You can adjust this value up or down, or even turn it off, which is good news.

And now the bad news: there are *two* locations for timeout values in Windows. Better check them both!

What's not nice is that there are *two* places to look in Windows for the timeout information. Better take these one at a time.

First come the modem timeout settings:

1. Bring forth the Phone and Modem Options dialog box.

From the Control Panel Home, choose Hardware and Sound, and then choose Phone and Modem Options; from Control Panel Classic view, open the Phone and Modem Options icon.

2. **Click the Modems tab in the Phone and Modem Options dialog box.**

3. **Choose your PC's modem from the list.**

   It's probably selected already, especially when there's only one modem in the computer.

4. **Click the Properties button at the bottom of the dialog box.**

   Another Properties dialog box opens, one specific to your brand of modem.

5. **Click the Change Settings button on the General tab.**

   You must do this or you cannot click the Change Default Preferences button, which you do in Step 8.

6. **Click the Continue button or type the administrator's password to continue.**

   The modem's Properties dialog box reappears, now with administrative goodness.

7. **Click the Advanced tab.**

8. **Click the Change Default Preferences button.**

   Finally, you hit pay dirt in the modem's Default Preferences dialog box, shown in Figure 17-4.

9. **Make the settings your heart desires.**

   To set an automatic disconnect, put a check mark by Disconnect a Call If Idle for More Than [blank] Mins. Then enter the amount of minutes.

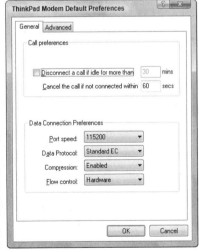

Figure 17-4:
The modem
timeout
setting is
buried way
down here.

10. **Click OK to close the Default Preferences dialog box.**

11. **Click OK to close the modem's Properties dialog box.**

12. **Click OK to close the Phone and Modem Options dialog box.**

    Okay! Okay! Okay!

    That's just the first location, and they hid it most effectively, don't you think? The second location deals with your ISP's connection information, which you can get to from the Internet Options dialog box:

13. **Open the Internet Options dialog box.**

    From the Control Panel Home, choose Network and Internet and then Internet Options; from Control Panel Classic view, open the Internet Options icon.

14. **Click the Connections tab in the Internet Properties dialog box.**

15. **If necessary, choose your ISP from the list.**

    If you have only one ISP, it's already selected for you.

16. **Click the Settings button.**

    A dialog box for your ISP's Settings appears. Believe it or not, you can check in *two* places for timeout values.

17. **Click the Properties button.**

    You're not there yet!

18. **Click the Options tab in your ISP's Properties dialog box.**

    There it is! Located in the Redialing Options area is the first idle-time-before-hanging-up item. It may be specific to redialing, but why take chances? Set the idle timeout value to a specific number of minutes or to Never (to not hang up automatically).

19. **Make your adjustments to the Idle Time Before Hanging Up value.**

20. **Click OK.**

    Now comes the second, more serious, timeout value setting for your ISP.

21. **Click the Advanced button.**

    Ah, the Advanced Dialup dialog box is just chock-full of timeout and idle values, as shown in Figure 17-5.

Figure 17-5:
The timeout options jackpot!

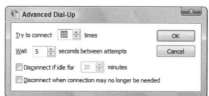

To disable the idle disconnect, uncheck the Disconnect If Idle for [blank] Minutes option, as shown in Figure 17-5. Or check that item and enter the number of minutes to wait before disconnecting.

In this dialog box, you also find the handy Disconnect When Connection May No Longer Be Needed item. That option tells Windows to automatically display the Disconnect dialog box when you close your last Internet application's window — a handy item to turn on.

22. **Make the necessary settings and adjustments.**

23. **Click OK to close the Advanced Dialup dialog box.**

24. **Click OK to close your ISP's Settings dialog box.**

25. **Click OK to close the Internet Properties dialog box.**

26. **Click any other button that says OK, just because you're in the mood.**

27. **Close the Control Panel window while you're at it.**

Be sure to bring in the trash cans before the neighbor's dogs get into them!

Obviously, if you have a broadband connection, you don't need to worry about timeout values; you're connected all the time anyway. Nya! Nya! Nya!

Chapter 18

Web Weirdness with Internet Explorer

Don't be so quick to point the fatal finger of blame at Internet Explorer. Often times, it's not the bad guy. You see, Internet Explorer is a *Web browser*. As such, it's merely a window through which you can view information on the World Wide Web. If a Web page screws up — which happens often — you really have to blame the Web page itself and not Internet Explorer for merely passing on the bad news. Still, Internet Explorer has enough quirks and oddities that warrant its own chapter in this troubleshooting book.

✔ Throughout this chapter, I use the abbreviation *IE* to refer to Internet Explorer.

✔ Though the information here is about IE (Internet Explorer — just checking to see whether you're reading all the bullet points), much of it applies to other Web browsers as well.

Internet Explorer Can Be Tamed

Internet Explorer is a relatively easy program to use and configure. It has only a few areas where it tends to frustrate people. I have listed the more popular frustrations and solutions in this section.

Changing the home page

The *home page* can be anything you want to see when you first start Internet
Explorer. Here's how to set the home page to something special or to nothing
at all:

1. **Start IE.**

   That's Internet Explorer, in case you were silly and skipped reading this
   chapter's introduction. The IE icon is often found on the Quick Launch
   bar or directly on the main Start menu.

2. **If IE opens several home pages on multiple tabs, close all but one of
   the tabs.**

   I've seen this multiple-tab trick on several new computers. Yes, you can
   set multiple home pages using IE version 7.0. For now, just set one home
   page.

3. **Visit the Web page you want as your home page.**

   For example, visit Yahoo! or my own Web page, www.wambooli.com.
   Displaying that Web page now makes choosing it as your home page
   much easier.

4. **Click the menu part of the Home button on the toolbar.**

   When you click the Home button, IE takes you to the home page. But by
   clicking the menu part of the button — the triangle to the right — you
   see a menu.

5. **Choose Add or Change Home Page from the menu.**

   A dialog box appears.

6. **Choose the option Use This Webpage As Your Only Home Page.**

7. **Click Yes.**

   Now that page is the first thing you see when you start IE.

The page shows up when IE first starts or whenever you click the Home
button.

IE version 7.0 introduced (well, introduced for *IE*) the concept of *tabbed
browsing*. It's possible to set several different home pages at once, each of
which appears on its own tab.

To create a set of multiple home pages, one on each tab, open the home
pages you want. Place each page on a different tab. (Use Ctrl+T to open a new
tab.) Then repeat the preceding steps, but in Step 6 choose the option Use
The Current Tab Set As Your Home Page.

Setting a blank home page

If you're like me and you prefer to have a blank home page, click the Home Page button and use the Remove submenu to clear your home page. (Or choose Remove⇨Remove All to zap multiple tab home pages.)

By removing the home page from the list, you let IE start its day with a blank home page. Or whenever you click the Home button, a blank page instantly appears.

You can summon a blank home page in IE at any time by typing the following URL:

```
about:blank
```

"I cannot change the home page!"

Sometimes, changing the home page may not be possible. This happens mostly because the home page has been hijacked by some malware, but it can also be accidental.

In Windows Vista, any program attempting to hijack the IE home page spawns a User Account Control (UAC) warning. When you click the Continue button or type the administrator's password, you're allowing that program to hijack the home page. That's why it's very important to *pay attention* to what you're doing on the PC and not consistently click the UAC's Continue button without checking.

If you end up installing malware that hijacks the home page, use the Windows Defender program to remove the malware. See Chapter 24.

"Why does it tell me that there's a new version of Internet Explorer?"

From time to time, Microsoft unleashes newer versions of its software and feels compelled to let the world know. When this happens, you don't see your regular home page when IE starts. Instead, you're redirected to an update page. That's normal; annoying, but normal.

✔ After you choose to update the software, your home page *should* return to normal. Sometimes it doesn't, in which case you can reread (or just read) the section "Changing the home page," earlier in this chapter, about changing the page back.

✔ It's up to you whether you want to upgrade to the newer version of any program. I generally don't do it unless the newer version offers me some feature that I think I need or fixes a problem I'm having.

✔ Other Web browser software also pulls this same home-page-direction stunt, so don't go off blaming Microsoft for being evil or sneaky.

Adjusting the temporary file size

IE stores megabytes and megabytes of temporary files on disk. Officially, this area is known as the *cache* (say "cash"). By storing images, sounds, text, and other information on your computer's hard drive, you make those Web pages you visit frequently load faster. After all, it takes less time to load an image from the temporary file cache than it does to squeeze that same image through the wires connecting you to the Internet.

The problem? The temporary file size can get huge! The bigger it is, the longer it takes IE to search through it, so cutting down on the size may truly improve your Web browsing performance.

Here's how to view or adjust the temporary file size for IE:

1. **Click the Tools button on the toolbar and choose Internet Options from the menu.**

   The Internet Options dialog box appears. The Browsing History area deals with temporary Internet files.

2. **On the General tab, in the Browsing History area, click the Settings button.**

   The Temporary Internet Files and History Settings dialog box appears, as shown in Figure 18-1. The key setting to adjust here is the amount of disk space used for storing temporary files.

3. **Set a new size value in the Disk Space to Use box.**

   Minimum and maximum values are a given: 8MB and 1024MB (1 gigabyte) in Figure 18-1. A recommended size range is also given: 50MB to 250MB, from Figure 18-1. If performance is slow, consider using the minimum recommended value. If it's still slow after making that change, set the value to the minimum value.

   Another item to change is the first one. I would select Every Time I Visit The Webpage to keep IE from wandering off to look for new copies of stored stuff.

   If you select Never from the list, which effectively disables the cache, you must use the Refresh command (or press the F5 key) to load a new version of a Web page. It's definitely an option *not* worth selecting.

4. **Click OK to close the Temporary Internet Files and History Settings dialog box and the Internet Options dialog box.**

Some folks say to delete the temporary files as another way to speed up Web performance. I'm not certain whether that method works, though it does increase disk space.

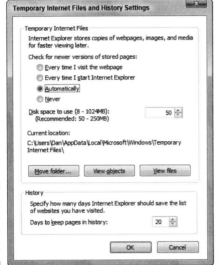

Figure 18-1:
Temporary
Internet file
control.

Common Puzzles and Solutions

Here are a few of my favorite and most common Web browsing puzzles and their solutions. Consider this the short list; the full list would consume many more pages — perhaps an entire book in itself!

Text size trouble

Grandpa: I don't know why some Web page designers seem hell-bent to make us old folks squint at the computer monitor!

Teenager: My finger scrolling muscle is bulking up, thanks to all that huge text on the Web!

Fortunately, IE has a solution for any Web page where you may find the text too teeny to interpret or too large to tolerate: Located in the lower-right corner of every IE window is the Zoom pop-up menu, shown in Figure 18-2. Use that menu to make the page appear larger or smaller.

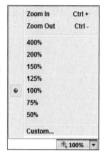

Figure 18-2:
IE's secret
zoom
controls.

✔ The keyboard command to zoom in is Ctrl++, which is really Ctrl+Shift+=.

✔ The keyboard command to zoom out is Ctrl+– (minus).

Robbery at the Louvre

Sacré bleu! Nos oeuvres d'arts est manquante!

A missing image from a Web page appears in IE as a red X icon, as shown in the margin. Technically, it means that the Web page refers to an image file that isn't there or the reference is bad. Either way, there's little you can do about it. Well, you can try:

✔ Refresh the page. Sometimes a simple refresh helps to find the image.

✔ Right-click the image and choose the Show Picture command from the pop-up menu.

If neither trick works, blame the Web page designer or programmer or the government for the problem.

You might also check to ensure that you haven't accidentally disabled *all* images. Although that seems silly, disabling images is one way to speed up the Web for slow Internet connections. To confirm, open the Internet Options dialog box and click the Advanced tab. Scroll through the list of options for the Multimedia header. Ensure that there's a check mark by the Show Pictures item. If not, check that item and click the OK button.

Full-screen mayhem

Pressing the F11 key directs IE to display the Web page in glorious full-screen mode. Yeah, that's cool, but often unwanted. To confine the Web page back into a window, press the F11 key again.

The F11 key also causes the "Hey! All my menus and tabs and other items are gone!" problem. Ironically, pressing F11 also solves the problem.

Print that Web page

What seems like one of the easiest things to do can confound Internet users like nothing else: that is, print a Web page. For some reason, this simple activity can drive people nuts. It's not the actual printing, or even finding the Print command. It's the *results* that drive people batty. Fortunately, the latest version of IE has made considerable progress toward printing sanity.

The key to printing in IE is to use the toolbar's Print button menu. Start by choosing the Print Preview command. Not only does that window let you preview how the page prints, but the bottom part of the window also describes how many pages are required in order to see the entire thing, as shown in Figure 18-3.

To best print, ensure that you chose the Shrink To Fit option from the Change Print Size menu, as shown in Figure 18-3. Or, if you're truly desperate to get the entire thing on a page, choose a low zoom value from the menu, such as 30%.

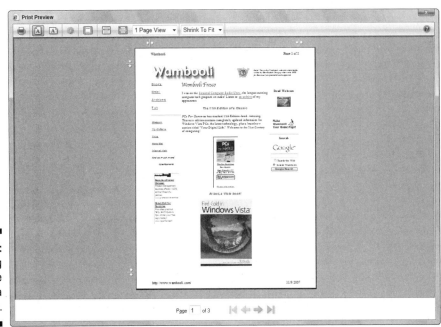

Figure 18-3:
Previewing before printing is a good idea.

Another trick to try is to print in Landscape mode; click the Landscape button in the Print preview window.

 Click the Print button in the Print Preview window to get the Web page down on paper.

Cookies

So it comes down to this! Cookies, huh? What do you think this chapter should end with — dessert? You are gravely mistaken! Cookies are nothing you eat. On the Internet, they're simply a bad name for a controversial Web browsing feature.

Understanding cookies

A *cookie* is merely information that a Web page saves to disk — and it isn't even that much information; it's more like random text. The information is stored on your computer in a special Cookies folder.

When you go to visit the same Web page again, programming code on the Web page can open the cookie that was previously saved. That way, for example, Eddie Bauer remembers your pants size and that you enjoy seersucker. Or, Amazon.com says "Hello, Dan Gookin! Welcome back! Boy, have we got some books for you!" I find that handy.

Some people, however, find the whole cookie thing annoying. They prefer *not* to have a Web page save anything. And that's fine because you can delete cookies, disable them, turn them off, and stomp them into cookie dust!

 ✔ Web pages can open only the cookies they saved. Cookies saved from other Web pages cannot be opened. (Even if they could, the content is usually so specific that no critical information would be compromised.)

 ✔ All cookies expire. Some are automatically deleted when you close IE. Some are deleted in several hours or in a day or so. Some last for up to six months. But they all have expiration dates, and they are, with few exceptions, automatically deleted on those dates.

Losing your cookies

You don't eat unwanted cookies; you delete them. There's a proper procedure to follow, which is outlined here:

1. **From the IE toolbar, click the Tools button to display its menu.**

2. **Choose Internet Options from the menu.**

   The Internet Options dialog box appears.

3. **On the General tab, in the Browsing History area, click the Delete button.**

4. **Click the Delete Cookies button.**

5. **Click the Yes button to confirm.**

   Lo, all your cookies have been smote. And you didn't gain a pound!

Preventing cookies in the first place

Why bother with cookies and deleting them? If they really bug you, turn them off at the source. Heed these steps:

1. **In IE, choose the Internet Options command from the toolbar's Tools button menu.**

   The Internet Options dialog box pops into view.

2. **Click the Privacy tab.**

   Yes, cookies are a matter of privacy, not security.

3. **Click the Advanced button.**

   The Advanced Privacy Settings dialog box appears (see Figure 18-4), but it should really be called the Cookie dialog box.

4. **Click to put a check mark by Override Automatic Cookie Handling.**

   You must do this step to enable the other options in the dialog box.

Figure 18-4:
Death to all
cookies!

5. **Choose Block for the Third-Party Cookies option.**

   That pretty much shuts down cookies from advertisers on any Web pages you visit. If you don't like cookies, this is an excellent option to take.

6. **Choose Block for the First-Party Cookies option.**

   This option is necessary only if you really, *really* hate cookies. Otherwise, I leave this option set to Accept.

7. **Click OK to close the Advanced Privacy Settings dialog box.**

8. **Close the Internet Properties dialog box.**

No more cookies!

- Cookies that are "stored on your computer" are any cookies that a Web page wants to save. They don't, however, include per-session cookies.

- *Per-session* cookies are deleted when you close the IE window.

- *First-party* cookies are cookies owned by the Web page you're viewing.

- *Third-party* cookies are cookies saved by the advertisements on the Web page you're viewing.

- Avoid choosing the Prompt option in the Advanced Privacy Settings dialog box (refer to Figure 18-4). Many, many Web sites use cookies. Being prompted for all of them can certainly drive you nuts!

Chapter 19

E-Mail Calamities

. . . .

In This Chapter

▶ Dealing with duplicate messages

▶ Finding the BCC field

▶ Making messages more readable

▶ Working in the Drafts folder

▶ Figuring out file attachments

. . . .

O! The joys of e-mail. Sending an e-mail is one thing, but the thrill of getting new e-mail is something that sells computers. Given that, you can understand how some folks can get really frustrated with their e-mail programs. Despite its simplicity and ease of use, e-mail can be a source of woe and can present puzzling predicaments for just about everyone. This chapter offers soothing solutions for everyone.

General E-Mail Nonsense

E-mail is such a simple thing, yet your e-mail program is perhaps the most complex application you will ever use. I could pack an entire book full of tips and tricks specific to any e-mail program, and not a single one of them would be considered advanced or obtuse. That's just the nature of the e-mail beast.

It was a tough task, but I was able to pinpoint a few key nonsensical issues with e-mail and stuff them and their solutions into this section.

Receiving duplicate messages

The main reason for receiving duplicate messages is that your e-mail program is leaving a copy of each message on your ISP's mail server. So every time you go to check mail, you grab the same message over and over.

The normal mode of operation in any e-mail program is to delete messages after they're retrieved from the server. But that option can be changed. For example, if you have your phone or laptop set to receive e-mail, you may want to leave messages on the server for later retrieval from your desktop PC. Either way, the setting is made in your e-mail program's Options or Properties dialog box.

In Windows Mail, you can check the server settings thusly:

1. **Start Windows Mail.**

2. **Choose Tools⇨Accounts.**

3. **Select your mail account from the list.**

   Or, it may be the only account on the list.

4. **Click the Properties button.**

   Your e-mail account's Properties dialog box appears.

5. **Click the Advanced tab.**

   In the bottom of the dialog box is a Delivery option, shown in Figure 19-1. If the option Leave a Copy of Messages on Server is checked, that explains your duplicate pick-up.

6. **Uncheck the box by Leave a Copy of Messages on Server.**

   That fixes it.

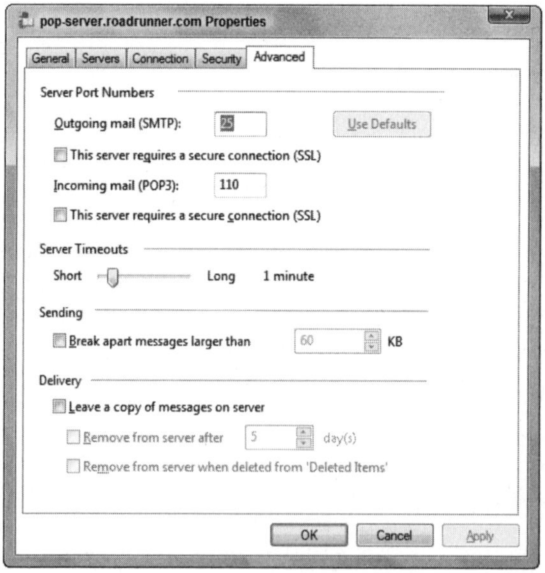

Figure 19-1:
Checking for that nasty Leave Mail on Server option.

If this trick doesn't work, check with your ISP to see whether a server "burp" or other problem happened on the other end.

Displaying the BCC field

Many e-mail programs don't normally display the BCC field when you go to create a new message. BCC, the *blind carbon copy* field, is used to send e-mail to people secretly; e-mail addresses put in the BCC field don't appear when the final message is received. The stealth nature of this feature makes the BCC field ideal for sending to a batch of people and not having each of them see the whole list of e-mail addresses — very tidy.

The solution: Choose View⇨All Headers from the New Message window. That command displays the BCC header, and away you go. This menu command is found in both Windows Mail and the older Outlook Express, which it replaced.

For more information on the BCC header, refer to my towering title *PCs For Dummies* (Wiley Publishing, Inc.).

Dealing with unreadable messages

Modern e-mail programs offer you a choice for composing your electronic epistles: plain or formatted text. Plain text is preferred by businesspeople. It's also the most common e-mail format, and plain text messages read identically on everyone's computer. Formatted text uses HTML to present graphics, fonts, and other formats in an e-mail message just as it does on a Web page. The downside is that not every e-mail program understands HTML-formatted messages, nor is the message displayed in the same way.

If you get an unreadable message, simply reply and ask the sender to resend the message as plain text.

When you get an e-mail message requesting that you resend something in plain text, change the message's format in your e-mail program. At that point, it's easier to copy the text from the original message (often found in the Sent folder) and then start a new message. In the new message window, choose Format⇨Plain Text. Then paste in the text from the original message.

Mail Folder Folderol

Folders are a great way to organize your e-mail — and I'm talking about folders beyond just the basic Inbox, Outbox, Sent, and Deleted (or Trash) folders. E-mail pros keep a host of folders: Work, Jokes, and Shopping, for example.

But that's a topic for another book. [*Insert Dan Gookin book plug here.*] The following sections cover some basic folder issues.

Understanding the Drafts folder

The Drafts folder should be called the I'm-not-quite-ready-to-send folder. But it's too late to change that now! Instead, the Drafts folder merely poses a puzzle to those who often find e-mail there.

How does a message get into the Drafts folder? The Drafts folder is the electronic dead-letter office. It holds e-mail you don't want to send. Rather than click the Send button for a message, you instead close the message's window. The program most likely asks whether you want to save the message and you say Yes. So the unsent message is stuck in the Drafts folder, where it lingers until you're ready to try to send it again.

How does one get a message out of the Drafts folder? Open the message, edit it if you will, and click the Send button. That sends the message off. Or, you can delete it if you think that's better. Or, you can drag the message out of the Drafts folder and stick it into any other folder.

Copying an e-mail folder to a "real" folder

E-mail folders aren't the same thing as real folders in Windows. They're *fake* folders. In fact, an e-mail folder is nothing more than a very large text file hidden somewhere on your PC's storage system. It only looks like a folder in your e-mail program.

This folder puzzle brings up an interesting issue: How would someone save all the messages in a folder to a real folder out there on the hard drive? The answer is "with much time and patience."

Although you can save any individual message to disk (choose File⇨Save As), you cannot save groups of them to disk at a time. You're stuck with going through the folder and individually saving each message in a "real" folder on the hard drive.

- An e-mail folder in your e-mail program is basically a long text file. The e-mail program works like a database, indexing and referencing the messages so that they appear separate.

- The location of the mail folder or text file is definitely not obvious in Windows; the software developer generally doesn't want you messing with the files.

✔ Okay: E-mail folders aren't *exactly* text files. But, they contain enough text that you can open them in Notepad or WordPad and be able to read some of the mail.

✔ Yeah, that Messages⇨Export command on the Windows Mail (and Outlook Express) File menu doesn't really transform your messages into text files that you can save. The messages are saved to disk, true, but in a specific file format.

Undeleting a deleted message

Messages you delete are put into a Deleted Items or Trash folder; they're not really deleted. To undelete the message, open the Deleted Items folder and drag the message to another folder. That's the idea behind keeping unwanted messages in a folder rather than just zapping them to kingdom come.

Of course, when you delete a message from the Deleted Items or Trash folder, it's *really* gone for good. Remember: The message was merely text inside a larger file. The message cannot be recovered. Pity.

✔ No, not even Norton Utilities or any other unerase program can recover e-mail deleted from the Deleted Items folder.

✔ You can, in theory, recover the original Deleted Items or Trash folder by using a PC Backup program. But the actual process is ugly and time consuming. It's just best to know *for certain* that you want to delete something from that folder, and to do so with gusto!

Attachment Adversity

Along with e-mail come . . . attachments. What a remarkable invention! Attachments make boring old e-mail all the more exciting. You can see pictures, hear sounds, send files, and do all kinds of other silly stuff. It's a thrill a minute with e-mail attachments!

This section gives you some attachment highlights for troubleshooting.

You just cannot open this attachment!

Try as you can, the attachment doesn't open. Either you have no option to open it or, when you open it, Windows presents you with an open-with-what? type of dialog box and no apparently obvious or useful choice is available. What to do? What to do?

My advice: *Give up.* I'm serious. If your computer cannot open the attachment, Windows simply lacks the necessary software. Other than rush out and buy that software (and remember that you don't exactly know which software it is), there's nothing you can do.

Well, not really nothing. You can do what I do: Respond to the message by telling the sender that you cannot open the attachment. Ask the sender to resend it in a more common format. For pictures, JPG (or JPEG) and PNG are common formats. For documents, HTML, RTF, and PDF are common.

✔ Those PSS files are PowerPoint Slide Show files, which people often e-mail to others without considering that not all of us have the PowerPoint program. (You can, however, pick up a free PowerPoint viewer from www.microsoft.com; follow the links for Microsoft Office downloads.)

✔ PSD files are Photoshop images. Have the sender resend the image in JPG format.

✔ WPD and WPS files are WordPerfect files: *Attention, WordPerfect users:* Save your documents as either plain-text (TXT) or RTF files. Thank you.

✔ MPG, MOV, and AVI are movie files. They represent three different movie file formats. Your computer is guaranteed to play at least two of them, and the third format is the one that everyone always e-mails to you.

"The attachment never got there!"

For a number of reasons, a file attachment may not make its way to its recipient:

✔ An attachment may be too large and get rejected (based on its size) by either your own ISP or the recipient's ISP.

✔ If the recipient is using AOL, AOL doesn't accept certain types of file attachments.

✔ The recipient's company or organization may filter out certain types of attachments.

✔ Antivirus software can prevent an attachment from arriving.

✔ The recipient may be using an e-mail program that doesn't allow or understand attachments.

✔ The recipient may not notice or may ignore the attachment.

In most cases, you can try sending the attachment again. If that fails, you have to use an optical disk and mail it through regular postal mail.

Avoiding humongous attachments

There are two issues with humongous attachments: sending and receiving.

For sending, please consider what the nerds call *bandwidth.* That's the bulk that information occupies as it zooms through the Internet. Lots of information consumes more bandwidth, which takes time and costs money. Less information uses less bandwidth. If more people send less information, it's better for everyone. Therefore, I admonish you to do the following:

Do not send the file, music, video, or picture. Instead, send a link to the item.

For example, if you see a funny video, spare your recipients the time and effort to download the entire monster 3.4MB attachment. Just send the YouTube or Google link to the video instead. Simple. Easy. Less annoying.

Now, if none of your friends buys this book (and the sales figures are telling me as much), you can easily avoid downloading bulky attachments by directing your e-mail program to prompt you before an attachment of a given size is retrieved from the server. For example, when any attachment over 500K comes in, you're asked whether you want to download it or just delete it. That's good news!

The bad news is that neither Windows Mail nor Outlook Express offers such a feature. The third-party freeware program Eudora has such a feature. Check out Eudora at www.eudora.com.

Printing an e-mail attachment

Most e-mail programs don't come with the facilities to print an e-mail attachment. Sure, you can print e-mail, but if you just want to print the attachment, you have to save the attachment to disk and open the program that views the attachment, from which you can print.

"I forward a message, and the image is replaced by a little red X!"

Two types of images can appear in an e-mail message: attached and embedded. When you see the red X, you're dealing with an embedded image. In that case, you cannot forward the image, and it cannot be saved to disk. That's just the nature of an embedded image.

The solution here is to reply to the message and have the original sender *attach* the image and not embed it.

Chapter 20

Shutdown Discontent

● ●

● ●

Do you ever get the feeling that the computer just doesn't want to be switched off? It's not that "please don't go" sentiment that I get from my PC. No, it's more of a "Why would you possibly want to turn me off?" kind of arrogance. I know that it's arrogance because sometimes the computer absolutely refuses to shut down. Hey! The party is *over*. Time to go!

This chapter answers the question of why your PC sometimes refuses to shut down. It dives into the computer conscience to determine which stubborn programs refuse to quit. Finally, it describes the best ways to really, seriously, turn off your PC when you need to. Honestly! Turning off a computer should not be a four-star ordeal.

What to Do When Your PC Doesn't Shut Down

Give the computer about two or three minutes before you're certain that it's stuck. Then just turn the sucker off. I know — that's "bad," but what else can you do?

Well, yeah: You can get the situation fixed. Windows is supposed to shut down and turn off the computer all by itself. When it doesn't work that way, you need to fix things, as covered in this section.

✔ If the Power button doesn't turn off the computer, press and hold that button for about three seconds. That usually works. See the section "Controlling the Power Button's Behavior," later in this chapter.

✔ If the Power button still doesn't turn off the computer, unplug it. Or, if your computer is connected to a UPS (*uninterruptible power supply*), turn off the UPS.

Solve common problems that stop up shutdown

Of course, it's not always the fault of Windows. Any of the following situations can also lead to shutdown constipation:

✔ Older, out-of-date, or conflicting device drivers may hang a computer on shutdown.

✔ Software you recently uninstalled that still has sad little pieces of itself remaining around to gum up the works may be the culprit.

✔ Any devices flagged as nonfunctioning by the Device Manager can also be causing the problem. See the appendix in this book for information on the Device Manager.

✔ A bad hard drive may be the problem.

✔ A virus or worm may be the problem.

✔ If your computer plays a sound file when it shuts down and the sound file is corrupted or damaged, that can also cause the system to hang; Windows just sits there and waits for the sound file to "fix itself."

If the shutdown problem is new, consider what you installed, removed, or updated recently. Odds are that the new software, the removed software, or changes in the hardware may be causing the conflict that's preventing the system from shutting down.

Close programs that refuse to quit

Windows refuses to shut down for the very same reason that some guests refuse to leave a party: rude behavior. Inside the computer, usually some stubborn program has been given the signal to shut down, but — like the guest who doesn't leave despite your walking around in your pajamas and bathrobe — it refuses to leave.

Get a hint, will ya?

The solution is finding that stubborn program and either forcing it to quit before you shut down or just not running the program in the first place. As luck would have it, the list of programs that could possibly not get the hint to quit is quite long.

✔ Windows Vista, as the Smartest Version of Windows Evar, shows you *which* stubborn programs are not quitting. You have a choice: Sit and wait, or click the End Now button. My advice: End Now.

✔ Most often the stubbornest of the stubborn software is the most ancient software you have on your computer. Though Windows is supposed to shut down all open programs before it quits, you probably should manually close older programs before you give Windows the command to shut down.

✔ A program that doesn't quit is said to be *hung* or *hanged.*

Try this first! (System Restore)

The first thing to do: Try System Restore. Odds are that restoring the system to a point where it shuts down properly fixes the problem. See Chapter 4.

Fix a problem with a corrupt shutdown sound

If the problem happens because Windows is playing a sound at shutdown and that sound is screwing things up, follow these steps to fix it:

1. **Open the Control Panel.**

2a. **From the Control Panel Home, choose Hardware and Sound and then choose Sound.**

2b. **From Control Panel Classic view, open the Sounds icon.**

   The Sound dialog box appears.

3. **Click the Sounds tab.**

4. **Scroll through the list of events until you find the Exit Windows item.**

   If no sound is listed there — and no icon is by the Exit Windows event name — you're okay. Skip to Step 7.

5. **Click the Test button.**

   The sound plays, showing your ears whether it's working. Even so, playing the sound at this point is no guarantee that the sound isn't the thing that's hanging the computer on shutdown.

6. **If the sound doesn't play, choose (None) from the drop-down list of sounds.**

   By choosing no sound, you effectively disable the sound playing at shutdown. That might fix the trouble. Or you can choose another sound, one that does play.

7. **Click OK.**

If the computer continues to hang when it's shut down, you know that the problem lies elsewhere. Continue reading in the next subsection.

Restart Windows quickly

Sometimes, the problem may be with a program you're running — one of those memory leak situations discussed in Chapter 11. If you're having that type of trouble, follow these steps:

1. **Start Windows as you normally would.**

2. **Wait for all the startup activity to settle down.**

3. **Shut down Windows.**

If Windows shuts down normally without any hang-ups, you're assured that it's probably some other program you're running and not Windows itself to blame. The job then becomes one of elimination to see which program or other software (such as a device driver) is hanging the system.

Try shutting down in Safe mode

One trick you can try is to start the computer in Safe mode. Once in Safe mode, try shutting down. If the computer shuts down successfully, you can be sure that the problem is not with Windows and most likely not with your computer hardware. No, the problem is either a device driver or a third-party program that's not shutting down properly.

See Chapter 24 more information on Safe mode.

Check logs and error messages

Refer to the Event Viewer to see whether any errors or troublesome events were logged just before shutdown. Also read the screen to see whether any programs displayed an error message just before the problem occurred.

After checking the messages, simply try to disable the program or service that's displaying the message. If you can kill the thing off, try shutting down. When shutdown is successful, you have found the bad program or service.

- ✔ Windows is quite good about writing error messages to the event logs, even right before it shuts down.
- ✔ Refer to Chapter 23 for information on the Event Viewer as well as instructions on how to stop a process in Windows Vista.
- ✔ Also see Chapter 8 for information on disabling startup programs.
- ✔ Defective programs should be reinstalled, or check with the developer for information on updates or new versions.

Hardware Things to Check

Three main areas cause woes in the modern PC:

- ✔ The graphics adapter
- ✔ The power-management hardware
- ✔ The networking hardware

Fixing any of these is easy: You just reinstall the software or update the software driver with a newer version. You can obtain the newer version from the manufacturer's Web page at no cost. The problem, of course, is to properly identify which of those suckers could be at fault.

Disabling the graphics adapter

To see whether the video driver is causing the problem, you need to disable the video hardware in your computer. No, this isn't bad, but it sounds scary. Obey these steps:

1. **Open the Control Panel.**

2a. **From the Control Panel Home, choose System and Maintenance and then choose Device Manager.**

2b. **From Control Panel Classic view, open the Device Manager icon.**

3. **Enter the administrator's password or click the Continue button when greeted with the User Account Control.**

Finally, the Device Manager window appears.

4. **Open the item labeled Display Adapters.**

   You see a list of graphics adapters installed in your computer. These are the hardware doohickeys that control graphics.

5. **Double-click your computer's graphics adapter item.**

   The graphics adapter's Properties dialog box appears.

6. **Check the General tab for signs of woe.**

   If the PC believes the graphics adapter to be cooperating, you see the message "This device is working properly"; continue with Step 7. Otherwise, you see a message attempting to describe the problem. If so, click the Check for Solutions button and continue there.

7. **Click the Driver tab.**

8. **Click the Disable button.**

   You see an intimidating dialog box.

9. **Click the Yes button to disable the device.**

   Because you're disabling the graphics driver, the screen's image changes; you soon find the display in low-resolution, or "dumb," mode. This is to be expected.

10. **Click OK to close the Properties dialog box.**

11. **Shut down the PC.**

If the system shuts down just fine, you need to update or upgrade your video driver: Repeat Steps 1 through 7 in this list, and then click the Update Driver button. Follow the directions on the screen.

If the system still refuses to shut down, the problem is *not* the video system. You need to repeat the preceding steps, but in Step 6, click the Enable button to restore your graphics hardware. Continue troubleshooting the shutdown problem in the next section.

Disabling power management

Turn off that power-management stuff and see whether that's the cause of your shutdown woe: Refer to Chapter 6 for information about fixing power-management software. Follow the steps there, but in Step 8 click the Disable button and then click OK. Shut down Windows to determine whether the problem is solved.

If operations shut down normally, you can continue to use the PC with its power-management software disabled, but most definitely contact your PC dealer or computer manufacturer about the problem. Most likely, a fix is available.

If the problem isn't solved, repeat the steps from Chapter 6, but in Step 8 click the Enable button. Continue troubleshooting in the next section.

Disabling the network

The final punk in the nasty trio of problem bullies is your computer's networking hardware. Though not as likely to be a problem as it was in the past (thanks to plug-and-play technology), the network can still be a source of agony and vexation.

The first way to check your networking hardware or software is to see whether any diagnostic programs are available. Check the All Programs menu (from the Start menu) to see whether it has a menu item for the networking hardware. If so, check there for a diagnostic tool or utility. That tells you right away whether there's a problem — though it probably doesn't tell you how to fix it. (Generally, the hardware needs to be reconfigured and reinstalled.)

Next, run a networking troubleshooter. Open the Device Manager as covered earlier in this chapter. Then open the Network Adapters item to see your network hardware listed. Double-clicking your network hardware displays the Properties dialog box, similar to the one shown in Figure 20-1.

As with the display adapter's Properties dialog box (see the section "Disabling the graphics adapter," elsewhere in this chapter), if there are any immediate problems, you see a description on the General tab. If so, click the Check For Solutions button to begin the troubleshooter.

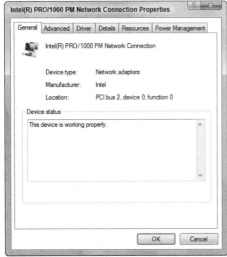

Figure 20-1: The networking hardware's Properties dialog box.

Finally, you can try disabling the networking hardware. This action works just like disabling the video hardware, as covered in the section "Disabling the graphics adapter," earlier in this chapter. The difference is that you're opening the Network Adapters item in Steps 4 and 5.

 Be very careful when disabling and reenabling your networking hardware. Setting up a computer for networking isn't the easiest or most pleasurable thing to do. If any of this causes pangs in your chest, definitely consider paying someone else to do it!

The Annoying Shutdown – Instant Restart Problem

The restart-after-shutdown problem was more of an issue for older versions of Windows. In Windows Vista, they pretty much have the problem licked, but perhaps not. So when the problem of an instant restart bugs you, consider perusing these steps:

1. **Open the Control Panel.**

2a. **From the Control Panel Home, choose System and Maintenance and then choose System.**

 2b. **From Control Panel Classic view, open the System icon.**

   The System window is displayed.

3. **Click the Advanced System Settings link from the left side of the System window.**

   You can open this icon from the Control Panel window, and also by right-clicking the Computer icon on the desktop and choosing Properties from the pop-up menu.

4. **When prompted with the User Account Control, click the Continue button or type the administrator's password.**

5. **In the System Properties dialog box, click the Advanced tab.**

6. **In the Startup and Recovery area, click the Settings button.**

   At long last, you see the Startup and Recovery dialog box. (You can go over to Figure 8-1, in Chapter 8, to see what it looks like.)

7. **Remove the check mark by the item labeled Automatically Restart.**

   This step effectively removes the restarting symptom.

8. **Click OK.**

9. **Close any other dialog boxes and windows that you opened.**

The symptom has been addressed, but the problem hasn't been cured. The next time you start Windows, immediately check the Event Viewer and review the system messages to see what exactly is going wrong at shutdown. That helps you nail down the problem, or at least arms you with enough information for tech support.

✏ Refer to Chapter 23 for information on using the Event Viewer.

✏ Also refer to Chapter 8 for information on the Boot menu. That helps you to stop the restart problem when Windows first starts.

Help Me, Mr. Microsoft!

Microsoft takes careful notes on all the problems that happen with Windows, by keeping a large database, or *Knowledge Base,* of all the trouble and the solutions offered. That's good. Even better is that Microsoft makes all this information available to anyone with Internet access. The Microsoft Knowledge Base Web site can be accessed at

```
support.microsoft.com
```

This Web site can be especially useful for diagnosing shutdown problems. After all, you're probably not the only person in the world who has had this type of issue. (Nope, no one is picking on you!)

Use the Search text box on the main Knowledge Base Web page. Type the word **shutdown**, plus any other words key to your problem. (If you cannot think of any extra words, **shutdown** is fine by itself.) Click the Search button and see what the Knowledge Base comes up with.

Controlling the Power Button's Behavior

In the old days — and I'm talking pre-1990 here — computers all came with an On-Off button or switch. Those were the days! That button did exactly what you would expect: On was on. Off was off. Today, with all the emphasis on power management and energy efficiency and *la-di-da,* the computer's On-Off button has become the *Power button.*

On all computers and laptops, the Power button most definitely turns the computer on. Good. But after that, the Power button's function is determined by *software.* Yes, that's weird, which is why I wrote this section.

Forcing the Power button to turn off the computer

Yeah, it may seem like the Power button isn't turning the computer off, but that's because you don't know the secret:

> Press and hold the Power button for about eight seconds.

Even when the computer seems locked up beyond all hope, the hardware is down in Hades playing rummy with a damned washing machine and an 8-track tape deck, and the software has taken your credit card number and flown Virgin Atlantic to Dubai (Upper Class), the Power button *always* turns the computer off if pressed and held for eight seconds. Magic.

Changing the Power button's function

When the computer is behaving nicely, you can program the Power button on many PCs to obey your whim. The options that are available depend on your computer's power-management hardware. To see what's available, as well as to change the Power button's function, comply with these steps:

 1. **Open the Control Panel.**

 2a. **From the Control Panel Home, choose Hardware and Sound, and then choose Power Options.**

 2b. **From Control Panel Classic view, open the Power Options icon.**

 3. **In the Power Options window, choose the link on the left, Choose What the Power Buttons Do.**

    The System Settings window appears, listing the console's Power and Sleep buttons. The buttons' functions are listed as two pop-up menus. You also see, on a laptop or a PC connected to a UPS via a USB cable, a column for the Power buttons' functions when the computer is running on battery power, as shown in Figure 20-2.

 4. **Choose a new function for the Power button from the drop-down list.**

    Four options are available, as described in Table 20-1.

    If you really want the Power button to turn off the computer, choose the Shut Down option. If you have a laptop and you want it to go into Hibernation mode when you press the button, choose that option.

 5. **Repeat your choices for the Power and Sleep buttons, as well as for the On Battery and Plugged In options.**

 6. **Click OK after making your choice.**

Figure 20-2:
Change
the Power
button's
function
here.

Table 20-1	Power Button Options
Option	**Pressing the Power Button Does This**
Do nothing	Nothing; ignores the Power button.
Sleep	Puts the computer into Stand By (Sleep) mode.
Hibernate	Puts the computer into Hibernation mode.
Shut down	Begins the computer shutdown process, by closing programs and shutting down Windows. When that's done, the computer turns itself off.

Even though you can change the function of the Power button, you still need to shut down Windows properly (or as best you can) whenever you're done working on the computer.

- ✔ If you set the Power button to Do Nothing, the only way to turn off the computer is to shut down Windows using the Start menu. If that doesn't work, you have to unplug the sucker.

- ✔ Selecting the Do Nothing option for the Power button doesn't affect the 8-second rule; no matter which option you choose for the Power button's function, pressing and holding it for 8 seconds turns off the computer.

Part III
Woes, Wows, Windows

The 5th Wave   By Rich Tennant

"How's the defragmentation coming?"

In this part . . .

*A*fter years of scientific study and billions of dollars in
government-funded research, it has been determined
that it's rare to have a computer crash or produce any
type of error — but only when the computer is turned off.
Yes, imagine the shock and consternation when that
detailed and technical report was delivered to the stunned
Congressional Subcommittee on Things You Can Switch On
or Off. The implications were clear: Turning the computer
on is one of the chief causes of computer problems.

Despite your urge to resist, you may occasionally switch
on your PC. If it can survive the boot process, the next
traumatic thing to happen is the loading of the computer's
operating system, Windows. Although hardware problems
may persist in the computer's On state, you may be
stunned to hear that many other problems can be a result
of the presence of the operating system, Windows itself. Sit
down and absorb that cold fact over a nice beverage, and
then ponder some potential problems and solutions in the
chapters that festoon this part of the book.

Chapter 21

Windows Is As Windows Does

· ·

· ·

The Windows operating system is graphical. Yes, people clamored for this. It was *easier*, they whined. Text? That's boring and ugly. Text reminds people that they're using a computer and not playing a video game. *Waa! We want Windows!*

Well, Windows you got. As a graphical operating system, Windows tosses a bunch of odd things into the computer mix. I'm referring to what computer scientists call "weird stuff on the screen." Perhaps it's not weird, but more like unexpected or unwelcome. It's like the computer is possessed at times. You may be in the driver's seat, but something else is definitely steering! This chapter helps remove your fear, superstition, and panic about various things in Windows, graphical or not.

"That Looks Stupid"

Sure, it looks stupid! And, calling something stupid is quite offensive. But, you know what? Stupid is easy to recognize. I know stupid when I see it. This section covers some of the most stupid-looking things in all of Windows.

Screwy colors

My 12-year-old son prefers using Windows with a black-and-purple color scheme. I cannot see *anything* on his PC. Yet he seems to function well with a black-and-purple system. Honestly, for a 12-year-old, black and purple colors on a PC are okay. If I spot him heading to his bedroom with buckets of black and purple paint, I'll probably calmly walk in and energetically stop him. But for a computer, odd colors make a statement. And they can be changed without dripping anything on the carpet.

Colors on the monitor can grow screwy in two ways. The first is the most definite way, which is when you go nuts inside the Appearance Settings dialog box, shown in Figure 21-1. Windows really doesn't care about your taste, so you can choose some truly odd combinations there — and live to regret it later.

Figure 21-1:
Don't go
nuts in
this-here
dialog box.

How to undo the nonsense? If you can *see* the screen just fine, follow these steps as written. If you're having trouble seeing things, start the computer in Safe mode to make your corrections (refer to Chapter 24 for more information on Safe mode):

1. **Right-click the desktop.**
2. **Choose Personalize from the pop-up menu.**
3. **Choose Themes from the Personalization window.**

   The Theme Settings dialog box materializes.
4. **Choose Windows Vista from the Theme drop-down list.**
5. **Click OK and, optionally, close the Personalization window.**

   That should fix it.

Well, it may not fix the screen, but it restores Windows to its standard screen setup. At least you can get work done or continue modifying the display settings.

✔ If you have your own set of custom colors defined, I recommend saving that set to disk as its own theme: Choose Themes in the Personalization window. Click the Save As button in the Theme Settings dialog box. Give your custom theme a name and save it to disk. That way, you can restore your favorite colors and screen settings whenever you like.

✔ For handling problems with the screen's resolution, refer to Chapter 16.

Fuzzy icon trouble

It's not that the icons get fuzzy, but rather that your desktop icons — and the Start button — seem to flash or rapidly change color — like the transporter effect from *Star Trek*. That's a sign of a bad or corrupted video driver, or your LCD monitor might be improperly set.

✔ LCD monitors have set resolutions. Ensure that you're using a proper resolution for the monitor. See Chapter 6.

✔ Also refer to Chapter 6 for information on upgrading or restoring your video driver.

Getting more stuff on the screen

You can't make the screen bigger. I wish you could! But no such thing as a screen-stretcher exists; a 17-inch monitor can display only so much information. If you want more stuff on the screen, the solution is to increase the screen's *resolution*.

Chapter 6 contains information on setting the screen's resolution. Look there for more information.

Resetting the screen's resolution to a higher setting makes things look smaller on the screen. You can do two things:

First, in your applications, you can take advantage of the Zoom command, usually found on the View menu. The Zoom command magnifies the contents of the window so that everything is easier to read.

Second, you can make the Windows icons appear larger: Right-click the desktop and choose View⇨Large Icons. In any folder window, choose Large Icons from the Views toolbar button menu. Or choose Extra Large icons for extra large visual goodness.

The window has slid off the screen

Moving a window on the screen is so easy that few beginning Windows books even bother to explain it in any detail: You use the mouse to *drag* the window around. Simple. But it's not so simple when you can't pinch part of the window by using the mouse. In fact, I have known some folks who get so desperate to get the window back that they just end up reinstalling Windows. Bad move!

The trick to getting any window to move when it's off the screen is the same trick you use to move a window when the mouse is broken: Use the keyboard!

These steps assume that a window you want to move is on the screen. Click that window to make it "on top" and selected, and then follow these steps:

1. **Press Alt+spacebar.**

   This command activates the window's Control menu.

2. **Press M, for *m*ove.**

   Now you can use the keyboard's arrow keys to move the window.

3. **Press the left, right, up, or down arrow to move the window in that direction.**

4. **When you're done moving the window, press the Enter key.**

The window is too large for the screen

Resizing a large window is next to impossible when you can't grab its edges with the mouse. The solution here is to use the keyboard to help resize the window:

1. **Ensure that the window isn't maximized.**

    You cannot resize a maximized window; click the Restore button (the middle button in the window's upper-right corner) to unmaximize the window.

2. **Press Alt+spacebar.**

   This keyboard command drops down the window's Control menu.

3. **Press S, for *s*ize.**

   You can now move each of the window's four sides in or out. You do that by first choosing a side and moving the side in or out.

4. **Press the left, right, up, or down arrow to move that side of the window.**

   For example, press the left-arrow key to choose the left side of the window.

5. **Use the left–right or up–down arrow key to move the window's edge.**

   For example, if you chose the left side of the window, press the left- or right-arrow key to move that side of the window.

6. **Press Enter when you're done resizing that edge.**

7. **Repeat Steps 2 through 6 to resize another edge of the window.**

   For example, to resize the bottom edge of the window, press Alt+space-bar, S, and then the down-arrow key to select the bottom edge. Then, use the up- or down-arrow key to move that edge in or out.

These steps may seem confusing, but if you work through them and mess with the window's size, they make sense. Just be thankful that such an alternative window-resizing technique exists.

The window is too tiny

Windows remembers the size and position of any window you open on the screen. When you return to a program or open a folder again, Windows sticks the window back in the spot in which it originally existed and at the same size as when you last used the window.

The problem is really a "feature." Windows is simply restoring a window that you have resized to be very tiny. Most people just maximize the window at this point, but the problem is that Windows doesn't remember maximized windows. No, instead, the window is opened again at its tiny size.

The solution is to resize the window *without* maximizing it: Use the mouse to drag out the window's edges (top, bottom, right, left) to the size and position you prefer on the screen. With the window larger — but not maximized — you can close it. Then, when that window is reopened, it opens to the larger size.

The taskbar has moved

On my long sheet of Windows regrets is the ability to move the taskbar. I'm certain that someone at Microsoft thought it would be handy to have a taskbar on the left or right sides or top of the computer screen. In practice, in my experience? I have never seen a taskbar anywhere except at the bottom of the screen. Even so, the ability to move the taskbar exists, and many people do accidentally move it — and then desperately want it back on the bottom.

You can move the taskbar just as you can move any window on the screen: Drag it with the mouse. The key, however, is to *close all open windows* so that you can easily grab the taskbar with the mouse.

The first step to moving the taskbar is to ensure that it's unlocked. Obey these steps:

1. **Right-click a blank part of the taskbar.**

2. **Choose Unlock the Taskbar.**

   This command sports a check mark by it when the taskbar is locked. Choosing the command removes the check mark and unleashes the taskbar.

To move the taskbar back to the bottom of the screen, follow these steps:

1. **Point the mouse at the taskbar (on a spot that has no buttons).**

2. **Press the mouse button.**

3. **Drag the mouse pointer to the bottom of the screen.**

If these steps don't work, you can try using the keyboard and mouse together:

1. **Click the taskbar once.**

   Click a blank spot that has no buttons.

2. **Press Alt+spacebar.**

   This step pops up a menu, shown in Figure 21-2. If not, start over again with Step 1.

Figure 21-2: Properly accessing the taskbar's control menu.

3. **Press M, for *move*.**

   If the Move command isn't available, the taskbar is locked; unlock it!

4. **Press and hold the down-arrow key until the mouse pointer is close to the bottom of the screen.**

   If this step doesn't move the taskbar, press the left-arrow key and hold it down. If that doesn't work, press the right-arrow key and hold it down.

5. **Click the mouse when you're done.**

The object is to use the keyboard to move the mouse pointer to wherever you want the taskbar. Use all four arrow keys — left, right, up, and down — to move the taskbar.

- ✔ Yes, you can accidentally move the taskbar. It happens all the time.
- ✔ Also, mean people move or hide the taskbar. They call it a practical joke, though there's nothing practical about it, nor is it funny.
- ✔ If the moving taskbar frustrates you, lock it down!

The taskbar has disappeared

The taskbar cannot disappear, but it can hide. It can also grow so thin as to seem invisible, although it's still there.

First, make sure that you're not using a program in full-screen mode, which would hide the taskbar. Most full-screen programs keep one button or menu item available to allow you to de-full-screen the program. Or, you can try pressing the F10 key to summon the menu bar and try to restore the screen. In Internet Explorer, press the F11 key to unzoom from full-screen mode.

Second, see whether the taskbar is simply too skinny to see. Check each edge of the screen for a thin, black strip. If you find it, you have found the taskbar: Point the mouse at the strip, and it changes into an up-down pointing arrow (or a left-right pointing arrow if the taskbar is on the side of the screen). Press the mouse button and *drag* the mouse toward the center of the screen. As you drag, the taskbar grows fatter. Release the mouse button when the taskbar is the proper size.

Third, the taskbar may be automatically hidden, which is one of its features. To check, point the mouse to where the taskbar normally lives and wait. The taskbar should pop right up. (If not, try pointing at the other three edges of the screen to see whether some joker moved *and hid* the taskbar.)

If the taskbar pops up, you can switch off its autohide feature:

1. **Right-click the Start button.**
2. **Choose Properties from the pop-up menu.**

   The Taskbar and Start Menu Properties dialog box appears.
3. **Click the Taskbar tab.**

   You see a dialog box specifically customized to deal with taskbar ways and woes, as shown in Figure 21-3.

Figure 21-3:
Control the
taskbar
by using
controls
in this
dialog box.

4. **Click to remove the check mark by the item labeled Auto-Hide the Taskbar.**

5. **While you're at it, click to select the item labeled Keep the Taskbar on Top of Other Windows.**

6. **Click OK.**

The menu or button or another element in the program is missing!

Without listing the 50,000 variations for every program and application, generally speaking you can fix missing visual elements by checking either the View or Window menu.

The View menu can contain commands that control which toolbars and buttons are visible.

The Windows menu controls which of the windows or palettes are visible.

Before giving up, consider checking the View or Windows menu for the missing items you yearn for.

The Big, Scary Question of Reinstalling Windows

At some point, reinstalling Windows became acceptable. And, I'll be honest: Reinstalling Windows works. It absolutely restores your computer to the way it was when you first got it or when Windows was last upgraded. It's a guaranteed fix, but it's a cheat.

It's a cheat because you usually have a simpler, easier way to fix the problem than to resort to reinstalling Windows. For example, consider going to the doctor for an irregular heartbeat, and he recommends a heart transplant. Or, go to a mechanic because your engine knocks, and he recommends replacing the entire engine. Reinstalling Windows is the same overblown, waste-of-time solution.

Fundamentally, an operating system should never need to be reinstalled. Just quiz a Unix wizard on how many times he has to reinstall Unix, and you get this puzzled, insane look. Even in the days of DOS, reinstalling DOS was never considered a solution. But, with 12-minute time limits on tech-support phone calls (refer to the sidebar in Chapter 5), suddenly reinstalling Windows isn't only a potential solution, most often it's *the* solution.

Poppycock!

✔ Reinstalling Windows is a solution only when the system has become so corrupted that no other solution exists. For example, if your computer is attacked by a virus or somehow major portions of Windows are destroyed or deleted, reinstalling Windows is an option.

✔ Reinstalling Windows is also necessary to recover from a botched operating system upgrade.

✔ Yes, often, reinstalling Windows fixes the problem. But it has also been my experience that it has caused more problems than it has solved. I feel that tech-support people who recommend it should be held personally and legally responsible for the consequences of such a drastic recommendation.

✔ No, reinstalling Windows isn't the same thing as rebuilding the kernel in Unix. The kernel is one file, similar to the Windows KERNEL32.DLL file. In fact, you can reinstall single files in Windows, which is one way to avoid reinstalling *every* file. You do this by using the System File Checker (SFC) utility, which is covered in Chapter 24.

"Are there any benefits to reinstalling Windows?"

I have been to various Web sites that tout the virtues of reinstalling Windows. It's almost a religious experience for them, like getting a high colonic but equally as dubious. The sites remind me of reading those ancient alchemy, or "medical," documents that enthusiastically recommend drinking mercury to cure a fever.

Argument 1: Reinstalling Windows removes much of the junk that doesn't get uninstalled when you remove programs. So (blah, blah, blah), you end up with a cleaner system.

Rebuttal 1: Well, yeah, you end up with a cleaner system *until* you reinstall all your applications, which reintroduces all the junk right back into the system. Cleaner system? No. Wasted time? Definitely!

Argument 2: Reinstalling Windows results in a faster system.

Rebuttal 2: No argument there. But the reason it's faster is that reinstalling has the marvelous effect of defragmenting the entire hard drive, especially nonmovable clusters. So, like, *duh!* The system is faster — for a time. Fragmentation eventually creeps back in.

Rebuttal 2½: Don't forget the time wasted reinstalling Windows. Count your computer system down for at least half a day.

Argument 3: Reinstalling Windows fixes a number of problems.

Rebuttal 3: You can fix problems without reinstalling Windows.

I could go on. And, I would love to, but I have run out of arguments in favor of reinstalling Windows. If you hear of any, please e-mail them to me for this book's next edition: dgookin@wambooli.com. Thanks!

"What about reformatting the hard drive?"

Reformatting the hard drive is another evil activity that's foisted on the computing public as a necessary task. It's not. In fact, you should never, *ever,* have to reformat your computer's hard drive. It's something they do at the factory. It's something a computer technician does. It's no longer anything a computer user has to do.

As with reinstalling Windows, in only one circumstance do I suggest reformatting a hard drive: when a virus has attacked the computer so thoroughly that the only solution to rid it of the virus is to reformat the hard drive. And, that's a pretty rare thing; an ugly thing; a thing that I hope never happens to you.

Repairing Windows

An alternative to reinstalling Windows is to repair it instead. This must be done with the original Windows installation disc. Sadly, most PCs today aren't sold with installation discs. If you don't have one, this trick doesn't work.

To use the installation disc to fix Windows, follow these steps:

1. **Insert the Windows installation disc into your PC's optical drive.**

2. **Restart the computer.**

3. **If prompted, choose to boot from the disc.**

   Refer to Chapter 8 for information on setting PC startup and boot options.

4. **Follow the directions on the screen.**

5. **After choosing language options, choose the option Repair Your Computer.**

6. **Choose your current Windows Vista installation.**

7. **From the System Recovery Options menu, choose Startup Repair.**

8. **Follow the directions on the screen.**

Chapter 22

Windows Versus Your Programs

● ●

In This Chapter

▶ Halting a program

▶ Stopping a service

▶ Shutting down all programs

▶ Disabling anti-malware software

▶ Configuring older programs

▶ Removing programs

● ●

*Y*ou probably didn't buy your PC for the joys of running the Windows operating system. Heavens, no! Forgiving Microsoft's battalions of attorneys, who insist that the operating system is anything and everything, an *operating system* is merely the main piece of software in a computer. An operating system has three basic duties: to control the hardware, to manage other programs and information, and to interact with you, the human.

The real reason you bought your PC was to run other software: to word-process, use the Internet, use Photoshop to make your thighs thinner, and play games, for example. The operating system has a big role in all that: Sometimes it's the hero; sometimes Windows is the villain. This chapter helps you determine which character the operating system is playing and how to deal with the consequences.

Programs Run Amok

Software can go loopy. In fact, loops are the main reason that software tends to hang up and go to town. In programming parlance, a *loop* is a section of code that repeats. Good programming mandates that at some point or under some condition, the loop gracefully exits. When a loop repeats endlessly without any possibility of exiting, it's known as an *endless loop* or *infinite loop*. Although it must be fun to observe at a subatomic level, it's not a very productive thing.

The following sections cover what to do when a program gets loopy or runs amok.

- ✔ The headquarters of Apple, makers of the Macintosh computer, are at 1 Infinite Loop in Cupertino, California. *Ha-ha.*
- ✔ Microsoft's headquarters are at One Microsoft Way in Redmond, Washington. Yes, there's humor there as well.

Stopping a naughty program

As Windows has improved over the years, so has its ability to deal with misbehaving programs. In the old days, such a program would topple down the entire PC house of cards. Today, with luck, only the one program will stop working. But how can you tell?

First of all, a nonresponsive program is exactly that: nonresponsive. Clicking the mouse does nothing. You might be able to move the window; you might not. But you still have control over the keyboard and mouse, and you can use other programs or Windows.

Despite any immediate frustration you may have, the first thing to do is *wait.* Programs get busy. Wait. How long? A few minutes should do it. Especially if the hard drive light is blinking like mad, there may be a sign of hope.

While you wait, you can check with the Task Manager to see whether the program is Not Responding. Here's how:

1. **Press Ctrl+Shift+Esc to summon the Task Manager window.**

2. **Click the Applications tab (if necessary).**

3. **Peruse the Status column to determine whether any program is not responding.**

   In Figure 22-1, you see that one of my favorite games, *Day of Defeat: Source,* is dead in the water. No chance of respawning, either. Also note that unless the Status column width is wide enough, you see only the first few letters of Not Responding.

4. **Click to select the unresponsive program with the mouse.**

5. **Click the End Task button.**

   Windows may respond with an "Are you sure?" dialog box, or it may confirm that the program is being silly and needs to be thumped.

6. **Click the Yes or OK button to dispense with the program.**

   The program is killed off.

7. **Close the Task Manager window.**

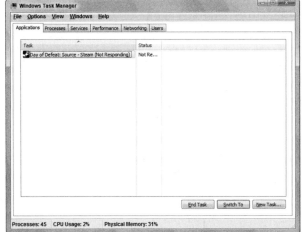

Figure 22-1:
A program
lingers in
bit limbo.

You can continue using your PC after killing off a useless program. In fact, you can start the program again and keep on using it. If it crashes again, however, I would suspect that it needs attention; contact the developer to see whether an update or fix is available.

The program has gone on strike

Sometimes you don't need to stop a program run amok; the thing may just stop on its own. What a blessing! Be thankful that you're using a computer in the 21st century because years ago such an offense would bring the entire PC to its knees.

Figure 22-2 illustrates what happens when a program (another game; I know — "Get back to work!") goes AWOL. In this case, Windows immediately recognizes the problem and displays a dialog box: Click the Close Program button and get on with your life.

Figure 22-2:
A program
goes quietly
into that
#FFFFFF
night.

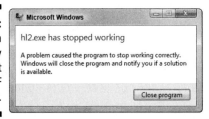

Why does this happen? Who knows? But the smell of death is ripe enough that Windows catches the program and kills the program by itself. Yeah!

Stopping a service

Windows runs both programs and services. The services are still programs, but they're specifically things that the operating system does to help control the computer. It's trivial stuff, but important when you need to stop a service.

Stop a service only when you're directed to do so, by either technical support or some other authority. Don't randomly stop services, or else you may change the behavior of your PC. That would be bad.

To stop a service, follow these steps:

1. **Press Ctrl+Shift+Esc to summon the Task Manager window.**

2. **Click the Services tab.**

   You see a list of all services running in Windows. The Description column helps clue you in to a service's purpose in life.

3. **Click the Services button.**

4. **Click the Continue button or type the administrator's password when prompted with the User Account Control warning.**

   The Services window appears, but may be hidden behind the Task Manager window.

5. **Close the Task Manager window.**

   In the Services window, shown in Figure 22-3, you see a list of all running services in your PC. Yep, there's a lot going on in there.

6. **Find the service you want to stop.**

   Scroll through the list and look for the service you were directed to halt.

7. **Double-click to open the service.**

   A dialog box appears for the service in question, similar to the one shown in Figure 22-4.

8. **To stop the service, click the Stop button.**

   This action stops the service, but it doesn't prevent the service from starting up again after the computer is restarted (or from causing another service to restart the service).

9. **To prevent the service from starting in the future, choose Disabled from the Startup Type menu button.**

10. **Click OK to confirm your choices.**

11. **Close the Services window.**

Don't just go randomly disabling services!

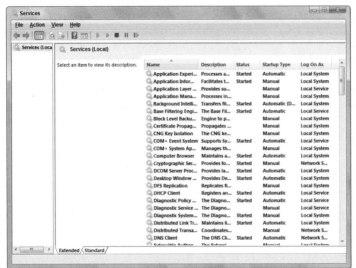

Figure 22-3:
Bunches of
services are
listed here.

Figure 22-4:
Services are
disabled
here.

Definitions to avoid: Program, process, service

Whether it's called a program, process, or service, it's all software that runs in your computer. Beyond that, the differences can be subtle and confusing, which is why this information is carefully shoved into a sidebar, where you can't accidentally read it:

program: A program is an executable file — instructions for the computer. Programs can be applications, like a word processor or Web browser, or part of the operating system, like Windows Explorer.

process: In Windows, a process is both a program that you run and a program being run by the operating system. Processes are listed in the Task Manager window, on the Processes tab.

service: A service is a specific program, or part of a program, that controls certain things in a computer. Sometimes one program is in charge of one service, but more often than not, one program runs several services. For example, the SVCHOST.EXE process in Windows runs many services, most of which deal with networking.

Shutting down all running programs

Do you ever get the message, most often shown when you install new software, that directs you to "Please quit all other programs now, before you install the Mondo Number Whacker 3000"? Of course, they don't tell you *how* to shut down other programs or even why.

The *why* I'm guessing at: Most new programs need to restart Windows to fully install. Because the computer is restarting, it's a good idea to save your documents. By quitting other programs, you're ensuring that your documents are saved. But that's just my guess.

The second why-reason is that some installation programs monitor what the computer is doing so that the software can be successfully uninstalled at a later date. Having a second program running, and writing stuff to disk during that operation may screw things up. It's just best to shut down your other running programs. Here's how:

1. **Press Alt+Tab.**

   This command switches your focus to the next running program or open window.

2. **If pressing Alt+Tab does nothing — you just return to the same Install or Setup program window, for example — you're done. Otherwise:**

3. **Close the program or window.**

4. **Start over with Step 1.**

By using Alt+Tab, you can successfully switch to each running program and shut it down, one after the other. When Alt+Tab doesn't appear to work any more, you're done shutting things down and can continue with the installation.

Don't bother trying to shut down any *processes.* No, the advice is to shut down other running *programs.* Windows has lots of processes going, and I don't recommend that you kill them all off just to install a new program. (Processes are killed on the Task Manager's Processes tab.)

Disabling antivirus, firewall, and so on

After you shut down any running programs, the next annoying thing you're requested to do for a new software installation is to shut down or disable your antivirus software. You may also be asked to disable the Internet fire-wall. Yeah, in other words, *strip naked and bare your computer's soul to the cruel universe!*

Well . . . it's not that terrible.

Most antivirus and firewall programs leave their marks as icons in the notifi-cation area. Shutting them down or disabling them is as easy as finding their tiny icons and right-clicking them. From the pop-up menu that appears, choose a Suspend, Disable, or even Shutdown command, to temporarily do away with that icon's papa program.

Immediately after installing the new software, be sure to restart Windows. That way, you ensure that your antivirus, firewall, and any disabled software are restarted as well.

The Compatibility Question

There will be issues anytime any operating system is upgraded. Compatibility is the topic. Developers try to make a new operating system compatible with existing hardware and software, but often the improvements wanted and updates needed just can't please everyone. So, there are incompatibilities. Dealing with those incompatibilities regarding your computer's software is the topic of this section.

The program has "issues"

Complain all I want, I admire Microsoft for keeping a database of programs that are truly troublesome for Windows Vista. These programs have *issues.* That means that if you install them, they probably won't work properly, or your computer may not function properly. That's a good thing to know beforehand!

When a program has issues, you're alerted to that fact when the program installs. A suitably scary error message appears. You're given the option to move forward with the installation: Don't. Instead, I recommend contacting the software developer and inquiring about when an updated, more compatible version of the software will be made available.

Tuning older programs to work in Windows Vista

One of the main reasons folks refuse to update an operating system is compatibility. There are just quite a few programs that don't work or that work incorrectly under Windows Vista. But don't give up after the first stab! Instead, consider playing the role of software mediator. Here's how:

1. **Locate the program's icon.**

   You need to modify the program itself, not a shortcut.

   If you find the shortcut icon, right-click it. From the pop-up menu, choose the Open File Location command. You next see a window with the program's icon highlighted. That's your baby!

2. **Right-click the program's icon and choose Properties from the shortcut menu.**

   The program's Properties dialog box comes into view.

3. **Click the Compatibility tab.**

   The Compatibility tab contains settings for controlling how the program sees Windows, as shown in Figure 22-5. It doesn't really modify Windows as much as it modifies the program. So, by making the proper settings, you can coax an older program into behaving in Windows Vista, but the program still may not function properly when it runs.

4. **Place a check mark by Run This Program in Compatibility Mode For.**

5. **Choose a version of Windows from the menu button.**

6. **If you constantly see the Administrator's User Account Control warning when you run the program, click to put a check mark by Run This Program As an Administrator.**

7. **Click OK and close the program's folder window.**

Setting the compatibility options is the best way to ensure that older programs behave, but it's no guarantee.

Figure 22-5:
Setting a
program's
compatibility
options.

Some programs just aren't compatible with the latest version of a computer operating system. This is true for Windows as well as for just about every other operating system ever developed.

Uninstalling Programs

You never delete a program from Windows. No, you're supposed to *uninstall* it instead. Here's how it works:

1. **Open the Control Panel.**

2a. **From the Control Panel Home, choose the link Uninstall a Program from beneath the Programs header.**

2b. **From the Control Panel Classic view, open the Programs and Features icon.**

3. **Choose a program to uninstall from the list that's displayed.**

4. **Click the Uninstall or Uninstall/Change button on the toolbar.**

5. **Heed any further directions that appear.**

   Uninstalling a program works differently, depending on the developer. Sometimes you're prompted (begged) not to uninstall, and sometimes the program is removed instantly with no prompts at all!

6. **Close the Programs and Features window when you're done.**

The preceding steps describe the *proper* way to remove the software.

Another way to remove software is to locate the Uninstall program that may have come with the software in the first place. Look on the Start button's All Programs menu for the folder containing the program you installed. Often, an Uninstall program dwells in the same folder as the software you want to remove. Simply run the Uninstall program and you're done.

The worst way to remove a program is to simply delete it. Despite however satisfying that method may be for you, it creates two problems. First, it's not your place to delete any file you didn't create yourself. Second, you can never be certain that you're deleting the entire program or whether your deleting actions will cause unintended consequences. Best be safe and do things properly.

✔ Don't delete any program remnants saved in the Windows folder or any of the subfolders beneath the Windows folder.

✔ Sometimes, the remnants are left around in the hope that you may reinstall the program later. For example, I uninstalled a game, but noticed that it kept personal data — saved missions and high scores — in the folder.

✔ You can freely delete remnants, such as shortcut icons: Right-click any shortcut icon and choose Delete from the pop-up menu to rid yourself of that icon. You can do that on the desktop as well as on the Start menu.

✔ Feel free to delete any .zip or .exe files you downloaded. After installing that software, you can delete the original download — if you like. (I tend to keep those files.)

✔ Sometimes, new computers come with folders full of yet-to-be-installed programs. For example, the Online or similar folders may contain icons for various online systems. Delete 'em all!

✔ Also consider checking with the System Configuration utility (MSCON-FIG) and its Startup tab to see whether bits and pieces of the program are still being started there. See Chapter 24 for more information on the System Configuration utility.

Chapter 23

Windows Can Be Your Friend

· ·

· ·

I am amazed at the various interesting tools and utilities included with Windows Vista. It's impressive. Yeah, I know: Lots of people like to complain about Windows Vista. But the more I use the operating system, the more I'm delighted — especially from a troubleshooting standpoint. There are so many useful things in Windows Vista, plus various ways to help you determine what's wrong with your PC, that I changed my mind and figured that Windows can be my friend! It might be yours as well (though I don't have high hopes), after you wade through the topics covered in this chapter.

O Windows, Please Do Tell

Windows can truly be informative — well, on its own terms. I find it curious that Windows, as the main piece of software in charge of your PC, can possibly *not* know something. After all, it's in charge! But then again, other things that purport to be in charge often don't know everything going on under their eyes. My seventh grade English teacher comes to mind. But anyway. . . .

This section lists a host of tools and places to visit to gather information about what's going on inside your computer.

Reading problem reports and solutions

Windows keeps track of all the missteps, mishaps, and misfortunes that befall your computer. One place to locate that information is in the logs, which are covered later in this chapter. But the most specific way to find out transgressions transpired is to use the Problem Reports and Solutions window, shown in Figure 23-1.

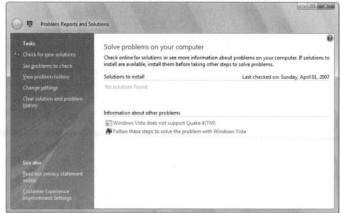

Figure 23-1:
The Problem Reports and Solutions window.

To summon the Problem Reports and Solutions window, follow these steps:

1. **Open the Control Panel.**

2a. **From the Control Panel Home, choose System and Maintenance and then choose Problem Reports and Solutions.**

2b. **From Control Panel Classic view, open the Problem Reports and Solutions icon.**

   The Problem Reports and Solutions window appears, as shown in Figure 23-1. You see listed any recent problems reported by Windows as well as any solutions available for installation.

3. **If you see any problems, click the link to get more information.**

   Clicking the link opens another window, where you can potentially discover a solution to the problem.

4. **Click the link on the left side of the window, View Problem History.**

   The window displayed after clicking the link categorizes the slew of problems you may have encountered in Windows Vista, along with the date and time, plus whether any information was sent to Microsoft to help fix the problem.

5. **Close the Problem Reports and Solutions window when you're done.**

The Problem Reports and Solutions window may tell you more about events run amok in your PC, but it doesn't tell you everything. For more detail, peruse the system logs, a topic that's covered in the next section.

Checking event logs

Windows makes a note of all activities taking place inside the computer, even items too trivial to place into a Problem Reports and Solutions window. The thing that keeps track of all those activities is the *event log*. Here's how to view the thing in Windows:

1. **Open the Control Panel.**

2a. **From the Control Panel Home, choose System and Maintenance, and then choose the link View Event Logs, found under Administrative Tools.**

2b. **From Control Panel Classic view, open the Administrative Tools icon, and then open the Event Viewer item.**

3. **If prompted, click the Continue button or type the administrator's password.**

   The Event Viewer window, shown in Figure 23-2, shows several of the logs or event entries monitored by the operating system. Yes, it's *too much* information!

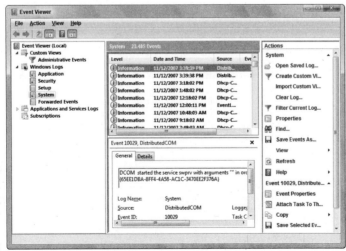

Figure 23-2:
The Event Viewer tells the tale.

4. From the left side of the window, open the item titled Windows Logs.

Five logs are listed on my PC: Application, Security, Setup, System, and Forwarded Events. When an application crashes or is working funny, check Applications. For security warnings, check Security. For Windows itself, check the System log. For example:

5. Choose the System item on the right.

The center part of the window now displays a list of events, such as the 23,485 events listed in Figure 23-2. Most events are of the Information type. That's okay. But there are other types as well, listed here:

- *Error:* Can indicate a major problem. Basically, an Error event means that something went wrong.

- *Warning:* For events not as serious as error events, but things you should potentially be aware of.

- *Information:* Indicates that a successful or normal operation has begun or has been completed or perhaps anything else that happens and is noted in the event log.

6. To view the details of an event, double-click the mouse to open that event.

For example, in Figure 23-3, you see the details of a surprise system shutdown. The date and time are given along with the other information. The Details tab lists the technical mumbo jumbo, but that information is good only for those who know the guts of Windows well. Still, it's an accurate report of the event. If UFO watchers had such data, there would be no doubt about the presence of extraterrestrials!

7. Close the various windows when you're done looking around.

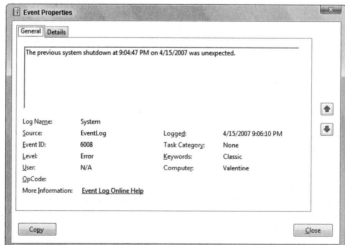

Figure 23-3: Details of a specific event.

The Event Viewer is good in two instances. First, when you suspect that there's a problem, you can quickly open the Event Viewer to ensure that you're not crazy. For example, when I recently experienced optical drive problems, a quick check of the Event Viewer confirmed that the computer was having trouble.

Second, the Event Viewer can alert you to certain problems you may not know about. For example, I recently had some network trouble, and the Event Viewer was crawling with related networking errors (though none of the errors helped me put the network back up).

Getting performance information

Windows Vista has a performance rating called the Windows Experience Rating. It's just a number, but numbers were designed to be compared, so the Windows Experience Rating has become something of an annoying curiosity.

To witness your PC's performance information, obey these steps:

1. **Open the Control Panel.**

2a. **From the Control Panel Home, choose System and Maintenance, and then choose System.**

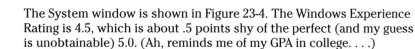

2b. **From Control Panel Classic view, open the System icon.**

The System window is shown in Figure 23-4. The Windows Experience Rating is 4.5, which is about .5 points shy of the perfect (and my guess is unobtainable) 5.0. (Ah, reminds me of my GPA in college. . . .)

Of course, the Windows Experience Rating is trivial. For more meaty information, you need to turn to the Performance Information and Tools window, shown in Figure 23-5.

3a. **From the Control Panel Home, choose System and Maintenance, and then choose Performance Information and Tools.**

3b. **From Control Panel Classic view, open the Performance Information and Tools icon.**

4. **In the Performance Information and Tools window, choose the link View and Print Details.**

Don't worry: Nothing prints. But you see a more detailed report about your system and how the hardware is holding up to the high standards of Windows.

5. **Close the Performance Information and Tools window when you're done.**

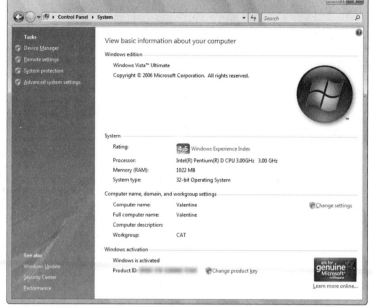

Figure 23-4:
A smidgen of performance information is shown here.

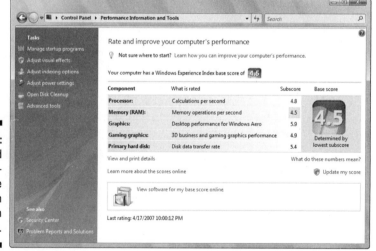

Figure 23-5:
Detailed performance information is shown here.

Running a system diagnostics report

The Reliability and Performance Monitor in Windows is capable of producing a system diagnostic. The information that's gathered tells you not only trivial

information about your computer but also detailed information about errors
and malfunctioning hardware. In fact, some of the incidental information
that's reported can be priceless (and not the silly kind of priceless, either).

To view the diagnostic information, obey these steps:

1. **Open the Control Panel.**

2a. **From the Control Panel Home, choose System and Maintenance and
    then choose Performance Information and Tools.**

2b. **From Control Panel Classic view, open the Performance Information
    and Tools icon.**

    You see the Performance Information and Tools window, shown in
    Figure 23-5.

3. **From the links on the left side of the window, choose Advanced Tools.**

    The Advanced Tools window immediately tells you whether anything bad
    has recently happened in your PC. Beneath the heading Performance
    Issues, you may see some warnings (yellow triangles) or errors (red stop
    signs) telling you that something is potentially or really wrong.

4. **Click any warning or error links beneath the Performance Issues
   heading to get more information about improving the performance
   of Windows.**

    A window appears, listing some approaches you can take to remedy the
    situation. Sometimes they're good suggestions; some suggestions you
    can write off as one-time blurps or as just plain silly.

    Click the Remove from List button in the suggestion window to remove
    the suggestion from the list.

    Meanwhile, back in the Advanced Tools window:

5. **Choose the link titled Generate a System Health Report.**

6. **If necessary, click the Continue button or type the administrator's
   password to continue.**

7. **Wait while the report gathers its data.**

    When the gathering is done, you see a detailed report listing any poten-
    tial errors, problems, and other information with which you can stuff
    your brain.

    Be sure to peruse the list for any failed tests!

8. **Close the various windows when you're done.**

Freshly Installed Updates

Hmmm. Nothing smells more like love than a freshly installed Windows update (see Figure 23-6). Don't you love it? Windows greets you in the morning and, golly, you just know something is new. Isn't that great? Nope? But it's a good idea to update, despite the smell.

Figure 23-6:
Fresh
updates!
Get your
fresh
updates
here!

Modern operating systems like Windows must be updated frequently. If you follow my advice in other computer books I've written, you configured Windows to automatically update itself. That's good! But often questions come up regarding one of the updates. The answers to those questions can be found in this section.

Reviewing Windows updates

When Windows is configured to update automatically, you're pretty much out of the driver's seat. Sure, you don't see those "Windows really, *really* needs to install updates. Why not stop everything and do that now or I will bug you like a 4-year-old begging a weak parent for candy in the grocery store" type of messages. Anyway. Follow these steps:

1. **Open the Control Panel.**

2a. **From the Control Panel Home, choose the link Check for Updates, found beneath the Security heading.**

2b. **From Control Panel Classic view, open the Windows Updates icon.**

   The Windows Update window appears.

3. **Choose the link on the left side of the window, View Update History.**

   A very long list of updates is shown in the View Update History window. Yikes! Look at all them updates!

4. **Close the window when you're done looking at all them updates.**

By looking at the list, you can confirm whether your PC received a vital update. Or, if you need to remove a questionable update, you can confirm that as well. Keep reading in the next section.

Undoing an update

Updates can be uninstalled just like any program can be uninstalled. Refer to the preceding section for information on reviewing the updates. And remove an update only if you're ordered to do so by an authority, such as your local block-watch captain or Commander Cody.

To remove an update — only when you must do so — follow these steps:

1. **Open the Windows Update window.**

   Follow Steps 1 and 2 from the preceding section.

2. **In the lower left part of the window, click the Installed Updates link.**

   The Installed Updates window appears, looking like the regular Uninstall Program window but listing only Windows updates.

3. **Choose the update to remove or uninstall.**

4. **Click the Uninstall toolbar button.**

5. **If prompted, click the Continue button or type the administrator's password, if prompted.**

   Prompting happens for *really serious* updates.

6. **Click the Yes button to confirm.**

At this point, you might return to the window or you might have to restart the computer. Whatever. Heed the directions displayed on the screen. In fact, I recommend restarting Windows in any event, just to ensure that the update is fully removed.

Don't remove an installed update unless you're certain that removing the update will somehow fix a problem that your PC is experiencing.

System Restore under the Hood

The System Restore control center is found in the System Properties dialog box. Here's how to get there from wherever you are:

1. **Open the Control Panel.**

2a. **From the Control Panel Home, choose System and Maintenance and then choose System.**

2b. From Control Panel Classic view, open the System icon.

The System window appears.

3. From the list of tasks in the left part of the window, choose Advanced System Settings.

4. Enter the administrator's password or click the Continue button to, well, continue.

Finally, the System Properties dialog box shows up. (It was easier to get to in the olden days.)

5. Click the System Protection tab.

Finally, you found the control center for System Restore, shown in Figure 23-7. In the Figure, Drive C has System Restore activated, and Drive E does not. (Drive E is an external drive used for backups; see Chapter 26.)

Figure 23-7:
System
Restore is
on and
running.

6. Ensure that there's a check mark by the drives in your computer on which you want to use System Restore.

Unless you're running an alternative System Restore-like utility, keep Windows System Restore on!

7. Close the dialog box and various windows when you're done with them.

The following subsections delve deeper in the System Restore tab of the System Properties dialog box.

✔ To disable System Restore, simply remove any check marks in Step 6 in the preceding set of steps, and then confirm your choice in the dialog box that appears. Even so, I don't recommend disabling System Restore unless you're doing something else on your computer that compensates for the lack of System Restore.

✔ When you turn off System Restore, Windows automatically deletes all restore points for that drive. Don't expect them to magically reappear if you decide to reenable System Restore later!

✔ Also, when System Restore is disabled, the Previous Versions feature in Windows is disabled.

✔ If you're backing up your hard drive regularly, you can go without System Restore, though it's easier to use than performing a restore from a backup. See Chapter 26.

✔ One alternative program to System Restore is the Go Back utility, sold by Symantec (the Peter Norton people).

Chapter 24

Useful Tools and Weapons

· ·

· ·

*N*othing beats charging into a troubleshooting battle when you're armed with an arsenal of appropriate tools and deadly weapons. Windows Vista does not disappoint. Included with your PC's operating system are interesting utilities, useful tools, and valuable programs that will help you on the road toward troubleshooting nirvana. Most of these tools are covered elsewhere in this book. What remains is covered here. Consider it an overview of those interesting and nifty programs you can use to help troubleshoot your PC.

Weapons within Windows

I could write a jolly good reference book on each of the various programs included with Windows. For some of the programs, I'd have to make up some stuff — you know, extra "padding" because writing 380 pages about Notepad would be a bit excessive. But for other tools, the information could easily fill a complete book, along with plenty of tips and tricks. Sadly, I don't have the time to do that (and I'm sure the notion would freak out the sales team), so instead I offer in this section some general overviews of the most helpful of the nifty programs you can use for troubleshooting your PC.

The System Configuration utility (MSCONFIG)

The System Configuration window, shown in Figure 24-1, is your main weapon in fighting the PC's startup battle. This handy window provides a platform from which you can view just about anything that goes on when Windows first starts up.

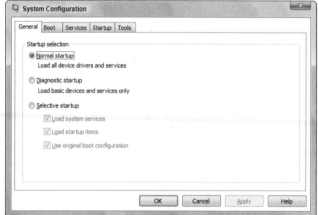

To start the utility, observe these steps:

1. **Summon the Run dialog box.**

   Choose the Run command from the Start menu or press Win+R on the PC keyboard.

2. **Type** MSCONFIG **in the Run dialog box.**

3. **If prompted with a User Account Control, click the Continue button or type the administrator's password.**

   The System Configuration window appears.

The General tab contains three options for starting Windows:

- **Normal Startup:** This option runs the normal Windows startup.
- **Diagnostic Startup:** Run the computer in Safe mode.
- **Selective Startup:** Choose various options to enable or disable during startup (used mostly by tech support).

The Boot tab contains startup information and some initial configuration options for Windows as well as other recognized operating systems.

The Services tab contains a list of services that Windows normally starts, which you can temporarily disable for diagnostic purposes.

Finally, the Startup tab contains programs that Windows automatically starts — programs you don't normally find by choosing Start⇨All Programs⇨ Startup. (Also see Chapter 8.)

Perhaps the most useful tab is the Tools tab. It lists the programs (along with their descriptions) that can help you configure, customize, and troubleshoot Windows. Included in the list are shortcuts to commands that would otherwise be difficult to locate or start.

The System Configuration utility is truly one of the most powerful PC troubleshooting utilities, providing a central location from which you can disable just about anything that happens when Windows starts or start a handy troubleshooting tool.

System Information

The System Information tool knows all, sees all, is all! Om!

The System Information window, shown in Figure 24-2, is where you go when you need to know the complete, honest details about your computer — the system. You can start it from the Tools tab in the System Configuration window; or, from the Run dialog box, type **MSINFO32** and click OK.

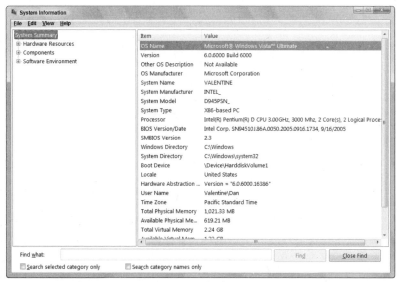

Figure 24-2:
The System
Information
tool.

The System Information window's main job is to report about your computer, as shown in Figure 24-2. This window provides a central location for listing all sorts of information about your computer's hardware, software, and environment and the various applications you run.

For example, to see whether your computer has any hardware conflicts, open the Hardware Resources item (click the [+] to its left) and then select Conflicts/Sharing. The System Information tool then lists any shared or conflicting devices in your computer. (Though there may be conflicts, they don't necessarily indicate that anything is wrong.)

The System File Checker

The System File Checker is perhaps the most powerful tool in Windows, one that is, sadly, neglected by too many people. In fact, if more of those tech-support wieners knew about it, they would rarely recommend reinstalling Windows. Ever!

SFC stands for System File Checker. What it does is verify the condition of the core files that make up the Windows operating system. When any file is missing or corrupted, it's replaced with a fresh new copy. So, in a way, running SFC is like reinstalling Windows, but only when necessary and without having to delete anything.

The SFC utility is a command-line program, and it must be run with administrator privileges. Follow these steps:

1. **Get a copy of the original Windows Vista CD.**

   You must have a copy of the CD to run SFC. This is the original CD you used to install Windows.

   If you don't have the Windows CD, don't run SFC! The program relies on the original CD for replacing files. No CD, no SFC.

2. **From the Start menu, choose All Programs⇨Accessories to display the list of accessory items.**

3. **Right-click the Command Prompt icon.**

4. **From the shortcut menu, choose Run As Administrator.**

5. **Click the Continue button or type the administrator's password to continue from the User Account Control prompt.**

   The command-prompt window appears.

To ensure that you're running the command-prompt window with administrator privileges, confirm that the window title reads Administrator: Command Prompt. If not, try again with Steps 2 through 5.

6. **Type** SFC /SCANNOW **and press the Enter key.**

   That's **SFC**, a space, a slash, and then **SCANNOW** with no space between SCAN and NOW. The line doesn't end in a period. Press the Enter key after confirming that you typed it all correctly.

   Follow the instructions on the screen.

   This operation can take quite a while!

7. **If any files need replacing, SFC asks for the Windows CD to be inserted. It does this so that it can read a replacement file from that disc.**

   Inserting the CD may start the Upgrade or Install program. Just close that window and continue.

   SFC may pull some false alarms and not recognize the CD after it's inserted. If so, click the Retry button. (This may happen several times.)

8. **When SFC is finished, you see another command prompt that's waiting for you to type another command.**

   SFC is done. You can close the command-prompt window.

9. **Type** EXIT **and press the Enter key.**

   The EXIT command closes the command-prompt window.

I recommend running SFC only when you suspect system trouble that even System Restore seems unable to fix. In that case, SFC may be able to pull needed files from the Windows CD and put the system back into order.

I don't recommend running SFC as regular system maintenance! Consider it a disaster-recovery tool only.

Feel free to recommend SFC to your friends who've been unwittingly told by some tech-support nimrod to "reinstall Windows." SFC does the job without having to reinstall Windows.

The Windows Memory Diagnostic

Windows contains a nifty memory-testing tool that's not really on the radar; it's not even mentioned in the System Configuration window's extensive list of tools! But you're reading about it here!

Use the memory diagnostic when you suspect that your PC is having memory issues. These issues include random errors, system crashes, and other weird activities. Windows cannot properly detect such malfunctions on its own because Windows itself must dwell in the same foul RAM that's causing the problem. But the Windows Memory Diagnostic tool can get to the bottom of the situation. Here's how:

1. **Save your stuff!**

    The Windows Memory Diagnostic procedure restarts your PC, so it's best to close up shop now.

2. **Press Win+R to summon the Run dialog box.**

3. **Type** mdsched **into the box and press the Enter key.**

4. **Click the Continue button or type the administrator's password to continue.**

    The Windows Memory Diagnostic Tool window appears.

5. **In the Windows Memory Diagnostic Tool window, choose the option Restart Now and Check for Problems.**

    The Windows Memory Diagnostic screen appears almost immediately when the PC restarts. Memory is checked thoroughly while a display keeps you amused and apprised of the program's progress. Wait.

    When the test is over, the computer automatically restarts.

6. **Log in to Windows as you normally do.**

    The test results are displayed from a pop-up bubble in the notification area, shown in Figure 24-3.

Figure 24-3:
All that late-night studying paid off for the memory test.

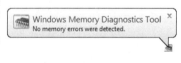

There's nothing you can do to fix bad memory other than replace it. Take the computer to the shop and get all new memory. Maybe even get more memory! Mr. PC would like that.

Welcome to Safe Mode

The only question I have is "Why does Windows need a 'safe' mode?" Shouldn't it be safe to use Windows all the time? And, if it's called Safe mode, does that make the normal mode of operation *Dangerous* mode?"

Once again showing a knack for improperly naming things, Microsoft gives Windows users Safe mode. (It's an industry-wide problem, not just a Microsoft problem, with naming things.) Safe mode really should be called Diagnostic mode or even Slim mode because in Safe mode you can run Windows with no extra drivers or options, which are often the cause of any trouble you may be experiencing.

Starting in Safe mode

You have many ways to get into Safe mode in Windows.

The first way happens under Windows own decree: The computer just starts up in Safe mode. You can tell by the low screen resolution plus the words *Safe mode* in all four corners of the screen, and you might even see the Windows Help system describing Safe mode, as shown in Figure 24-4. When that happens, Windows is telling you that something is wrong. Indeed, it may even announce why it's going into Safe mode before you even see Safe mode.

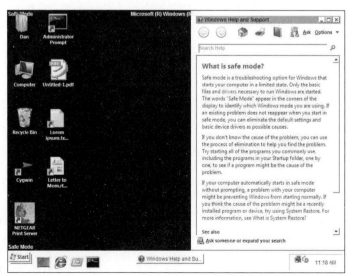

Figure 24-4: Safe mode.

The second way you can enter Safe mode is manually, when the computer starts. Immediately after the *Starting Windows* text message appears, you can press the F8 key to see a Startup menu. (I cover this subject in Chapter 8.) You can select one of the Safe mode options from that menu to start your computer in Safe mode.

Finally, you can direct the computer to start in Safe mode from the System Configuration utility. On the General tab, if you select the Diagnostic startup, Windows starts in Safe mode the next time around. (Conversely, if you would rather have Windows not start in Safe mode, select Normal from the list in the System Configuration utility.)

Accept and realize that you use Safe mode to *fix things*. That's it. You don't work on projects there. You don't gather and reply to e-mail. You fix something and then start the computer in Normal mode.

Fixing things in Safe mode

The idea behind Safe mode is that it's easier to figure out what's wrong with your computer when only Windows itself is running the show. That's because in Safe mode, only Windows is running. No other programs, device drivers, services, or processes are running. Nothing fancy.

In the bare-bones Safe mode environment, you can instantly determine whether Windows is at fault: if the problem persists, Windows is to blame. (Or you have a hardware issue.) But if the problem is gone, you know that it's not Windows but rather some other piece of software or device driver that's crippling your PC.

Another way to put Safe mode to use is in fixing problems that make using your PC impossible. For example, I recommend using Safe mode when someone has changed the settings on the Appearance tab in the display properties so that the text is very small or has changed the graphics so that they're very big or the text is black on a black background. You can fix all these problems in Safe mode and restore those settings.

When the computer just spontaneously goes into Safe mode, check the Device Manager. If your computer has a problem, the disobedient gizmo appears flagged in the hardware list. Open that device by double-clicking it and then read what the problem is. Follow those instructions to fix the problem.

Generally speaking, disabling a device in the Device Manager or reinstalling ("rolling back") an older device driver is the solution that puts the computer back to normal.

Note that you can change just about any Windows settings in Safe mode. Those changes may not appear immediately, as they would when Windows is run normally. The changes are made nonetheless; you see their effects when you restart the computer and return to Normal mode.

✔ Yes, many operations don't work in Safe mode. Those things, such as networking, are disabled to provide a better environment for troubleshooting.

✔ Refer to Chapter 4 for more information on running System Restore to fix problems in Windows.

✔ The changes you make may not have any visual effect in Safe mode, but they have an effect when you return to Normal mode.

Leaving Safe mode

When you finish making Safe mode corrections, simply restart your PC. Do this part properly! Even Safe mode must be restarted in the same manner as you would normally restart Windows.

When your computer comes back to life, the problem should be fixed. Then you can get on with your duties.

If the computer continues to boot into Safe mode, check the Device Manager. Read any startup messages that appear. Open the System Configuration utility (which is covered elsewhere in this chapter) and switch back to the Normal Startup option to see whether that helps.

As a next-to-last resort, connect to the Internet and visit the Microsoft Knowledge Base (refer to Chapter 5) to see whether you can find a solution to your predicament there.

Internet Tools

Hooking your computer up to the Internet is like leaving your car unlocked with the keys dangling in the ignition. Truly, the Internet is a hostile place for the uninformed computer user. It's best to be safe on the Internet, but being safe requires knowing what the potential threats are. After all, cars have keys because doors should be locked and you don't want just anyone starting your car and driving off — especially a teenager!

The main thing you're protecting yourself from on the Internet falls under the category of *malware,* or *mali*cious soft*ware.* For each category of malware, there's a corresponding utility designed to prevent and fight it:

- ✔ Viruses and Trojan horses are fought with antivirus software.

- ✔ Spam and junk e-mail are dealt with by anti-spam tools.

- ✔ Spyware and Internet tracking software are defended against by anti-spyware.

- ✔ Hijacking and home-page-stealing programs are dealt with by anti-hijacking utilities.

- ✔ Probing and infiltrating programs are stopped by firewall protection.

Windows deals with all these problems in the Windows Security Center. The Windows Defender program provides even more help, as does the Windows Firewall. The following sections cover each of these tools.

Windows Security Center

The Windows Security Center is home plate for all things regarding security in Windows — locally, on the network, and on the Internet. To open the Security Center, mind these steps:

1. **Open the Control Panel.**

2a. **From the Control Panel Home, click the link Check the Computer's Security Status beneath the Security heading.**

2b. **From Control Panel Classic view, open the Security Center icon.**

The Security Center window appears, as shown in Figure 24-5. Note that some of the options shown in the figure definitely need attention! (I don't use Windows Firewall because I have a hardware firewall installed.)

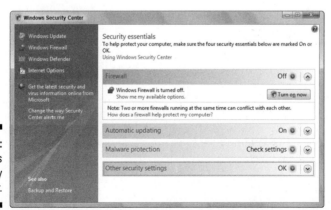

Figure 24-5:
Windows
Security
Center.

3. **Check the status of the firewall.**

   Click the Show Details button to see the firewall status displayed. Also refer to the later section "Windows Firewall."

4. **Check the status of Automatic Updates.**

   I recommend keeping the Automatic Updates option *on.*

5. **Check the status of malware protection.**

   Malware protection involves two different programs: antivirus and, well, "other." Antivirus protection isn't included with Windows, but refer to the section "Aunty virus," later in this chapter. The Windows Defender program provides other malware protection and is covered in the section "Windows Defender."

6. **Check the status of other security settings.**

   The last two items to check are Internet Explorer settings and the User Account Control option.

7. **Close the Windows Security Center window when you're done checking your PC's security.**

   Might I suggest leaving the window open if you continue with the next several sections in this chapter?

Note that the Security Center window also sports a number of handy shortcuts on the left side. Those shortcuts lead to handy locations in Windows where you can continue the battle for your PC's security.

> ✔ The only protection not offered in the Windows Security Center is spam protection. That's really a function of your e-mail software, though a section later in this chapter is devoted to fighting spam: "Anti-spam."

> ✔ If you tire of the Security Center warnings, click the link on the left side of the Security Center window: Change the Way Security Center Alerts Me. From the window that's displayed, choose one of the Don't Notify Me options.

Windows Firewall

The Internet was designed by people who were very trusting of each other. Picture the Internet as a big neighborhood where all the neighbors originally liked each other so well that they not only left their doors and windows unlocked but also left them all open all the time and welcomed guests at all hours. In a trusting environment — and especially one in a nice warm climate where everyone is fit and attractive — that's a perfectly acceptable thing to do. But not these days.

The Internet is still designed with all open doors and windows. To close those doors and windows, you need protection in the form of a firewall. The firewall guards those open doors and windows — officially called *ports* — to limit access both in and out to only those programs you allow.

Windows comes with a firewall called, surprisingly, Windows Firewall. It's a fairly decent program, which you can witness by pursuing these steps:

1. **Open the Control Panel.**

2a. **From the Control Panel Home, choose Security and then choose Windows Firewall.**

2b. **From Control Panel Classic view, open the Windows Firewall icon.**

The Windows Firewall window is shown in Figure 24-6, though again I mention that my PC's firewall is disabled. I explain why in a few paragraphs.

3. **Click the link on the left side of the window, Turn Windows Firewall On or Off.**

The Windows Firewall Settings dialog box appears.

4. **Choose On to turn on the firewall, or Off to disable it.**

5. **Click OK.**

6. **Close the Windows Firewall window when you're done.**

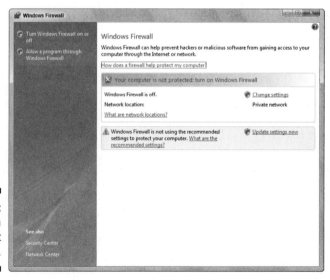

Figure 24-6:
Come on baby, light my firewall.

The idea behind using a firewall is to train it to recognize which programs are okay to use the Internet and which are not. This is done as you use the firewall software. As you do, you see a pop-up window asking whether such-and-such a program can access such-and-such a service on the Internet. You then click a button to allow or deny access. That's how the firewall is trained, and how it works.

The reason I disable the Windows Firewall is that I have another firewall. My Internet connection comes through a router, which includes a hardware firewall. That firewall works just fine, and if you're using a similar setup, you can also disable the Windows Firewall. (There's no point to running two firewalls for your computer; it doesn't make you twice as safe, and it may even cause more problems than it prevents.)

✔ You can also open the Windows Firewall from the Windows Security Center window, as discussed in the preceding section.

✔ When you get a request for Internet access — in or out — from an unknown or unlikely program, the firewall warns you. Click the Deny button. Deny! Deny! Deny! That's how you keep the bad guys out of your computer.

Aunty virus

Viruses are nasty programs that come into your computer to do evil things. They may, for example, program your computer to relay spam, pornography, or unwanted e-mail. The virus may program your computer to attack other computers. Or, it may simply propagate itself, by sending out more viruses to everyone in your e-mail address book. Viruses are nasty!

To protect yourself against viruses, your PC needs antivirus software. This software isn't a part of Windows, though many computer dealers often bundle either the Norton AntiVirus program or the McAfee VirusScan program. Many other sources of antivirus programs are on the Internet. Table 24-1 lists some popular ones.

Table 24-1	Antivirus Programs and Sources
Program	*Web Site*
Avast	www.avast.com
AVG	www.grisoft.com
Kaspersky	www.kaspersky.com
McAfee Virus Protection	www.mcafee.com
Norton AntiVirus	www.symantec.com/avcenter

Use antivirus software to scan your system, but not all the time. Some antivirus programs allow you to manually scan the system every so often. That's good. But, antivirus programs that constantly scan the system waste resources. Unless your computer is in a high-risk situation, such as in a very public place, don't bother with a constant scan.

Configure your antivirus software to scan all incoming files, such as e-mail attachments and programs downloaded from the Internet. Those two doorways are the most common paths for viruses and other nasty programs to mince into your PC.

With antivirus software installed and running on your PC, you have one less thing to worry about and one less major problem to troubleshoot.

- ✔ Cleaning up after a computer virus requires great effort and lots of time. It's not something you want to do. In fact, many folks pay huge sums of money to others to clean up virus messes.

- ✔ Virus programs generally require you to subscribe to a service to keep your computer up-to-date when fighting the latest viruses. Do not neglect to pay for these services! They're worth every penny!

- ✔ You can have two antivirus programs installed on your PC, though you don't run both at the same time. For example, use Norton to do a full system scan, and then use Kaspersky to do the same thing. Often times, one antivirus program catches something the other one misses.

- ✔ Avoid Web-based antivirus scans. Sure, some of them may be good and legitimately do their job. I just don't feel right recommending such a thing to you.

Windows Defender

The Windows Defender program is designed to prevent the hostile takeover or infiltration of your computer system by the forces of evil. I'm proud to say that it does a pretty decent job of that. And if one of the bad guy's henchmen does make it in, it's easy to use Windows Defender to snuff the guy out, James Bond style!

To view the Windows Defender window, regard these steps:

1. **Open the Control Panel.**

2a. **From the Control Panel Home, choose Security and then choose Windows Defender.**

2b. **From Control Panel Classic view, open the Windows Defender icon.**

The Windows Defender window is rather humble, so no illustration is needed. But it should immediately inform you of its last scan for nasty programs. That information should indicate that the computer is running normally. Whew!

3. **To scan for nasty programs at once, click the Scan button on the toolbar.**

   It takes a few minutes for the computer's guts to be scoured. Be patient, and remember that Windows performs a scan automatically. So scan for nasty programs only when you suspect that something is up.

   The real power behind Windows Defender lies in its tools.

4. **Click the Tools button on the toolbar.**

   The Tools and Settings part of the window lists half a dozen nifty things you can do to help protect your computer. One of the handiest things is the Software Explorer, which was also covered over in Chapter 8.

5. **Choose the Software Explorer.**

   The Software Explorer window lets you examine programs running on your PC.

6. **From the Category button menu, choose Currently Running Programs.**

   The list of programs shows only those programs running in your computer. It's a big list, but if your computer has been infected with spyware or has other programs lurking about that shouldn't be, they show up on the list. To kill off a program you believe to be causing trouble, select the program and then click the End Process button.

7. **Close Windows Defender when you're done defending your PC.**

You can also open the Windows Defender window from the Windows Security Center window, as discussed in the section "Windows Security Center," earlier in this chapter.

Anti-spam

I suppose that spam is a common enough term these days that I don't need to explain it, but I will anyway: *Spam* is unwanted e-mail. Or, call it junk e-mail. It floods the average computer user's e-mail inbox every day. In fact, they say that more than 90 percent of all e-mail that's sent is spam, or unwanted and unrequested advertising.

The best way to deal with spam is to create *e-mail filters,* which Windows Mail (and its ancestor, Outlook Express) calls *Mail Rules,* to help weed out which messages are advertising and which are legitimately intended for your own eyeballs. This task can be tough because spam-senders are often very clever at disguising their messages.

How you can tell whether your computer has spyware

The frustrating thing about spyware is that you cannot really tell what is spyware and what isn't. Consider this: Most spyware isn't advertised as such. It's given away freely on the Web, often as some friendly tool or shopping helper. Though some spyware sneaks into your computer, most of it is downloaded by invitation: shopping assistants, calendar minders, free utilities, free wallpaper or desktop backgrounds, free screen savers, or any of a number of seemingly innocent programs.

The problem occurs, and you probably first notice that you have a problem, when you try to uninstall the software you downloaded. That's when you discover that the program keeps coming back — like an unwanted cat! Nothing you try removes the program! You complain to the developer, and it claims that you agreed to keep the program on your computer when you downloaded it — which you did, but who reads all those software licensing agreements?

The next step you need to take is to remove the program. Uninstall it by following the directions in Chapter 22, and then kill the program's process as covered in this chapter's "Windows Defender" section. That should eliminate the problem. Restart Windows and confirm that the program is gone. And in the future, mind what you download from the Internet!

✔ I recommend avoiding those e-mail verification services that require legitimate e-mail users to do a puzzle or reply to a secret message before they can send you e-mail. Although such services work and are popular, many people (such as myself) who are very busy don't have time to deal with such things.

✔ Legitimate e-mail that is misinterpreted as spam is referred to as *ham* by the computer geeks.

Anti-phishing

Here's another problem you need to defend yourself against: phishing scams. Say "fishing" for phishing, and then don't bother asking me where the term came from, though maybe you can pull something from this description: A phishing scam lures people into a false sense of security by baiting them with a phony Web site or e-mail link.

For example, you get a notice that looks like it's from your bank. The notice is alarming: You need to contact the bank (or mortgage broker or credit card company) immediately, or else you will lose *everything!* So you click the link and go to a Web page that looks like your bank. You have to fill in all sorts of information, such as account numbers, Social Security number, and other vital info. But the Web page isn't run by your bank. It's run by the bad guys who collect the information to abuse or sell, costing you time and money.

Internet Explorer helps fight phishing scams by identifying misleading links and known phishing Web sites. To turn on the phishing filter, follow these steps:

1. **In Internet Explorer, use the toolbar's Tools button menu to choose Phishing Filter⇨Turn On Automatic Website Checking.**

   If the submenu says Turn Off Automatic Website Checking, you're done.

2. **In the dialog box that appears, click OK.**

   You're done.

In addition to turning on the phishing filter, you should be careful! The bad guys use *human engineering* to trick you into doing something you normally wouldn't. No bank, mortgage company, government, or any other responsible agency uses the Internet to send important information. Important stuff comes through the mail, or you may get a phone call. Do not let yourself be fooled!

Part IV
Preventive Maintenance

The 5th Wave   By Rich Tennant

"I know my modem's in the microwave.
It seems to increase transmission speed.
Can you punch in 'defrost'? I have a
bunch of e-mails going out."

In this part . . .

Truly, isn't all maintenance preventive? The entire idea behind maintaining anything is to keep it in good operating order. Even more, good maintenance is designed to address those specific issues that most likely will turn into problems when not addressed. It just makes so much sense! Yet people are sadly conditioned not to maintain their stuff.

Let me tell you a secret about your PC: It's a *computer*. True, you can be up on the Internet in minutes. You can create digital photography. You can listen to music. But it's still a computer, and it requires the same type of maintenance as was done to those behemoth computers back in the 1960s. Maintenance is necessary! The chapters in this part of the book explain how it's done.

Chapter 25

Maintaining the Hard Drive

• •

In This Chapter

▶ Finding hard drive tools

▶ Fixing hard drive problems

▶ Defragmenting the hard drive

▶ Saving hard disk space

▶ Running the Disk Cleanup program

▶ Reviewing scheduled maintenance

• •

*Y*our PC's storage system is more than disk drives. That's because storage on a PC (and I'm talking *permanent,* or long-term, storage, not computer memory) is growing more and more solid state. But in the bad old days, everything was a disk: floppy, hard, or CD. Even so, among all this storage, the most important place where you put stuff is the hard drive. Obviously, maintaining that hard drive is the key to being a happy computer owner. This chapter helps show you how that's done.

Hard Drive Maintenance Tools

Windows gives you two tools for maintaining your hard drive and helping its performance: Check Disk and Defrag.

 The Check Disk utility is used to scan a hard drive for errors, potential problems, and damage. It then tries to fix the situation as best it can.

 The Defrag utility is used to optimize the hard drive's performance.

A third disk maintenance tool is Backup. It's covered in Chapter 26. But Check Disk and Defrag are covered right here, in this chapter and in this section.

- ✔ Check Disk and Defrag aren't the best tools available for maintaining your hard drive. You can find better versions of these tools in third-party utilities, such as the Norton Utilities Disk Doctor and Disk Optimization tools.

- ✔ Another good alternative for the Defrag tool is Vopt ("vee-opt"), from Golden Bow Systems:

  ```
  www.goldenbow.com
  ```

- ✔ Hard disk performance decreases as the amount of stuff on your hard drive increases. You can't do anything about this; it's just a simple truth. It takes longer to access and sift through more information than it does for just a little information.

Accessing the tools

Windows keeps all its hard drive tools near the bosom of your PC's hard drives. Here's how to get at that common tool chest:

1. **Open the Computer window.**

   You can open the Computer icon on the desktop or choose Computer from the Start menu.

2. **Right-click the icon for hard drive C.**

   Or, you can open any hard drive's icon, such as Drive D, if you want to use the tools on that hard drive instead.

   Note that these tools are available for use only on a hard drive.

3. **Choose Properties from the pop-up menu.**

4. **Click the Tools tab.**

   You see a list of the three common disk maintenance tools, as shown in Figure 25-1. The error-checking tool is Check Disk. The defragmenting tool is Defrag. And then you see a button for backup, if your version of Windows has Backup installed.

The following subsections cover the tools found on the Tools tab in the disk drive's Properties dialog box.

Figure 25-1:
Where
Windows
hides the
disk tools.

Is not the hard drive riddled with errors?

The Check Disk program is designed to check for and repair common errors on a hard drive. It's not really a performance-enhancing tool. And, unlike previous versions of Windows, this Check Disk program is *serious*. It works only when you first start your computer, not on the fly. This is a good thing. Follow these steps:

1. **Click the Check Now button in the hard drive's Properties dialog box.**

   Refer to the preceding section for details.

2. **If prompted, type the administrator's password or click the Continue button.**

   The teeny Check Disk dialog box opens, as shown in Figure 25-2. Feel free to check either option in the dialog box, which merely expands upon the problems that Check Disk looks for (and adds time to the total operation).

3a. **For any drive other than drive C (or any drive in use), click the Start button.**

   The Check Disk operation proceeds. Skip down to Step 4.

Check Disk Local Disk (C:)

Check disk options

☑ Automatically fix file system errors
☐ Scan for and attempt recovery of bad sectors

Start   Cancel

Figure 25-2:
Starting
Check Disk.

3b. For drive C, or any drive in use, click the Start button.

Windows is unable to check drive C at once; the check is scheduled for the next time the computer starts: Click the button to schedule Check Disk when the computer restarts. You can then restart Windows and watch Check Disk in action at startup. Yes, it will be in text mode, as are any warnings.

When Check Disk is done, the computer restarts. Log in to Windows as you normally do; you're done.

4. Review the summary information.

5. Click the Close button.

You can close the Properties dialog box and Computer window as well.

Does Check Disk increase performance? No. It fixes errors. So, if the errors are stopping up performance, Check Disk improves things. For the most part, running Check Disk doesn't make anything run faster.

✔ You have to check each hard drive in your system individually. Keep in mind that just checking Drive C, for example, doesn't ensure that Drive D has also been checked.

✔ Oh, yeah, choosing that option to scan and recover bad sectors causes the operation to take a *really* long time to complete.

✔ Sometimes, Check Disk runs automatically when the computer first starts up, especially if the computer was suddenly, unexpectedly, or improperly shut down. This is a good thing.

✔ The Norton Disk Doctor utility does some of the same things as Check Disk, but in a more cautious and thorough manner. Disk Doctor is also capable of recovering from some errors that seize Check Disk cold.

Fragment me not

Defragmenting a hard drive isn't only a necessary maintenance tool, but also a performance-boosting one. By eliminating most fragmented files and reshuffling popular files to the beginning of the disk (like the head of the line), you see a modest performance improvement.

File fragments aren't bad things. Windows tries to make the best use of the hard drive, so what it does is to split some files into smaller pieces — *fragments* — so that disk space is used more efficiently. But, all those little pieces require overhead to keep track of and to reassemble when the file is accessed. After a while, disk space may still be used efficiently, but disk performance drops like the GPA of two teenagers in love. To fix the problem, you need to run a tool like Defrag every so often.

The good news is that Windows automatically defrags your PC's hard drives. You really don't have to do a thing. But if you feel compelled, you can pull a manual defrag. Here's how:

1. **From the Start menu, choose All Programs⇨Accessories⇨System Tools⇨Disk Defragmenter.**

2. **If prompted, type the administrator's password or click the Continue button.**

   The Disk Defragmenter window appears, as shown in Figure 25-3. It confirms what I just wrote — defragmentation is a regularly scheduled activity in Windows. If you're happy with that, you can skip to Step 5. Otherwise, continue with Step 4.

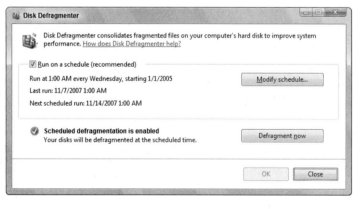

Figure 25-3: Thrill-a-minute disk defragmenting goes on here.

3. **Click the Defragment Now button.**

Oops! Now it tells you: This may take from a few minutes to a few hours. Go grab some cocoa.

Yes, unlike in the olden days, there's no graphical display to entertain you while the disk defragments.

It's best to do nothing while the disk is defragmented. In fact, that's why Windows schedules defragmenting for late at night, when the computer is supposed to be doing nothing (but I have my doubts).

When the process is over (and it took three hours on my PC), you see . . . nothing! The window just returns to normal, and you get that same feeling you have after watching your first "art film" upon realizing *that was it.*

4. **Close the Disk Defragmenter window.**

Refer to the later section "Regularly Scheduled Maintenance" for information on how the defragment process is automated.

Increasing Hard Drive Storage

Another potential problem with a hard drive is that disk space quickly runs dry! At first, this situation is suspect with me because today's hard drives can hold oodles of information; it would take a busy person lots of time to fill things up. But, with popular graphics files, videos, and especially online music, you can see the free space on a 150GB hard drive dwindle like you would watch ice melt in the sun.

Checking disk space

To quickly peek at your hard drive's disk usage situation in both numerical and graphical terms, use the disk drive's Properties dialog box, as shown in Figure 25-4.

To see this dialog box, comply with these directions:

1. **Open the Computer window.**

Open the Computer icon on the desktop or choose Computer from the Start menu.

2. **Right-click a hard drive icon in the Computer window.**

For example, choose the famous drive C.

3. **Choose Properties from the pop-up menu.**

4. **Click the General tab in the Properties dialog box.**

   The Used Space and Free Space information details disk usage down to the last byte. And that lovely pie chart (I'm guessing it's grape pie, though it could be blueberry pie with an Iron Chef-worthy grape crust), graphically details how much space is used and remaining on your PC's hard drive.

5. **Click OK to close the Properties dialog box when you're done.**

6. **Oh, and also close the Computer window.**

7. **And clean those baseboards! My! Imagine what my mother would say about that.**

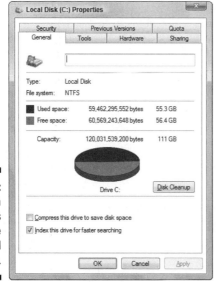

Figure 25-4: Gauging a hard drive's available and used space.

Some space-saving suggestions

If you're collecting more than one type of a specific file — such as graphics, video, or music files — consider putting all that stuff on recordable optical discs: CD-R or DVD-R. Archiving is the name of the game! Just wait until you have a collection of enough files (more than 500MB, for example), and then burn 'em all on a CD-R.

If you absolutely must have all that stuff on a hard drive, however, consider getting a second hard drive for your computer. External USB hard drives are cheap and easy to install. A second hard drive is a valuable addition, specifically when space is scarce.

Finally, *do not* use disk compression on your hard drive to get more space. In the hard drive's Properties dialog box (refer to Figure 25-4), note the item labeled Compress This Drive to Save Disk Space. Avoid it! Do not put a check mark there! Compressed hard drives are something I never want to troubleshoot. Please buy a second hard drive before you dream about compressing.

✔ You can also buy a second, internal hard drive for your PC, which is often cheaper than the external model. Installing it is something your dealer can best do for you.

✔ After you burn your stuff to an optical disc, you can freely delete it from the hard drive and save yourself oodles of space.

✔ The most common disk compression troubleshooting question I get is "How can I uncompress 95GB of data from my 80GB drive?" My answer is "Only by getting a second, larger hard drive" — which, incidentally, is one of my earlier suggestions. That would have saved some time.

Disk cleanup

Your greatest weapon in the hard drive space battle — the Death Star laser, if you will — is the Disk Cleanup tool. It puts several handy features in one place, which allows you to instantly reclaim lots of hard drive space in one easy step. Here you go:

1. **Click the Start button thing.**

2. **From the Start menu, choose All Programs⇨Accessories⇨System Tools⇨Disk Cleanup.**

   Windows modestly asks which files you want to clean up. (Yes, that sentence ends with a preposition, but keep in mind that they're programmers and not copy editors.) My advice is to clean up your files if you're just in a spring-cleaning mood, but otherwise you want all the space you can grab, so:

3. **Choose Files from All Users on This Computer.**

4. **Type the administrator's password or click the Continue button to continue.**

5. **Click OK to select Drive C, or choose another drive from the drop-down list.**

   A brief analysis is made. Sit and hum.

   Eventually, results are posted in a dialog box, as shown in Figure 25-5. Note the items you can select *plus* how much disk space is freed by selecting them. In the figure, you see that 1.67 gigabytes of crap is waiting to vanish. Wow!

Figure 25-5:
A few of the
many items
needing
cleaning.

6. **Click to check off those items you want to delete, and thereby clean up disk space.**

7. **Click the More Options tab.**

   Holy smokes! More options. Who would have guessed?

   The Clean Up button in the Programs and Features area opens the Programs and Features window, where you can remove programs you seldom use. Refer to Chapter 22 for more info.

   The Clean Up button in the System Restore and Shadow Copies area displays a dialog box that lets you wipe out all recent restore points (except for the most recent one). I recommend that operation only when disk space is really, *really* tight.

8. **Click the Disk Cleanup tab.**

   You're now ready to roll.

9. **Click the OK button.**

   Are you being serious? Actually, I think the Delete Files message comes from the Recycle Bin, but I'm not really certain.

10. **Click the Delete Files button.**

    And you're done. That's it.

Now go back and check your disk space pie chart, as covered in the section "Checking disk space," earlier in this chapter. You should see more pie, and more pie is good!

✔ Click the View Files button to review what's being deleted before you click the OK button. This button appears only when certain file categories are chosen from the scrolling list.

✔ The Downloaded Programs option refers to internal upgrades (add-ons or plug-ins) for Internet Explorer. The option doesn't refer to any shareware or other utility you have downloaded.

Other things to try

Please, O, please, don't sit and stew over your disk space usage. The disk is there for you to use, and Windows works fine with a nearly full hard drive. In fact, if space gets too low, Windows lets you know. If you're like most people, your computer will most likely die before you get a chance to fill up its hard drive.

Even so, and even with Disk Cleanup and all that, you can try a few more things to keep disk space usage low:

Decrease the size of the Internet cache. See the section "Adjusting the temporary file size" in Chapter 18.

Decrease the space used by the Recycle Bin. Here's how you can change the disk space allocation for your deleted files:

1. **Right-click the Recycle Bin icon on the desktop.**

   Or, choose Recycle Bin from the menu button on any address bar in any folder window and then right-click in that window.

2. **Choose Properties from the shortcut menu.**

   The Recycle Bin Properties dialog box is displayed, as shown in Figure 25-6. Settings for each disk drive in your system are listed, but they can be changed to help save disk space.

3. **Enter a new value in the Maximum Size text box.**

   The less space you allocate for the Recycle Bin, the more room you have for your junk. I suggest simply cutting in half whatever value is currently displayed. That's a good start.

4. **Click OK after making your adjustments.**

Remove the Online Services folder. Many new computers come with a folder named Online Services. It may be on the desktop directly, or it may be a folder in the Program Files folder. Wherever — it's something you can freely delete.

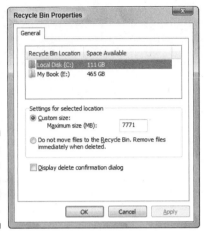

Recycle Bin Properties

General

Recycle Bin Location	Space Available
Local Disk (C:)	111 GB
My Book (E:)	465 GB

Settings for selected location

◉ Custom size:
Maximum size (MB):   7771

◯ Do not move files to the Recycle Bin. Remove files immediately when deleted.

☐ Display delete confirmation dialog

[OK]   [Cancel]   [Apply]

Figure 25-6:
Setting the Recycle Bin's allocation.

The Online Services folder contains program stubs that let you sign on to various online services, such as AOL, CompuServe, and whatever else is out there. If you don't plan on using those services, zap that folder.

If you get a warning about deleting program files, it's okay. Those programs install only larger programs that you don't plan on using anyway. Yes, you have my permission to delete them — despite my constant admonition never to delete any file you didn't create yourself.

Regularly Scheduled Maintenance

Windows Vista is quite smart when it comes to hard drive maintenance. It's automatically configured. There's really nothing more that you need to do, though I recommend taking a peek to see what's up with the schedule. Here's what you can do:

1. **Summon the Run dialog box.**

   Press Win+R on the keyboard to bring forth the Run dialog box in an expeditious manner.

2. **Type** mmc taskschd.msc **and click the OK button.**

3. **Click Continue or type the administrator's password to proceed.**

   The Windows Task Scheduler appears, as shown in Figure 25-7.

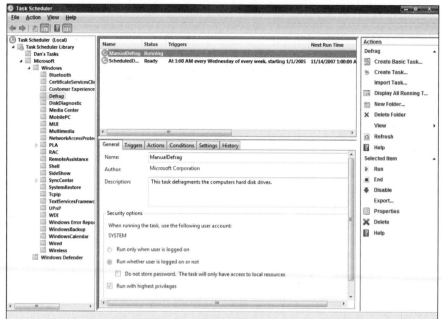

Figure 25-7:
See? Defrag
does run
automati-
cally.

4. **From the folder tree on the left, open Task Scheduler Library, Microsoft, Windows, and finally Defrag.**

   Information about the scheduled Defrag task is listed in the center part of the window, as shown in Figure 25-7. There's really little you can do here other than look.

5. **Close the Task Scheduler window when you're done looking.**

If you really want to schedule your own disk maintenance or modify whatever Windows set up, consider buying another one of my books! I recommend *Find Gold in Windows Vista* (Wiley). Not only is it a page-turner, but you also learn even more about Windows Vista than I could possibly put in this book.

Chapter 26

The Benefits of Backup

1’ve been writing about backup longer than any other computer topic. Backup is an ancient, tried, and worthy technology — simple, really — and it can save your butt better than just about any other digital butt-saving trick. Nothing beats backup as far as reliability is concerned. In fact, backup’s number-one enemy is *you*. Writing about backup is easy. Getting people to actually back up their computers is a task from which even Hercules would flee.

Are you one of the few who backs up computer data? Probably not. Keep reading anyway. Thanks to advancing technology, and cheap external hard drives, backing up today is simple and effortless. Despite that simplicity and all the benefits of backing up, I still consider it a vain task to write *another* chapter on backing up your computer. If you’re still reading, count yourself among the few and blessed.

> ✔ This chapter covers backing up using the Windows Vista Backup and Restore Center, though the general philosophy applies to any PC backup program.
>
> ✔ This chapter does not cover using Backup’s productive half, Restore. Refer to Chapter 4 for information on Restore.

The Backup Philosophy

As far as software goes, the basic backup program is pretty simple. It’s merely a file copying program. The reason for making copies is safety: After backing up, you have two copies of all your stuff — one for using and one “just in case.” Imagine how backing up stuff in your personal life would come in handy if you were able to duplicate your car keys, glasses, homework, and furniture, for example. In fact, backing up everything in real life would probably devastate the insurance industry overnight.

Backing up your stuff

When you back up, you're making a duplicate copy of all your computer stuff: operating system, programs, files — all of it. The duplicate, or *backup* copy, dwells outside your computer system, on digital media, on optical disc (CD or DVD), or perhaps on a network or external hard drive. That way, the data is free from the confines — and potential perils — of dwelling inside your PC.

After you have the safety copy of your stuff, you can continue working. As long as you adhere to a regular backup schedule, you know that a copy of your stuff exists, safe and elsewhere. If disaster strikes (take your pick of disaster), you can rest assured that a safety copy of whatever was destroyed still exists and is available for recovery.

In fact, even the most fatal disaster — a complete hard drive failure — isn't a problem for Backup. Just replace the old hard drive with a new one, and then use the backup program to *restore* everything. (The topic of restoring from a backup is covered in Chapter 4.)

The Backup program

You don't need to use a backup program to perform a backup. Because a backup is simply a secondary copy, you can use Windows itself to simply drag folders and icons over to a waiting DVD-R. That's really all there is. But with a backup program, you get more.

Modern backup programs not only copy files, they can also

- Choose to back up only files created or modified since the last backup
- Schedule backups to happen when you're away from the computer
- Compress backed-up files so that they occupy less disk space

The backup program also provides a restore tool for resurrecting backed-up files or even restoring your entire computer if the unthinkable happens.

A backup program is included in Windows Vista. It's not a specific program, but rather a Control Panel item that oversees backups and restores. The Backup and Restore Center is covered later in this chapter.

Third-party backup programs exist, some offering fancier features and more flexibility than what comes with Windows Vista. These backup programs all work the same, though only the Windows Vista way of doing things is covered specifically in this book.

The backup routine

To make backing up work, you must establish a routine. It works like this:

Full backup: Once every week or month (depending on how much you use your computer), you do a full backup. You back up every dang doodle file on the computer.

Incremental backup: Every day you back up only those files that have been created or modified since the last full backup.

The philosophy here is that all your bases are covered without wasting any time or storage. To recover a file, you find the file in either an incremental backup set or back in the full backup set.

Of course, there are variations on this theme. For example, it's probably impractical to back up the *entire* storage system. You really need to back up only your data; the operating system and your program files can be restored from the original discs or from a set of recovery discs. Still, not every PC comes with recovery discs, so maybe a full backup of everything is required once, and only a full backup of just your stuff is required after that.

- ✔ There's no need to back up the applications installed on your computer; it's easier just to reinstall them. No, the most important thing on your computer is your data — the stuff you created and stored.

- ✔ You can restore Windows and your software only if you have a copy of the original installation CD or a reinstall disc that came with the computer. Don't throw that stuff out!

- ✔ Keep copies of all the software you install on your computer. I keep the original CDs in the boxes the software came in.

Backup media

The main storage media being backed up in a computer is the hard drive. Many backup programs, including Windows Vista Backup, refuse to let you back up to the same device you're backing up. That may sound confusing, but look at it this way: You cannot save money when your wallet is stolen by simply moving the bills around within your wallet. Nope, you need a different storage place. Backup does, too.

Various backup terms

Backup programs may use some interesting terminology. Sometimes the backup manual explains the terms; sometimes it doesn't. If not, here are my own handy definitions of various backup terms.

@#$%&*!: You utter this phrase when you realize how useful backing up could have been to save your butt, but you were lazy and thought not to back up.

Archive bit/archive attribute: This is information about a file that's used primarily for backing up. The archive bit, or a file's archive *attribute,* is *on,* or *set,* when the file has been created or modified since the last backup. The backup program itself resets the archive attribute, turning it off, which means that the file has been backed up.

Archive: This word is a more professional-sounding term for a backup copy.

Copy: Files are backed up, but they're not marked as having been backed up, as they would be for a full backup.

Differential backup: This type is the same as an Incremental backup, where only files modified since the last backup are archived; however, unlike an incremental backup, the backed-up files are *not* marked as having been backed up.

Full backup: This term refers to a complete backup of the entire PC storage system, which generally means the main hard drive plus any other hard drives. All the backed-up files are marked "backed up" by the computer. That way, you can easily spot new files created after the backup was made.

Incremental backup: This term refers to a backup of only those files created or modified since the last full backup.

Specific backup: Only those files that are selected are backed up.

Backup programs spin their digital duplicates onto separate media — hopefully, media located outside the computer box. Traditionally, removable media is used for backing up. The variety of devices describes a wee bit of computer history:

Floppy disk: Way back when, floppy disks were used to back up a computer. This method made sense when the typical hard drive was 20MB and each floppy disk stored about 1.5MB of data.

Tape: Tape drives predate personal computers, but for a while, having a tape drive in your PC for backup purposes made sense. Tapes are still available for backup, but they tend to be for high-end computers and not for PCs.

Optical media: For a while, the CD-R or CD-RW was popular, but now the optical backup media of choice is the DVD-R or DVD-RW (or the +R variations).

Network or external disk drive: Having a second disk drive *outside* the PC is preferred for backup. An external drive can be connected by a USB or IEEE cable, or it may be a hard drive attached to your computer network.

The best choice for backing up is an external hard drive or a hard drive on the network. The top reasons are that the drive is roomy and fast and always available. The other choices are fine as well, but you may find yourself filling up a CD or DVD and having to replace it several times to complete the backup. That's one of the pains that prevents most people from ever backing up their PCs. No, an external disk drive or disk drive on the network is the preferred choice.

Windows Vista Backup

Windows Vista doesn't really have a backup program. No, it's more of a backup procedure than a separate program. In fact, there are two locations in Windows Vista where you find backup:

✔ The Backup and Restore Center in the Control Panel, shown in Figure 26-1.

✔ A program named Backup Status and Configuration, which is found on the Start menu: All Programs➪Accessories➪System Tools, as shown in Figure 26-2.

Both windows serve overlapping purposes, and it's rather confusing to have the two separate locations. Even so, my experience shows that the Backup and Restore Center is where you want to go.

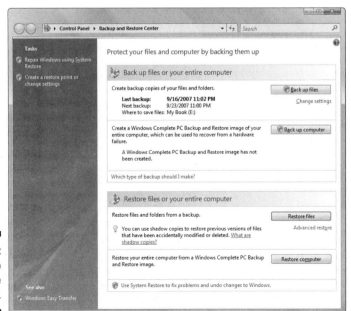

Figure 26-1:
The Backup and Restore Center.

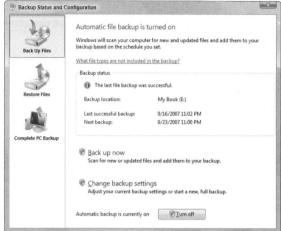

Figure 26-2:
Backup
status and
configu-
ration.

Visiting the Backup and Restore Center

The Backup Status and Configuration window (refer to Figure 26-2) may look like it's a good place to start your backup adventure, but most of the things you do there lead back to the Backup and Restore Center window (refer to Figure 26-1). So why not start there?

Open the Backup and Restore Center window in the Control Panel: From the Control Panel Home, click the link Back Up Your Computer, found beneath the System and Maintenance title. From Control Panel Classic view, open the Backup and Restore Center icon.

Note that the Backup and Restore Center window is divided into three parts. On the left is the traditional task list. On the right, at the top, is the Backup area. On the bottom is the Restore area.

The Backup area lists information about any recent backups performed on your computer. It also lists when the next scheduled backup will occur, if regularly scheduled backups have been configured.

The Backup and Restore Center is where you conduct most of your backup and restore operations. Before starting anything, however, you should configure the backup program.

Configuring Backup

To ensure that Backup is doing what you want it to do, you need to step through some configuration options. Obey these steps:

1. **Summon forth the Backup Status and Configuration window.**

   Specific directions are found earlier in this chapter.

2. **Choose Back Up Files on the left side of the window.**

3. **Choose Set Up Automatic File Backup.**

   If this item isn't visible, then Backup has already been configured. You can choose the option Change Backup Settings to make modifications, if necessary.

4. **If necessary, enter the administrator's password or click the Continue button.**

   The Backup Files window appears.

   Your first step is to set the backup media, the location for the archival copy of your stuff. You have two main choices:

   - On an external hard drive or optical media (CD or DVD)

   - On a hard drive located on the network

   My recommendation is to choose an external hard drive or the network drive. Optical discs are okay for quick backups, but large backups require you to "sit and shuffle" discs as the backup occurs — which also implies that you cannot do an automatic backup late at night unless you plan on sitting there. Nope, external drives are best.

5. **Click the Next button.**

6. **If prompted, enter the network drive's password.**

   Don't get frustrated here. If the drive isn't password-protected or you just can't seem to enter a password, go out and buy an external hard drive and start the process over again using the external drive.

7. **Choose which types of files to back up.**

   I choose everything on the list, except for TV Shows I've Recorded from Windows Media Player. They occupy too much space, and, honestly, if I really want a backup, I'll go out and purchase the series DVD.

8. **Click the Next button.**

9. **Set the regular backup schedule.**

   Choose how often you want Windows to perform an automatic backup. Again, when you use an external hard drive, the backup can take place automatically and unattended. (And that's as long as you keep your PC on all the time, as I do.)

10. **Click the button Save Settings and Backup.**

    If you're making modifications to existing backup settings, then the button is titled Save Settings And Exit.

11. **Close the Backup Status and Configuration window.**

You're done.

The backup is configured and ready to go, but I recommend that you create a full backup before relaxing into your "I'm safe because I have regular backups scheduled" comfort zone.

> ✔ You can check the progress of your backups by opening the Backup and Restore Center window to review the time, success, or failure of the most recent automatic backup.
>
> ✔ If you (against my advice) choose to back up to a DVD or CD, ensure that the proper disc is in the PC's optical drive, waiting and ready to accept the regularly scheduled backup.

Running a manual backup

After configuring automatic backups (refer to the preceding section), you really don't have to worry about backing up your computer; the backups happen automatically on the schedule you specify. But if you feel the need to create a manual backup *right now,* you can do so by following these steps:

1. **Open the Backup and Restore Center window.**

2. **Click the Back Up Files button.**

Instantly, the computer performs a regular backup. (Yes, you can continue using the computer while the files are backed up.)

The reasons for performing an unscheduled backup or a manual backup are many. For example, if you just finished a huge project and want to ensure that you have a backup, you can create a manual backup.

When the backup is complete, an annoying pop-up bubble alerts you.

Backing up a project

One area where the Windows Vista Backup falls short is backing up a specific clutch of files. For example, you may want to back up only one set of folders, say, containing your current project. If so, you're out of luck using Backup.

For an alternative solution, you can perform a regular file copy instead. Although it's not automatic, and it lacks some of the bells and whistles of a true backup, the file copy gets the job done for you. See the section "Backing Up without Backup Software" later in this chapter.

Doing a Full Backup (Windows Complete PC Backup)

At least once in your lifetime, you should back up your entire PC. All of it. Every ding dang byte. To accomplish that, Windows Vista comes with the Windows Complete PC Backup program. But take heed! Windows Complete PC Backup is available only with the Ultimate, Business, and Enterprise versions of Windows Vista. Yep, that means if you have Windows Vista Home — even Home Premium — you don't have the Windows Complete PC Backup feature.

Providing that you do have the proper version of Windows Vista, follow these steps to completely backup your PC's data:

1. **Open the Backup and Restore Center.**

2. **Click the button aptly named Back Up Computer.**

3. **If necessary, enter the administrator's password or click the Continue button.**

   The Windows Complete PC Backup program begins.

4. **Choose the backup media.**

   Again, I highly recommend an external hard drive. Note that the drive must be formatted with NTFS, or else the backup program gets all bitchy.

5. **Review the settings.**

   The most important setting in this case happens when you choose to back up to DVDs: the program specifies how many DVDs you need. On my PC, the number is between 7 and 12. That's a lot of DVDs, and it implies a lot of time that I'll need to spend sitting there and swapping DVDs during the entire process. Again — it's ample reason to use an external hard drive rather than DVDs.

6. **Click the Start Backup button.**

   Heed the advice on the screen and begin your backup.

The Windows Complete PC Backup is not the same as the regularly scheduled backup that the Backup and Restore Center normally performs. It's a special type of backup — one that may truly save your butt someday if ultimate disaster strikes your PC.

You can also run Windows Complete PC Backup from the Backup Status and Configuration window: Click the big Complete PC Backup button on the lower-left side. (Refer to Figure 26-2.)

Converting an external drive to NTFS

Most external drives come preformatted with the FAT32 file system. That's okay for most uses, but for backup, you need to convert the file over to the NTFS format. Doing so is easy, and it doesn't destroy your data. In fact, I'm curious about why it's not an easy option that's present in the Backup program window itself, but Microsoft doesn't pay me to think outside the box for them.

To convert the external hard drive to NTFS, follow these steps:

1. From the Start menu, open All Programs⇨ Accessories.

2. Right-click the Command Prompt item.

3. Choose Run As Administrator from the pop-up menu.

4. Type the administrator's password or click the Continue button to continue.

   An administrator command prompt window appears.

5. Type the following command:

   `convert n: /fs:ntfs`

   Replace *n* with the drive letter of the hard drive to convert. For example, if the external hard drive uses drive letter D, you type this command:

   `convert d: /fs:ntfs`

6. Review what you typed.

   If you made a mistake, press the Backspace key to erase and carefully type the command again.

7. Press the Enter key.

   The conversion process takes a few minutes, but not that long.

8. Close the Command Prompt window when you're done.

Backing Up without Backup Software

To merely *copy* a group of files (to back up without using backup software), you just need to drag and drop the clutch of icons from one disk to another — from the hard drive to an optical disc or to an external hard drive, network drive, or any other storage media that can handle the load. It works.

The manual backup process has two limitations. The first is that it's up to you to determine whether all the files will fit on the destination media. For example, you cannot copy 1,300MB of your stuff to a 720MB CD-R disc. It just doesn't work. Ditto for copying 3GB of music to a 1GB flash drive. No amount of suitcase-sitting gets those extra bytes on the disc. No way!

The second limitation is simply automation: "Real" backup software automates the process. Plus, it may even let the backup span across multiple discs, which certainly saves some time.

Part V
The Part of Tens

The 5th Wave   By Rich Tennant

"Well, that's the third one in as many clicks. I'm sure it's just a coincidence. Still, don't use the Launcher again until I've had a look at it."

In this part . . .

On the planet Zwlnyx, the sentient beings have 14 fingers on each hand. Therefore, the Zwlnyxian translation of every *For Dummies* book contains a Part of Twenty-Eights. Those poor Zwlnyx authors have to come up with 18 more items for their lists, more than we human authors do. And you should hear them complain! At the last Dummies Author Festival, they went on and on in their screeching twang. I felt so badly for the Wiley Publishing reps who had to sit through it all.

Fortunately, humans have only ten fingers, and our *For Dummies* books feature a Part of Tens. As an author, I consider this a blessing. Therefore, the chapters snuggled in this section contain ten tips, tricks, suggestions, or ideas, all of which are geared toward troubleshooting your PC.

Chapter 27

The Ten Rules of Tech Support

1 believe that you'll find the task of phoning tech support made all the easier if you keep the following rules in mind.

Don't Use Technical Support as an Excuse for Not Reading the Manual or Using the Help System

Always look up your problem first in the online help. Second, visit the company's Web site and look for a Technical Support link, FAQ list, or troubleshooter. If you can find the answer there, great! Even if you don't, the tech-support people will appreciate that you have made the effort.

Have Something to Write On

This advice not only gives you a pad to doodle on while you wait on hold, but having something to write on also means that you can take down notes and instructions as you're given them. You may also need to write down a case number when your issue is unresolved and you need to call back. That saves a great deal of repetition later and helps serve as a record of your tech-support call.

Be Nice

Each new call is a mystery to the tech-support person. The person doesn't know you, doesn't know your problem, and doesn't know how long you have been waiting on hold. None of those things is that person's fault, and he doesn't need to hear you scream about any of it.

The tech-support person is there to help you. That person didn't cause the problem and isn't out to get you. The friendlier and more informative you can be, the better for the other person.

Be Sure to Get the Person's Name and a Number Where You Can Call Back

Before diving into the problem, get some basic information about your tech-support person. Generally speaking, the person says his name when he answers the phone: "This is Rajanikant in technical support. How can I help you?" Write down *Rajanikant* on your notepad.

If possible, ask for a direct line on which to call back in case the call breaks off. Sometimes they have it, and sometimes they don't. Accept whatever answer the person gives you.

✔ If a tech-support person says that he doesn't have a direct line or that he cannot be contacted directly, it's most likely a lie. Don't get mad! The company typically has a policy not to give out direct lines, so he's being forced to lie on purpose. This is policy, not an excuse to ignore you.

✔ You can also try to get an employee number up front.

Prepare: Do the Research before You Call

Exhaust every possibility and potential solution on your own before you phone tech support. Ensure that you're referring to items by their proper terms. If not, carefully describe what they look like.

Have These Items Handy: Serial Number, Order Number, Customer Number

Often, tech support needs confirmation of who you are and that you have a legitimate product before you can continue. You should get items like serial numbers beforehand — especially if the serial number is on the computer's butt and the computer's butt is up against the wall under your table.

It also helps to know which version of Windows you're using. Do this:

1. **Click the Start button.**

2. **Choose the Run command.**

   Or, press the Win+R key combination, which summons the Run dialog box.

3. **Type** WINVER **into the text box.**

4. **Click OK.**

   The WinVer program displays a dialog box that details which version of Windows you're using.

You may also see which is your PC's optical drive, whether it's D or E or whatever.

Don't Spill Your Guts

The tech-support person needs to know about the problem, not about the doom and peril that await you if you can't get your computer working in time. Remember that most tech-support people are under the clock; they may have only 12 minutes to deal with you, so be as direct as possible.

Be Patient

Tech support always assumes that you don't know anything about your computer. Don't bother saying, "But I really know computers. My wife calls me a 'computer genius.'" That doesn't speed things up!

Often, tech-support people must follow a script and check things off despite your insistence that you have already done such a thing or another. Just follow along and eventually they catch up with you.

Get a Case Number

Before the call is over, try to get a case number, especially if the result is inconclusive or doesn't meet with your liking. The case number ensures that the next time you call, the support person can read over the incident, and you have less repeating and reexplaining to do.

- ✔ You don't need a case number if the problem is solved.
- ✔ Some tech-support people give case numbers whether the problem is solved or not. Write it down and keep track of it for later.

Thank the Person

Whether your tech-support person solves the problem or not, thank the person for her time and effort in assisting you. I'm not sure why, but it's just one of those things that was beaten into me as a child. (Heck, I even thanked the bullies who stole my lunch money.)

Chapter 28

Ten Dumb Error Messages

*H*oo, boy, this could be one long chapter! If only computers had just ten dumb error messages. But they don't. They have thousands. Back when I wrote the original *DOS For Dummies* (in 1991), I asked for and received from Microsoft a list of all possible error messages in DOS version 5 — all 20,000 of them. And, that was only DOS! Over the evolution of Windows, I can imagine that several *hundred thousand* error messages are possible — so many that I doubt Microsoft has them all listed.

This chapter lists what I consider to be the most popular, annoying, or just frustrating dumb error messages. Obviously, it's not the entire list. That would take too much room to print — and too much booze for me to write them all down.

User Account Controls

Oh, I could go on. . . .

The *User Account Control* (UAC) warning should not be a surprise. When it is, you probably have something going on that shouldn't be; click the Cancel button. Otherwise, you can expect a UAC, as shown in Figure 28-1, whenever you click a button or choose an item flagged with the shield icon, as shown in the margin. Then the warning is expected.

The reason the UACs are "dumb" is that it's too easy to condition yourself to click the Continue button. Or, when you use a Limited account, to type an administrator's password. Taking advantage of your comfort level is something called *human engineering,* and believe me, the bad guys will take advantage of that.

Figure 28-1:
The
ubiquitous
User
Account
Control.

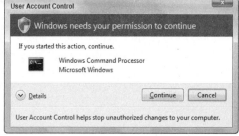

The Blue Screen of Death

When it's a big and important error, Windows doesn't mess around with a dialog box or cute graphics and icons. No, it goes straight back to its text-based soul: The error message is displayed on a text screen with white text on a blue background. The wags call it the *Blue Screen of Death.* Generally, these errors are either fatal or important enough that they require immediate attention.

- If the error message says something along the lines of "Wait for window or press any key (or Ctrl+Alt+Delete) to reboot," then reboot. You can try waiting — especially if you feel that you can fix the problem or that the problem will fix itself — but it's normally Ctrl+Alt+Delete+Pray.

- Sometimes, the error message is simply urgent and not life threatening. For example, you may be asked to reinsert a disk that the computer was using. If so, obey the instructions, and the computer continues working.

The Program Has Performed an Illegal Operation or Stopped Responding or Is Just Being Stupid

In our modern "What is legal?" society, this error message often induces uncalled-for terror in the bosom of its victims. What is *legal,* anyway?

Relax! In the computer world, the word *illegal* is used to describe a programming operation that isn't allowed. The computer programmers could have used the words *prohibited* or *corrupt* instead, but they didn't.

Another popular word to use is *invalid,* as demonstrated by the next several error messages. The word is pronounced "in-VAL-id," as in "not valid." It's not "IN-valid," as in "incapacitated by illness."

Anyway! The program has done something beyond your control. Too bad. Shut down the computer. Restart Windows. Start over.

Don't bother contacting the "program vendor." Odds are that the vendor knows about the bug but doesn't want to hear from you and won't fix it. You can try if you want, but my experience has shown that the vendors really, really don't care. And, that's too bad.

Faults Various and Sundry

Whose fault is it? And who is this General Protection Fault? Is he related to the San Andreas Fault?

Fault messages are numerous. You may see a specific fault message, such as Invalid Page Fault (which relates to the way Windows controls memory), or you may see a nonspecific fault message, or General Protection Fault. That pretty much means that a program did something it shouldn't have done. If so, Windows responds by immediately killing the offending program and issuing this error message.

When fault errors become numerous, it's a sign that something big is looming, perhaps even a hardware problem. Consider having your dealer or another professional take a look at Mr. PC.

What KB Means in an Error Message

Some error messages contain the letters *KB* followed by a number. That's good news! The KB stands for knowledge base — specifically, the Microsoft Knowledge Base. It's a very large database full of problems and (yes) solutions. So what you need to do when you see the KB error message is visit the Microsoft support Web page and search for the given article.

For example, you see an error message with KB555474 in it. That means you're not getting any sound in Internet Explorer. Weird. But Microsoft has some solutions handy, so you follow these steps:

1. **Browse to the Microsoft support page:**

   support.microsoft.com/

2. **Locate the Search box.**

   On my screen, it says "Search Support (KB)." Hey! There's the KB again.

3. **Type the number following *KB* and press the Enter key.**

   Type a number such as 555474.

4. **Press the Enter key.**

   There's the article in the search results page. On my screen, it says "No Sound in Internet Explorer."

5. **Click the link.**

6. **Peruse the solutions offered.**

   You might also want to print the results — unless, of course, you're experiencing printer woes.

7. **Close Internet Explorer when you're done.**

If you're an aspiring computer nerd, you don't have to plow through these steps. Simply plug the number into the following address:

support.microsoft.com/kb/######/

Replace the ###### part of the address with the KB number and you see the proper article.

This information is time sensitive. This book goes to press in early 2008. The Web page addresses and KB numbers might change in the future. (And, if you're reading this book in 2019, please let me know where I can finally get my flying car. Thanks!)

The Activation Period Has Ended

Windows Vista requires that you *activate* the product with Microsoft. Activation can be done over the Internet or telephone. After Windows is activated, you have full control over it. But if you choose not to activate, Windows offers only limited (read "stupid") functionality and you'll be eternally frustrated.

My advice: Activate the product! As long as you legally acquired it, there's no problem.

When activation fails, you need to either fess up and buy a legitimate copy of Windows Vista or let Microsoft know who you bought the computer from so that someone there can pursue those folks for violating Microsoft's license and illegally distributing Windows.

Don't worry about security concerns. Heck, if that really bothers you, you're probably a good candidate for using the Linux operating system. *Bon chance!*

A Disk Read Error Has Occurred

And you thought librarians were strict! Honestly!

Disk read errors happen all the time. In fact, for the computer to report a disk failure, it takes a series of errors multiple times. Yet when this error happens, you must *immediately* back up your computer and especially your important files. Buy another hard drive. Use it. Remove the defective hard drive.

 ✔ Disk read errors are more popular on floppy disks and optical discs than on hard drives. But for diskettes and discs, just toss out the defective media and try again.
 ✔ See Chapter 26 for vital information on backing up your PC's data.

Stack Overflow

Technically a programmer's error, a *stack overflow* happens when a program runs low on a specific type of memory. The memory is called the *stack,* and it's used to store information for the program — like a scratch pad.

The problem is that the stack has only so much room, and a sloppy or damaged program consumes that room quickly. When that happens, the microprocessor must take over and rescue the program, lest it bring down the entire computer system. The microprocessor steps in by halting the program and issuing a Stack Overflow error message.

There's nothing you can do about it other than complain to the program developer.

Divide By Zero

Another error caught by the microprocessor is the *divide-by-zero* error. When you try to divide something by zero on your pocket calculator, you get an *E* to indicate an *error*. The computer equivalent of the E is that the microprocessor steps in, stops the program, and issues a divide-by-zero error message.

No, there's nothing you can do about this error message either. You can try complaining to the software developer, but it usually blames you for it.

Unknown Error

Yes, the Tomb of the Unknown Error is a favorite place for folks to visit, especially around the holidays. Seriously, there are so many errors and potential mishaps that it would be impossible to catalog them all. But that's really no excuse! I mean, even a cryptic number error message is better. At least you can potentially look up the message number in a reference.

To me, unknown errors are the sign of a lazy programmer. Rather than be specific, or waste time concocting error messages for each possible flaw, the programmer merely displays the same message: Unknown Error. Or, perhaps the program is too complex and often errs in ways the programmer doesn't imagine? Either way, I find the Unknown Error message a true disappointment.

Chapter 29

Ten Things You Should Never or Always Do

- -

In This Chapter

▶ Never work in Safe mode all the time

▶ Never reinstall the operating system

▶ Never reformat the hard drive

▶ Never delete random files

▶ Never let other people use your computer

▶ Never steal software

▶ Always shut down Windows properly

▶ Always back up

▶ Always set restore points

▶ Always scan for viruses

- -

*Y*ou should always wash your hands before eating. And after eating. And between eating. And any time you touch a filthy door knob. According to my mother, filthy door knobs exist all over, lurking with the potential to infect and transmit diseases to unsuspecting hand washers all over! Better wash your hands again after you leave the lavatory.

Oh, boy! I hate lectures. But, I thought that I would end this book with one just because I have been really good this time and haven't done much finger wagging. You see, it really isn't your fault! If you still have shame, consider reading through these ten things you should or shouldn't do. That should sate your guilt gland.

Never Run Your Computer in Safe Mode All the Time

Safe mode is for troubleshooting and fixing problems. It's not the computer's standard operating mode. And though you can get work done in this mode, it's not what this mode is there for.

- ✔ I know that this advice makes sense, yet I get e-mail from people who run their computers all the time in Safe mode.

- ✔ Perhaps it's the name. Maybe it should be called Fixing mode or Troubleshooting mode.

- ✔ See Chapter 24 for more Safe mode stuff.

Never Reinstall Windows

Reinstalling Windows is a bad idea, especially considering that most problems can be fixed without having to reinstall. Only if your computer is ravaged by a virus or some other catastrophe is reinstalling the operating system ever necessary.

- ✔ Lazy tech-support people suggest reinstalling Windows just to get you off the line. Don't give up that easily!

- ✔ Also refer to Chapter 20.

Never Reformat the Hard Drive

You have no reason to reformat. It's not a routine chore. It's not required. It's not a part of owning a PC.

As with reinstalling Windows, reformatting a hard drive is necessary only if the system is utterly destroyed by a catastrophe. Otherwise, this task is a rare and unnecessary thing to do.

Never Randomly Delete Files You Didn't Create

I think that the emphasis in this heading is more on "randomly" than on "files you didn't create." In many instances in this book, you have permission to delete certain files that you didn't create or cause to come into being. My point is merely to be careful with what you delete. Don't be hasty. Don't assume just because you don't know what something does that it's okay to delete it. That gets people into trouble.

Never Let Other People Use Your Computer

Windows is designed for multiple people to use the system — as long as all users have their own accounts. So give them their own accounts! Don't let them use your account. There's no point in that!

Treat the computer like you would treat your wallet: Never loan it out to anyone unless you expect to have it returned in a different condition. Your computer is a private thing. Keep it private.

- ✔ Especially avoid letting visitors — relatives, specifically — use your computer. All it takes is one grandnephew to infect your computer with all sorts of viruses.

- ✔ If visitors really want to use a computer, they can bring their own or go to the library.

- ✔ Be firm. Say "No."

- ✔ Okay, when you're weak, you can set up a new account for the other person. Ensure that it's a Limited account and not an Administrator.

Never Use Pirated Software

Pirated or stolen software — or any software you didn't pay for — is often the source of computer viruses. Sure, it may be "free." But, who knows what idiot put what virus on that disc?

Pirated games are perhaps the single greatest source of viruses in the PC world. You just run a terrible risk — not to mention that it's legally and morally wrong to steal.

Always Shut Down Windows Properly

Use the Shut Down Windows dialog box to make the operating system die a peaceful death. The idea is to try to avoid the situation where you just turn off the computer. That leads to major problems down the road.

Of course, if the system doesn't let you shut down properly, you have to just flip the power switch. Refer to Chapter 20 for some help.

Always Back Up

Whether it's just copying today's files to a removable disc or using real backup software, you would be wise to have a spare copy of your data handy (refer to Chapter 26).

Always Set Restore Points after Installing New Software or Hardware

The System Restore utility is a must-use tool for whenever you upgrade your system. Remember that change introduces problems in many computers. Having the ability to "go back in time" with System Restore is a blessing. Set those restore points!

Refer to Chapter 4.

Always Scan for Viruses

I highly recommend using antivirus software. It's a must. In fact, it's shocking that such a utility isn't a part of Windows. (Oh, but I could go on. . . .) Instead, I recommend investing in a good antivirus program, such as Norton AntiVirus or any program that offers updates via the Internet.

Computing in this decade is a dangerous thing. Make it safer. Use antivirus software. See Chapter 24.

Keep your antivirus subscription up-to-date! New viruses are introduced all the time. Be safe! Protect yourself.

Index

• E •

• S •

• *U* •

• *V* •

• *W* •